Frank

P9-DEA-162

800
(XL)

BILLY GRAHAM

BILLY GRAHAM

The Authorized Biography

by John Pollock

McGraw-Hill Book Company

NEW YORK   TORONTO   LONDON   SYDNEY

Contents

Part III · "To God Be the Glory": 1954–1955

Part IV · The Wide World: 1956–1959

Part V · The New Age: 1960–

Preface

Billy Graham has already preached to some 50,000,000 people in person. Countless millions have heard or seen him by radio, television or film. Nearly one million have "come forward" during the Billy Graham crusades. He is the confidant of statesmen and rulers, and his opinions are quoted across the world. His actions, motives and achievements have been debated, attacked and defended as those of few contemporary religious leaders.

The present book is the first major biography to have the full cooperation of Graham and his associates. It is primarily based on his private and unpublished papers, and on transcripts (which run to nearly half a million words) of many hours of tape-recorded conversations with him, and of interviews with a wide range of people in North America, Europe, Australia and New Zealand. More details of sources are given as an appendix.

Before I accepted this assignment in 1963 I had met Billy Graham for personal conversation only three times: during the London crusade of 1954, at Cambridge in 1955, and in South India in 1956. I have been interested to discover, as I researched, how many misconceptions I held about him, and I believe this to be true of many who have strong opinions on the man. The point was well put by Dr. Helmut Thielicke, professor of systematic theology and social ethics at Hamburg University, in a letter which he wrote to Graham after attending the Los Angeles crusade in August 1963: "How different it is when men encounter each other face to face, rather than just hearing about each other! I am ashamed that we Christians—including myself—are always susceptible to preconceived opinions. . . . The evening beneath your pulpit was a profound 'penance' experience for me in this respect."

My hope is that this book will prove for many readers a genuine encounter with the real Graham, that it will provide the means for an assessment which is accurate, whatever the reader's verdict may be. In the course of a BBC (London) program, July 1, 1964, the late

Canon Stanley Evans of Southwark Cathedral said of Billy Graham's preaching: "It is not the Gospel at all. It never speaks of anything other than a sentimental relationship between the individual and God. . . . The mind and the will are left out of this completely. This is not the Gospel, this is the Gospel degutted and individualized."

Is this an *accurate* assessment of Billy Graham?

Or an example from another angle. General of the Army Dwight D. Eisenhower, the former President of the United States, very kindly sent me a letter on February 8, 1965, in the course of which he refers to Billy Graham as "an evangelist who can relate his basic spiritual beliefs to the tough problems of the day. . . . By word and action he has been a splendid influence in the United States, indeed in other areas of the world also."

Is this opinion prejudiced by friendship, or is it an *accurate* assessment?

A book, however objective, about a man in the full flood of his work cannot be written in the same way as the definitive biography of a figure of the past. On the other hand, a critique of a contemporary tends to reveal more about its writer than about his subject—this has certainly been true of interpretive studies on Graham—and is worth little more than its author's opinion happens to be worth.

I have sought therefore to give the straightforward story of Billy Graham, set in the pattern of his times; to tell of his origins and preparation, of what he has done and how he has grown: the first forty-seven years of a man whose greatest days and most substantial achievements may well lie ahead.

My warmest gratitude naturally goes to Billy Graham, his family and his Associates, for all that they did for this book. I am also extremely grateful to the staff of the Billy Graham Evangelistic Association. It would be quite invidious to single out any names, but in Minneapolis, London, Sydney and elsewhere there are many people without whose special help I would never have been able to gather and prepare the material. The illustrations in the book are also all by courtesy of BGEA unless otherwise stated.

I would like to thank the following who, together with Mr. and Mrs. Graham, read the book in manuscript and made many valuable suggestions:

Dr. L. Nelson Bell
Dr. Robert O. Ferm
Dr. Frank E. Gaebelein
Mr. George M. Wilson
Dr. Sherwood E. Wirt

I am most grateful to those who have allowed me to quote private letters, and who provided memories and impressions. Finally, I would specially thank those who helped with itineraries and gave my wife and me hospitality and encouragement in all our traveling.

The quotation from *The Young Church in Action* is by kind permission of Canon J. B. Phillips and The Macmillan Company, New York. The quotation on page 170 is by kind permission of Mr. Malcum Muggeridge, that on page 181 by kind permission of Mr. David Frost and the *Daily Mail*.

John Pollock

ROSE ASH
DEVONSHIRE, ENGLAND

I

The Country Boy
1918-1949

Crook Graham, a Confederate veteran with a bullet in his leg, who died in 1910, had a patriarchal beard and a large family, but nothing else Biblical about him. "He'd get drunk and he'd stay drunk pretty much over Sunday," tells a son-in-law. "He didn't abuse his family, but I don't hardly think he ran his farm." He would not pay his debts, swore lustily, and had a habit of shooting fowling pieces in the general direction of his daughters' young men.

He had been born across the state line at Fort Mill in South Carolina, and after the Civil War bought the land near Charlotte, North Carolina, which on his death he left to two of his sons, William Franklin and Clyde. Together old Mr. Crook Graham's sons built up a three-hundred-acre dairy farm of rich red soil, with woods and streams and gently rolling contours, and delivered milk in the city.

William Franklin Graham and Morrow Coffey of Charlotte were married in 1916. Their eldest son, William Franklin Graham, Jr., Billy Frank to his family, was born in the frame farmhouse on November 7, 1918, three days before his father's thirtieth birthday and four before the Armistice.

All four of Billy Graham's grandparents were descended from the Scottish pioneers who settled in the Carolinas before the Revolution. His mother could claim kinship with a signatory of the Declaration of Independence, Ezra Alexander, and a President, Charlotte's James K.

Polk. Her father, Ben Coffey, had fair hair and blue eyes (like his grandson) and the tall, clean-limbed, strong-jawed physique immortalized in the North Carolina monument at Gettysburg, where he fell badly wounded in Pickett's charge. A one-legged, one-eyed veteran, he was a farmer of intelligence, spirit and sterling honesty, with a tenacious memory and a love for Scripture and literature which he imparted to his daughters, whom he managed to send to Elizabeth College in Charlotte for a year.

In the frame farmhouse and then in the red brick home nearby which they built when Billy was ten, with its pillared porch, paved paths, and shade of oaks and cedars, Morrow Coffey Graham kept the books, did the cooking and housework and chopped the wood, with the aid of Suzie, her Negro maid. A blend of determination with gentleness and affection won Morrow the complete devotion of her two sons and two daughters: Billy Frank, Catherine, Melvin, and Jean, who was fourteen years younger than Billy.

Their father, Frank Graham, was an equally strong character. Six feet two, dark haired with a fine bass voice, he was a farmer through and through. In early manhood he had experienced a religious conversion as vivid as that of St. Paul on the Damascus road, but his faith had long since lost urgency, though it remained the foundation of his integrity. He was as straight as his back in business dealings, adored and a little feared by the farm hands and his children. His scanty education was offset by shrewdness and a lively curiosity. He had a dry wit and a warm and generous nature kept in close control because agricultural bankruptcies were frequent in the Carolinas, and he must husband land and assets, and deny luxuries to the family and himself. His one indulgence was the smoking of large cigars. He scorned relaxation and hated travel. To Frank Graham, Yankees were suspect; a neighbor or stranger not Presbyterian, Baptist or Methodist he rated peculiar. His world was the South—placid, sunny, but smarting from the Civil War.

In Billy Graham's boyhood the defeat of 1865 and the era of Reconstruction, which only old folk remembered, dominated the South. Poverty prevailed and resentment springing from the belief that the former Confederate states were still discriminated against and punished by an unforgiving North was widespread.

The Graham farm, however, was comparatively prosperous. Billy Frank's hero was the foreman, Reese Brown, an army sergeant in World War I, a splendid Negro who could hold down a bull to be dehorned, had a wide range of skills, was tireless, efficient and trust-

worthy. Billy crammed down Mrs. Brown's delicious buttermilk
bread, the Brown children were his playmates and Reese taught him
to milk and herd.

Billy was a bit too prankish to be of much use at first. Whether for
pulling up lettuce heads, tugging Catherine's hair, teasing her, or en-
dangering his girl cousins' safety in daring escapades, off came his
father's belt, or out came his mother's long hickory switch. His father
never whipped in anger or desperation except once—the oft-told occasion when excessive fidgeting in church led to summary punishment
in the vestibule. "Billy was rowdy, mischievous," sums up an older
cousin, "but on the other hand, he was soft and gentle and loving and
understanding. He was a very sweet, likable person." His parents
were strict but fair, and the house was full of laughter and the
melodious North Carolina accent.

Billy Graham's early education was almost as poor as Abraham
Lincoln's. A primary reason was the low level of teaching. At Sharon
High School, deep in the country, two or three of the teachers had
never been to college. Yet if the teaching had been better he would
have made little use of it, for by the age of ten or eleven he reckoned
horse-sense enough for a future farmer, an attitude slightly abetted by
his father, stoutly resisted by his mother.[1]

His chief interest was baseball. He had been taught the game early
by the McMakins, three sons of the sharecropper on his father's farm,
a red-headed man of high temper but strict Christian principles, who
had once been a Southern champion bicycle racer. When Billy was
ten Frank Graham secured him a handshake with that immortal slug-
ger, Babe Ruth. At Sharon High School Billy Graham's keenness for
baseball was not matched by his skill. In running, throwing and field-
ing he was fair; in batting he was weak, being too tall for his strength.
He barely made the Sharon team as a first baseman and dreamed of
being a professional. Out of Graham's later tendency, in sermons for
youth, to emphasize his athletic ambitions has grown the legend of a
young man who trained to be a professional but became an evangelist; even the handshake with Babe Ruth has been blown into a
serious interview. If Billy Graham never had the remotest chance of

---

[1] Stories of his pranks at school are numerous. More unusual was the habit,
each day before the school bus came, of bicycling slowly down the road followed by a small black goat, a large brown goat, and a collie. (The wild white
cat, which he alone could handle, lay purring on his lap during homework, but
would not join the procession.) If a car passed and the passengers laughed,
Billy would be pleased.

becoming a professional (and the dream died before he left high school), baseball influenced him by interfering with his studies.

The one redeeming feature of Billy's early intellectual life was an exceptional love of reading history books. By the time he was fourteen he had read about a hundred.

When Billy was small, Sunday was rather like an old Scottish Sabbath, its highlights the five-mile drive by automobile to the small Associate Reformed Presbyterian Church, which sang only psalms, in Charlotte, a city then rated the most churchgoing in America.

He never thought of his parents as particularly religious: "They went to church, but beyond that they never talked religion. They never acted religious."

Then, when Billy was about fifteen, a succession of events led straight to the most profound experience of his boyhood.

In 1933 Mrs. Graham joined a Bible class at the urging of her sister, Lil Barker, and learned "that the Lord has come in and lives in our hearts. I had never known that truth before." Her husband remained indifferent. His energies were absorbed by the farm, especially since he had lost all his savings in the recent wave of bank failures.

Three weeks after Mrs. Graham had joined the Bible class Frank Graham's head was smashed by a flying stick of wood from the mechanical saw. The surgeons believed he would die. Mrs. Graham, after calling her Christian friends to pray, went up to her bedroom "and just laid hold of the Lord. I got up with the assurance that God heard my prayer." Both the Grahams believed that in Frank's accident and full recovery "the Lord really spoke to us," and that they should find more time for Bible study and prayer.

Mrs. Graham began to read to the children devotional writings like those of Donald Barnhouse. The adolescent Billy Frank "thought it all hogwash." He was also in confused, mild and barely acknowledged revolt against accepted standards, though his chief wildness was to borrow his father's car (there was no minimum age for a driving licence in North Carolina in those days) "and drive it as fast as I could get it to go," turning curves on two wheels, and racing other boys on the near-empty roads of North Carolina. "One night I had driven 200 or 300 miles in races and my father looked at the speedometer the next morning and said, 'Where in the world have you gone?' He had checked the speedometer! And once I got the car stuck in the mud, and I had to call my father. He was more angry than I had ever seen him. He had to get mules to come and pull it out."

Physically Billy Graham had developed fast, like most Southern country boys. At high school he was much the ladies' man, with his height, wavy blond hair, blue eyes and tanned skin, his neat clothes and fancy ties. He was in and out of love, sometimes dating two girls successively the same night, but did not fall into the immoral practices of some of his school pals. Fortunately for Billy his heroes, the McMakins, were clean-living youths; furthermore the Graham parents expected their children "to be clean and never doubted that we would be. They trusted us and made us want to live up to their confidence."

Had Billy Graham been a city boy such good intentions might have failed. Farm labor gave him release of physical energy. Every day he was milking before dawn. All the Grahams were light sleepers who found early rising no hardship, and Billy milked fast and smoothly, then helped pour the Holstein, Guernsey and Jersey milk into the big mixer before bottling. From school he hurried back to the afternoon milking. He reveled in sweat and exertion, whether cleaning out cow stalls, forking manure or pitching hay.

In May 1934 Frank Graham lent a pasture to some thirty local businessmen who wanted to devote a day of prayer for Charlotte because the Depression had spread spiritual apathy in the city. They had planned, despite the indifference of the ministerial association, to hold an evangelistic campaign later that year. During that day of prayer on the Graham land their leader, Vernon Patterson, prayed—as Frank Graham would often recall between Billy's rise to fame in 1949 and his own death in 1962—that "out of Charlotte the Lord would raise up someone to preach the Gospel to the ends of the earth."

The businessmen next erected in the city a large "tabernacle" of raw pine on a steel frame, where for eleven weeks from September 1934 a renowned, fiery Southern evangelist named Mordecai Fowler Ham, and his song leader, Walter Ramsay, shattered the complacency of church-going Charlotte.

Ham was highly literate, with old Southern courtesy, yet a man of intense convictions who charged full-tilt at scandals and prejudices and was a mighty protagonist for Prohibition. He tended to "skin the ministers," as his phrase was, and cared not at all that Charlotte's most powerful clergy opposed, or that newspapers attacked him. In later years the relish for controversy hurt his ministry, but in 1934, for all the brimstone and a tendency to frighten men into heaven by dangling them over hell, Ham's passionate preaching left hearers with an overwhelming realization that Christ was alive.

The Frank Grahams did not attend the Ham campaign's first week or ten days—a curious sequel to the prayer meeting on their land, possibly explained by their minister's guarded neutrality toward Ham and the tabernacle's distance. Some neighbors then took them. After that "we couldn't stay away."

Billy Graham, too old to be ordered to attend, was "definitely antagonistic," until the Ham-Ramsay campaign exploded new controversy when Ham flung at his audience a charge of fornication among the students at the Central High School. Infuriated students marched on the tabernacle, the newspapers featured the sensation, and Billy Graham was intrigued.

Albert McMakin, the second of the sharecropper's sons, now twenty-four and newly married, had been attending the campaign regularly because a few months earlier, at one of the small preparatory meetings on Tenth Avenue, he had discovered that an upright life was not enough. He filled his old truck with folk from the Graham neighborhood, both whites and Negroes, and determined that Billy should jump on it too. "I figured he was the same way that I had been, a moral boy with a head knowledge taught by his own people, but not having come face to face with the Lord Jesus Christ."

Albert told Billy that Ham was no "sissy" but a fighting preacher. Albert invited Billy to drive the truck to the meetings.

They sat at the back of the largest crowd Billy had ever seen. Far away up the "sawdust trail" of wood shavings sat the choir, and on the pulpit, vigorous, white-haired Mordecai Ham. Ham began to preach, and Billy was "spellbound," as he wrote thirty years later. "Each listener became deeply involved with the evangelist, who had an almost embarrassing way of describing your sins and shortcomings and of demanding, on pain of divine judgment, that you mend your ways. As I listened, I began to have thoughts I had never known before."

That night in the room he shared with Melvin, Billy Graham gazed at the full moon and felt "a kind of stirring in my breast that was both pleasant and scary. Next night all my father's mules and horses could not have kept me away from the meeting."

His sixteenth birthday passed. Albert McMakin detected that Billy's self-righteousness was crumbling. "He didn't know really what was wrong with him. He moved around from one place to another. I could tell he was under conviction, but I kept my mouth shut because I felt God was handling this affair, and I could very well cause him to not want to go with me if I said much." Ham had a habit of pointing his finger. His analysis cut so close to the bone that once Billy ducked behind the hat of the woman in front, and to escape the accusing finger applied for a place in the choir. Though he could not carry a tune and his vocal efforts in the bath were a merriment to all the Grahams, he was accepted and found himself next to Grady Wilson, a casual acquaintance from another school.

The maneuver was futile. By now Billy had "a tremendous conviction that I must commit myself. I'm sure," he recalls, "the Lord did speak to me about certain things in my life. I'm certain of that. But I cannot remember what they were. But I do remember a great sense of burden that I was a sinner before God and had a great fear of hell and judgment."

The more he struggled to assert his own goodness the heavier grew his burden. He had no doubt now in his mind that Christ had died on the Cross to bear the sins of Billy Graham; and each night the conviction grew that Christ, whose Resurrection he had never doubted in theory, was actually alive, wanting to take away the burden, and in its place to bring Himself to be Savior and Friend, if only Billy would commit himself unreservedly. Billy was far less conscious of Mordecai Ham than of Christ. Yet the price of Christ's friendship would be total surrender for a life-long discipleship; Billy would no longer be his own master. That price he was not yet prepared to pay. When Ham invited those who would accept Christ to move toward the pulpit in an act of witness and definition, Billy Graham stayed in his seat.

The inward struggle continued, at school desk, in the gymnasium at basketball, in the cowbarn milking. He did not tell his parents ("We suspected, and we were hoping and praying"), but talked with a first cousin, Crook Stafford, who encouraged him to go forward although Crook had not yet done so himself. Billy moved again next night and sat near the front. Ham's smile seemed consciously directed; Billy, quite wrongly, was certain Ham knew about him and quoted specially for him, "God commendeth His love toward us in that while we were yet sinners, Christ died for us."

Ham made the appeal. Billy heard the choir sing, "Just as I am, without one plea," verse by verse, as people gathered round the pulpit. Billy stayed in his seat, his conscience wrestling with his will.

The choir began "Almost persuaded, Christ to believe." Billy could stand it no longer and went forward.

"It was not just the technique of walking forward in a Southern revival meeting. It was Christ. I was conscious of Him."

A short man with dark hair and eyes approached him. Billy knew and liked J. D. Prevatt, who kept a tailoring shop and was English-born. They talked and had a prayer. Billy had a "deep sense of peace and joy," but around him many were in tears and he worried a bit because he felt so matter-of-fact. His father, as McMakin well remembers, "came clear across from one side to throw his arms around him and thank God for his decision."

That night Billy Graham walked upstairs past the old family clock ticking loudly the time, day and month, and undressed in the dark because Melvin was already asleep. The moon rode high again and Billy looked out across his father's land, then lay for hours unemotionally checking over in the context of his adolescent world what should be the attitudes of a fellow who belonged to Christ. He drifted into sleep content and at peace, with just a grain of doubt: "I wonder if this will last?"

In the next months it was more obvious to Billy Graham than to anyone else that "something tremendous" had happened inside him. His school principal, Connor Hutchinson, noticed, and his mother: "Billy was more thoughtful, he was very kind, he was quieter. . . . In just little things it was very evident." Deep within, scarcely understood, not yet formulated beyond a sensing that a friendship had begun with Someone as real as the flesh-and-blood people around, Billy Graham was aware of new appetites, new standards. The whole world looked different, and he had no doubt that this was what the Bible called "the new birth."

---

2 · *The Eighteenth Green*

Early in 1936, a young Alabama evangelist named Jimmie Johnson, with good looks, flashing eyes and potency of speech, took the seventeen-year-old Billy Graham to a service in Monroe jail, about thirty miles from Charlotte. In the middle of preaching Johnson suddenly said on impulse, "Here's a young fellow who can tell you what it is like to be converted." A surprised, aghast Billy began falteringly, and according to his recollection, "Three or four sentences were all I could manage." Johnson remembers differently: "We were all surprised at his ability to speak. He did a very commendable job right there in that prison."

Jimmie Johnson did not remotely consider Billy a candidate for fame, but a "typical, unpredictable, gangling tall young man," though with "great personality. He was a most likable person." When Grady Wilson, a jolly fellow who had followed Billy up the sawdust trail that night at Ham's, started preaching, Billy remained in tongue-tied admiration. With Grady's current girl friend he had gone to the 18th Street Mission across the tracks in Charlotte. Some twenty people were present. From a book Grady borrowed a theme, "God's Four Questions." From Billy he borrowed a watch. He started on "God's first question," and in nervousness wound and wound the watch. After fifteen minutes Billy was so worried for the watch that he lost interest in the sermon, but after thirty minutes he had forgotten the watch in admiration: "My, what a tremendous thing this is. Here's Grady, my friend and pal, up preaching. How does he learn all this? How can he say all that?" After an hour Grady paused: "Now we come to 'God's second question.' "

Occasionally Billy testified with others of his Bible club when they held impromptu services on sidewalks. But he was, in Grady's memory, "just scattered and rattling. He'd stand there and twist his coat, very nervously. He appeared to me to be awfully shy and timid."

Billy had started a Christian group in Sharon High School, despite scorn and kidding, somewhat muted because he was gay, athletic, and not in the least sanctimonious.

A school contemporary whose religion, by his own definition, is nominal, has not forgotten how Billy "had such a wonderful feeling about it all that he wanted to share it with all of us." The coach, Clinton Eudy, now an attorney in Salisbury, North Carolina, remembers Billy in his last years at school as an "interesting, challenging and inspiring mixture of saint and devil, with a predominant measure of saint."

After 1934 Billy Graham had settled down to his studies, but had now too much ground to recover and Sharon High School was unable to teach him academic discipline. He was happier on his own. Before he graduated he had read through Gibbon's *Decline and Fall of the Roman Empire* as well as Charles and Mary Beard's earlier works on American civilization. Except that he no longer wanted to farm, he had no ideas about a career, but aimed to enter the University of

North Carolina. His mother, however, had such admiration for Jimmie Johnson that she chose his college, Bob Jones College at Cleveland, Tennessee, as a strongly Christian institution. Grady Wilson would be going too, and Grady's older brother, T.W. (Thomas Walter) was already there. Until the Ham campaign T.W. had been a boy of violent temper who had habitually socked Grady's nose for disobedience! Several other of their friends had enrolled.

The Grahams did not realize that Bob Jones College was not accredited.

Before entering Bob Jones, Billy had the summer of 1936 free. Albert McMakin had become a field manager for the Fuller Brush Company in South Carolina and needed temporary door-to-door salesmen. Billy was enthusiastic, his parents a little dubious, and Uncle Clyde laughingly gave Billy two weeks to wire for money.

After an uncertain start at Darlington (and a near miss when an irate female emptied a pitcher of water from an upstairs window), Billy earned $17. Then accidentally he lost all the dollar bills and begged a loan from Albert, saying he would sleep in the open before wiring for money. He repaid the loan in a week, "and from then on his sales were good. Fact is," says McMakin, "I had a time keeping up with him. Some weeks I couldn't. He beat any salesman I had." Graham reveled in imparting to South Carolinians his genuine, if very recent, conviction that a Fuller brush was a necessity of life.

By now Grady and T. W. Wilson had joined the summer sales staff. Whenever they were together the Wilsons, Graham and Mc-Makin would spend the evenings hard at Bible study and in prayer. At Florence they went on the streets with the Salvation Army. On business rounds Billy learned before each call to pray for sales success and, if he could make opportunity, would at each call unfold the thrills of knowing Christ.

Once, back in Charlotte for a weekend, the four young men took a puncture to Robinson's at Diamond Point on the Pineville Road. When changing the tire the new garage hand hammered his thumb. "Christ!" he swore.

"Sir," said Billy sharply, "don't do that! Don't ever do that again!"

"This is a free country. I can do what I please and say what I please!"

"Not around me you can't!"

At that the garageman lost his temper and nearly hit Billy with a length of iron.

Bob Jones, the Methodist minister and evangelist of fifty-three who dominated the college he had founded, was a rugged frontiersman whose boast that "nobody leaves this school who ought to stay," was often made good surreptitiously from his own pocket. He was a man of extremes who, as Graham found, could be as tender as a child or as rough as an infuriated bull. Bob Jones College was run as if a cross between a high school and a recruiting barracks: hours were long, rules rigid, discipline administered by monitors (in 1936 nicknamed "the Gestapo") on a system of demerits. The dormitories with their two-tier bunks displayed a notice to end all grumbles and grouses: *Griping Not Tolerated.*

Although Billy Graham was disappointed to find no athletic contests were held with other colleges, his first letters—he wrote home three times a week until nearly the end of his entire education—were enthusiastic. "I have gained exactly twelve pounds since I've been here," he claimed on September 24. "My gray pants to my gray suit will hardly meet. It's great here. I'm making fair in my work, and I think my grades will be good this month, but next month should be better. I'm studying all the time I have." He was stirred by the Sunday vespers arranged with almost operatic dignity by young Bob Jones, Jr., and by the deep convictions and homespun philosophy of old "Dr. Bob" as he preached in his curious, strangled voice from the side of his mouth. "I loved to hear him," recalls Graham, "and it made a great impact on me."

Enthusiasm for Bob Jones College, however, waned fast. T. W. Wilson says that Graham at this point "didn't have any purpose or goal in life. He felt that he ought to preach. And yet he didn't know how to go about it." He needed careful handling if latent intellectual and spiritual powers were to be drawn out. But Bob Jones College ran in fixed grooves. "Dr. Bob" knew exactly what was true and false in faith, ethics and academics. He often stated publicly that his institution had never been wrong. Independent thought was so discouraged that many alumni say in retrospect that there was almost thought control.

All this, together with a bout of flu, made Billy reluctant to return to Bob Jones College after Christmas. Mrs. Graham put her finger on the trouble, in a letter early the next year: "It was not so much the studies as the all-round strenuous schedule put in practice there from early morning until late at night which will sometimes detract very greatly from the deepening of spiritual things." She wanted a "quiet, spiritual atmosphere for Billy Frank."

Billy Frank caught flu again, which led to the beginning of a long battle with respiratory trouble.

Afterward the family visited relatives in Florida, where Billy raved about the sunsets and the oranges, and although the Grahams doubted the wisdom of changing schools, a Charlotte doctor pronounced Billy's need of sunshine.

The Grahams had discovered a small but highly recommended Bible school in Florida. When Billy returned to Cleveland to finish the semester, he found that his roommate Wendell Phillips, a thickset Yankee, had also heard of the Florida Bible Institute at Tampa, and he too needed sunshine. Dr. Bob Jones sent for the boys and looked sternly at Billy, who, remembers Wendell Phillips, sat "biting his nails and hanging his head sheepishly as Dr. Bob began censuring him for his wavering and fickle attitude toward school, particularly his school."

"Billy," said Jones, "if you leave and throw your life away at a little country Bible school, the chances are you'll never be heard of. At best all you could amount to would be a poor country Baptist preacher somewhere out in the sticks."

The Florida Bible Institute's elegant cream-colored building in Spanish style at Temple Terrace, near Tampa, faced the eighteenth tee of a golf course. It had been a country club, picked up for a song at the height of the Depression. In 1937 the Institute had between thirty and forty men and about fifty women students. The remainder of the rooms were used as a hotel and Bible conference center: the Florida Winter "Keswick" Convention was held there.

The entire Graham family drove up in a new Plymouth on a January morning of 1937. All the school was out except the Reverend John Minder, the giant, ginger-haired dean. Frank and Morrow Graham were very favorably impressed, as she wrote to the president, Dr. W. T. Watson, with the "homelike, restful Christian atmosphere." They left after lunch. The lady caterer, "Gibby," came out to Billy and said, "Say, can you drive a car? I have a station wagon full of tourists who are supposed to be taken on a tour of Tampa, and I have nobody to drive them. Will you do it?"

Billy said, "But I've never been to Tampa. How can I take them on a tour of Tampa?"

"Well, tell them something."

So, Billy recalls, "I drove these tourists into Tampa and spent the afternoon explaining the virtues of Tampa, which I didn't know anything about, and brought them back, and they all seemed happy!" That evening Roy Gustafson, a senior in the music department, was highly amused to see Billy Graham, an overgrown schoolboy with a large scout knife, running out with Wendell Phillips, "like an animal that had been in captivity and had finally got its freedom. He and Wendell Phillips ran all over the golf course!"

Billy Graham quickly relaxed and burgeoned in the freedom and family spirit, the sunshine and scenery—the beginning of what he was to call "three and one-half glorious, happy, character-building, life-changing years." "Mother," Billy wrote home, "words can't express Florida Bible Institute.... I never felt so close to God in my life. This is the first time I have enjoyed studying the Word of God.... I love it here. I am stronger and feel so much better." And in Charlotte, every day after lunch, Frank and Morrow Graham "went to our bedroom upstairs and got down on our knees by our bed" and prayed that Billy would fulfill the Apostle's charge to young Timothy: "Study to show thyself approved unto God, a workman that needeth not to be ashamed, rightly dividing the word of truth."

The school was too small for baseball, though convenient for watching (through a hole in the fence) the big league training sessions. On the golf course Billy began to caddy, then to play. The others said rudely that "he played golf like baseball—he whacked it." There was tennis and volley ball and the Hillsboro River for swimming and canoeing. Billy and his roommate, a senior named Woodrow Flynn, one Sunday went canoeing in their best clothes before a date. Billy was "standing up and clowning, and he raised his oar up and said, 'I see an Indian—bang!' And he leaned backward and we both went in the water."

The students worked their way, but Frank Graham, having rebuilt his assets, settled the modest fees and sent Billy pocket money. Billy worked, though, to be like the other students, and as an outlet for his unceasing energy. He sought grass cutting, hedge trimming and jobs to develop his wiry strength. He could wrestle a roommate under the bed, and when a bully picked up a heavy stone to settle an argument, Billy knocked him down.

The work he liked best was dishwashing, for "the fellows would wash the dishes and all the girls would dry," recalls one of them, "and we always had a good time." Billy claimed to wash so fast that he could keep four girls busy—"the first automatic dishwasher the college ever had," as Dr. Watson remarks. At Bob Jones, restrictions on meeting the girls had been galling. Here with his natty clothes, suits regularly sent to the cleaners, bright bow ties for the evenings, Billy Graham was again a favorite. A good fellow to have around: vital, generous, clean-limbed, clear-eyed.

Yet he was aimless, lacking serious application to lectures or study. At an ordinary school these virtues and defects might have left him, after three and a half years, a charming incompetent.

The school at Temple Terrace did not pretend to be a college of liberal arts, or attempt a general education; nor was it a seminary. It aimed to give a thorough grounding in the English Bible, with courses in related subjects—Greek, Church history and missions, hermeneutics and pastoral theology, etc.—and practical training in Christian service. Unlike Bob Jones it did not impose a rigid intellectual system. The lecturers made their positions clear but encouraged the students to think. What distinguished it from other Bible schools was the exceptional emphasis, made possible by the small size, on individual instruction; the faculty worked from the belief that the latent possibilities of each student must be fostered. As the Christian and Missionary Alliance (of which Watson and Minder were members) was among the first of the overseas mission field to promote the idea of the indigenous church, so Tampa applied the same principle: that the Holy Spirit, if allowed to operate in His own time and way, could make of a man what He would.

John Minder, with his humorous eyes, endless patience, and exceptional gift for encouraging students, applied this principle to Billy Graham.

Having heard Graham give his testimony outside the dog track at Sulphur Springs, Minder invited him to stay at the little conference center he had developed on the shores of Lake Swan near Melrose in northern Florida, during the Easter vacation of 1937. On Easter Sunday evening they drove to Palatka above the broad St. John's River to call on Minder's close friend Cecil Underwood, an interior decorator who was a Baptist preacher. They found him setting out to supply a pulpit at the nearby country community of Bostick. In the car Underwood suggested Minder might preach. Minder replied: "Billy's preaching tonight."

"No, sir," said a horrified Billy, "I've never preached before."

"Well, you are preaching tonight," said Minder. "When you run out, I'll take over."

At Bob Jones every boy had to compose sermons, and Billy had recited one borrowed from a book, with his own embellishments, before a small mountain congregation. This had been merely a "preacher boy" exercise. He had since, however, secretly prepared and practiced four sermons on themes taken from the sermons of Lee Scarborough, the famous Baptist preacher, each schemed to last forty-five minutes.

They drew up at the clapboard church, stepped through the beagles and hounds that had accompanied their masters, and joined a congregation of twenty-five or thirty cowboys and ranchers. The song-leader, a man of odd jobs from junk collecting to fishing, led off in a raucous marching hymn, pausing occasionally to spit tobacco juice into the boiler. Underwood introduced Billy, whose knees knocked and palms and brow were sticky. Billy began loud and fast. "He had a bit of difficulty," remembers Underwood, "but he got through all right. He ran out of words. He ran out of thoughts. His delivery was impressive, even that first sermon, because of his sincerity." Billy had worked through all four of his sermons in eight minutes!

On a Saturday, back at Temple Terrace, Minder asked Billy to preach to the young people the next evening at Tampa Gospel Tabernacle, of which Minder was pastor. Billy rushed to Woodrow Flynn: "I've got to preach and I haven't got a sermon." Flynn sat up in his bunk and preached him a sermon on Belshazzar's feast. That night Billy could scarcely sleep. He studied, prayed and sweated, and next morning crept out for a practice preach to the squirrels and rabbits. Sunday evening left Billy Graham sure he would never make a preacher. His audience, however, so appreciated this dramatic, forceful youth that before the 1937 summer semester was over, Minder invited him to take charge of the young people's department.

By the early months of 1938, when Graham had been a year at Temple Terrace and was nineteen, he was still an overgrown undisciplined boy. "I had no purpose, I was interested in the Bible, I had been converted, I wanted to know the Bible. But I was still carefree, happy-go-lucky." In a phrase he has often used about himself at that time, "I didn't amount to much."

Three major upheavals turned him into a man of overriding purpose and intense conviction.

Two Christians whom Billy Graham had admired and learned from were accused of serious moral defections, and he was shaken to the core. He learned that a man may talk piously and help others, and yet be himself a castaway. Graham determined that nothing should ever be allowed in his life, known or unknown, that could harm the name of Christ. Furthermore, he realized that this could happen unless he took his vocation seriously. The scandals "caused me to look to God rather than to men. I realized that any man could have feet of clay. Paul said, 'Put no confidence in the flesh.' This was an early lesson that helped me tremendously through the years."

The second upheaval began in great happiness. He became engaged to be married.

Emily Regina Cavanaugh, one class senior to Billy, was a sparkling personality, intelligent, musical, vivacious, dedicated. Billy had "loved her from the moment I saw her." They partnered each other at tennis, rivaled each other at table tennis and worked together for the Tabernacle youth, often returning afterward to her parents' home in Tampa for Billy's favorite fruit Jello.

In the summer vacation of 1937, when Emily was in Toronto, Billy wrote asking her to marry him. As late as January 29, 1938, he told his parents, "Emily thinks a great deal of me and I believe she loves me, but she is not sure. She won't give me a definite answer yet as to whether she loves me enough to settle it for life. Of course I can't even think about getting married for three or four years anyway." A week or two later they had gone to a Negro church and on the way back stopped to buy ice cream cones. Emily said: "I have something to tell you. I want to say 'yes' to your letter last summer."

He could not afford a ring yet, but their friends understood and rejoiced. Emily encouraged Billy to study and think. He began to settle down.

At this time an even stronger influence began to shape him. Temple Terrace had become a vacation attraction to prominent evangelicals from North and South, whom Dr. Watson would invite to lecture to his Bible conferences for a small fee and their board and lodging. Billy had the inestimable benefit of rubbing the shoulders (or at least wiping the boots) of the great. He listened attentively as Gypsy Smith and Homer Rodeheaver, who had been song leader to Billy Sunday, described the great days now gone when thousands flocked to mass meetings. W. B. Riley of Minneapolis (name and place being then of no significance to Billy Graham) would discourse on the grievous decline of religion in America—church budgets low, church buildings emptying, church preaching blunted and confused. The veteran William Evans, giving Billy a whole dollar for carrying his bags, reminisced about D. L. Moody who had brought him into the ministry. These old stalwarts who had seen the fires die down had one theme: we need a prophet. We need a man to call America back to God.

A "tremendous burden" began to weigh on Billy Graham. On

walks at night across the golf course and along the open streets, laid out for housing estates never built, he faced his future. He believed he would not make a preacher: he was too poorly educated. Yet he began to sense an unmistakable call. Praying aloud as he walked the empty countryside he answered that call in Moses' words at the burning bush: "They will not believe me, nor hearken unto my voice. . . . I am not eloquent."

During these days the president's secretary, Brunette Brock, would often say, "Billy, God has called you to preach." In the night walks alone he tussled with excuses. His indifferent background would indeed keep him a mediocre preacher "somewhere out in the sticks." Yet any sacrifice appeared trivial beside Christ's sufferings or the world's needs. As for eloquence, the Lord had told Moses, "Go, and I will be with thy mouth, and teach thee what thou shalt say." Billy hesitated because for him the call was absolute. If he accepted, he must henceforth have no other ambition, no other occupation but the proclaiming of God's message, everywhere, to everybody, always. God was already his passion. "I can truly say," he had written home, "I love Him, the Lord Jesus, better every day." When driving with a fellow student Billy had often slipped out at a filling station to testify to the garage hand: "Mister, I want to tell you what happened to me back in Charlotte a few years ago. . . ." This had not implied intention to devote his life to the ministry.

Once the call was accepted, half measures would be impossible. One night in March 1938 Billy Graham returned from his walk and reached the eighteenth green immediately before the school's front door. "The trees were loaded with Spanish moss, and in the moonlight it was like a fairyland." He sat down on the edge of the green, looking up at the moon and stars, aware of a warm breeze from the south. The tension snapped. "I remember getting on my knees and saying, 'O God, if you want me to preach, I will do it.' Tears streamed down my cheeks as I made this great surrender to become an ambassador for Jesus Christ."

In the days following, "I used to walk those empty streets in Temple Terrace praying. I would pray sometimes three or four hours at a stretch. And then," he recalled a quarter of a century after, "in the most unusual way I used to have the strangest glimpses of these great crowds that I now preach to." He certainly did not see himself as the preacher, and scarcely believed great crowds would ever come together again to hear the Gospel, but the daydreams or visions flashed across his consciousness. "I think I saw myself as participating in some way in what Billy Sunday and D. L. Moody had witnessed—big stadiums, big meetings."

For himself, "I felt something like Jeremiah when he said, 'I am a child.' But I also heard the still, small voice of God saying, 'Be not afraid, for I am with thee to deliver thee.'"

He wanted a seal to his call. A Mr. Corwin, an elderly part-time faculty member who could speak seven languages and ran a little mission in the Spanish area, would choose a student helper for each Sunday, but never Billy. Despite prayer to God and judicious placing of himself in Corwin's eye, week after week passed until Billy grew discouraged, even enough to doubt his call. One Saturday he was cutting grass by the Hillsboro River and saw old Corwin ambling around the main house. Billy dropped on his knees behind a bush, "Dear Lord," he prayed, "please let me preach at his mission tomorrow." He looked up and saw Corwin heading in his direction.

Early in May, Emily told Billy that she was again uncertain whether they were meant for each other, and asked him to pray.

In a basement room, every day for a quarter of an hour, Billy would pray that they should marry—if, and only if, it were God's will. Emotional suspense bred spiritual development, for hitherto he had seldom related prayer to specific matters, as distinct from the wide sweeping vistas of the world's need; never before had he seen such answers.

Emily found herself deeper in love with Charles Massey, a senior classman about to graduate, whom Billy admired. Before Class Night in May 1938 all the boys ordered from Larson the florist a twenty-five-cent corsage for his girl. Billy exclaimed: "I'll buy a fifty-cent one. Emily must have the best."

Emily did not wear it.

During the party she asked Billy outside. They sat on one of the swings on the riverside, and she told him gently that she was going to marry Charles.

They parted friends. Billy sought John Minder, who consoled him by the scripture verse, "The God of all comfort comforteth us in all our tribulation, that we may be able to comfort them which are in any trouble." Billy bravely rejoined the social evening. The other students saw him undimmed in gaiety and zest. He remained close friends with Charles and Emily, attending the wedding and keeping touch through the years as Charles Massey rose to distinction in the Army chaplaincy.

"One of two things can happen in a time like that. You can resist and become bitter, or you can let God break you. And I determined to let God have His way."

---

3 · The Girl from China

Old timers say that last night's meeting in East Palatka was the greatest meeting of the history of the church. Rev. Cecil Underwood and his Peniel Fellowship Club Choir gave a song service with choruses and guitar duets. Billy Graham, the young 19-year-old student evangelist of the Florida Bible Institute . . . is causing quite a sensation, according to Cecil Underwood. Young Graham does not mince words when he tells church members that they are headed for the same hell as the bootlegger and racketeer unless that they get right and live right, Underwood said.

The faded clippings from Florida reveal the new Billy Graham of the summer of 1938. "I now had a purpose, an objective, a call. That was when the growing up began, and the discipline to study."

At first he had been forced to create most of his opportunities. "I was getting no invitations from anybody to preach. I would take two or three students with me, or somebody that would sing, and go down on a street corner. I couldn't get a church; nobody would take me. I tried to get in at the Sulphur Springs Baptist Church. I asked them to let me preach, and they wouldn't do it. And I went out to a little United Brethren church outside of town that had about seventy-five members and asked them—they didn't have a pastor—if I could preach, and they said, 'No.' So I just went to the streets."

On Sundays he would hold seven or eight street-corner services. Once he began preaching in front of a saloon, full of alcoholics and prostitutes, on Franklin Street, in those days Tampa's worst. "I stood right in the door, preaching to the people sitting at the bar. The barkeeper came out and ordered me away, and I wouldn't go. He just shoved me down, and I half fell and half tripped into the wet street. I got my clothes messed up. I remembered the words of Jesus, and felt that I was suffering for Christ's sake. It was quite tactless the way I went about it, zeal with no knowledge; but those were experiences that helped develop."

Soon Billy secured a regular invitation to the Tampa City Mission. John Minder departed for six weeks in California, leaving Billy in charge of the Tampa Gospel Tabernacle as assistant pastor, where he learned the hard labor of ministry to the poor. He was made a chaplain to the trailer parks, and when the "Tin Can Tourists of the World" rolled into the municipal trailer park on Columbus Drive for their annual convention, Billy was there. He visited the prisoners at the Stockade (Tampa's jail was still a stockade in the old style). "That's where I started my discussion groups. I had them ask me questions. A lot of them I couldn't answer, but I did it deliberately not only to help them, but to try to sharpen my mind."

Billy Graham rose from the ranks, as it were. Most ministers acquire learning and qualification, and then, from the inevitable superiority of pastorate or priesthood, begin to impart. Graham learned to preach while his fund of knowledge was limited. "I had one passion, and that was to win souls. I didn't have a passion to be a great preacher; I had a passion to win souls. I'd never been trained as a public speaker. I had to learn in the best way I knew." His stock of sermons was small, the outlines generally looted from eminent preachers heard or read, but he knew exactly what he would say, to the last word. He did not write them out except in skeleton, but he practiced them, even to cypress swamps and alligators.

He made full use of unrivaled opportunities to hear famous evangelical preachers of different denominations. John Minder noticed some of their gestures and phrases reappearing in Billy (Dr. A. B. Winchester of Toronto used the phrase, "My Bible says. . . ."), but Billy did not model himself deliberately nor attempt to perfect a technique. "It was all unconscious. I wasn't practicing gestures. I was practicing my material, learning my material. I felt I was not prepared to preach a sermon until I had practiced it many, many times." Dr. Watson heard the sound of preaching in a dormitory, and through a door ajar saw Billy with wee Bobby, the Watsons' four-year-old son, a captive audience on the dresser. Billy used the old garage too, and Ponzi Pennington, Billy's roommate that year, sometimes saw fellows creep up "and all of a sudden let out a big shout or an amen in fun. Billy would turn around with that wonderful smile of his and just grin real big at them and go right back to preaching."

He preached too loud. He preached too fast. He dramatized and was dubbed "the preaching windmill." An Episcopal bishop wandering unawares into Tampa Tabernacle might have withdrawn hurriedly, but the tramps, alcoholics, prisoners, and the northern winter visitors in the trailer parks knew what Billy meant.

Apart from muddled pronunciation (such as referring to the writing on the wall at Belshazzar's feast as "Meany, Meany, Tickle,

Upsharn") many of his mistakes were recognized only in retrospect. "I didn't relate my message sufficiently to social concerns and every-day life," he wrote in 1965. "I placed too much emphasis on judgment and hell. I didn't temper my message with love as much as I should have." But a contemporary clipping shows that God's love was the theme of his sermon on hell: "The road to hell is blocked with many Godly interferences," Billy Graham told a congregation. Speaking on the theme of God's Blockade, the young student told the people, "If you go to hell, it will be your own deliberate choice, as God is doing His best to keep you out of there. Before a person can sink there," he declared, "he must climb over the Bible, a mother's influence in prayer, the Holy Spirit, the mountain of reason, and the Cross of Christ."

Graham's chief fault in Florida was his lack of balance. He practiced and prayed so hard by day that he mounted an evening pulpit worn out. His mind refused to relax at night. Light sleeping became the insomnia which has troubled him ever since.

But nothing made Graham grumpy. "He thoroughly enjoyed living," is the memory of Pleasant Cavanaugh, Emily's younger sister. He was not considered the school's outstanding student, but a natural leader. One of his Florida contemporaries puts it charmingly: "He could walk into a crowd, and within a few seconds it seemed that every eye would be upon him. Whereas I could walk through the crowd and step on their toes or kick their shins and no one would ever notice me!"

While war was coming to Europe far away, Billy Graham was in growing demand at obscure churches and chapels in different parts of Florida. To get around he bought with a loan from kindly Mr. Furstenberger an ancient Chevrolet coupé, and when too shaken and sore after a ride to Miami bought a five-year-old Oldsmobile before fully paying off the loan! His aim, whether preaching or speaking with individuals, was not to promote an idea but to bring them to know the living Christ. Dedication to a cause or an idea might have hardened or narrowed Billy Graham; dedication to a Person sweetened him.

The first time he himself gave the "invitation" or altar call (which the pastor of a church does normally) was at Venice on the Gulf shore, in the only church, a converted meat market. The parents of a girl at the Bible Institute had telephoned for a supply preacher and Graham was sent, with Ponzi Pennington to sing. Their morning service seemed to them sluggish, so the two boys spent the afternoon praying on the dirt floor of the garage at their hosts', who were out encouraging the local youths to attend.

The church that evening was packed with nearly a hundred people. Billy thought his sermon indifferent, but when he gave the invitation, thirty-two young men and women came forward. Billy was astonished —yet paradoxically he had expected it. The superintendent of the Sunday school, Mr. Baird, remarked afterward, "There's a young man who is going to be known around the world!" [1]

On the way back to Tampa, "every mile in the old car was a mile of rejoicing and praising God." "Ponzi," said Billy, "I've learned my greatest lesson. It's not by power or might or any fancy sermon, it's wholly and completely the work of the Holy Spirit."

He was always learning, reaching forward. The custom in the Christian and Missionary Alliance is for the pastor at the close of a service to invite anyone with a problem, or who wants to pray, especially to come forward to the altar. At Tampa Tabernacle, when Minder preached, Billy Graham on many occasions came forward. Sometimes he would stay two or three hours with others so moved. Several times he and a group of students prayed right through the night.

Because of this spiritual intensity, wedded to an outstanding gift for communicating the Gospel, Graham was in danger of not developing into a fully rounded personality. One lifeline to a wider understanding was his interest in current affairs; he was never a Christian who would not read a newspaper. Another lifeline was his zest for educating himself, not only in history. It was at Florida that he first bought a set of encyclopedias—an old set for three or four dollars—and acquired the habit of reading them through. If not a scholar's way, it laid one of the foundations of his inexhaustible fund of facts.

Billy in truth needed a more substantial education. Early in 1940, among the winter visitors to Temple Terrace were the mother of Dr. V. Raymond Edman, the newly appointed president of Wheaton College near Chicago; her other son, Elmer, a wholesale coal merchant; and an attorney, Paul Fisher, brother of the chairman of Wheaton's board of trustees. Billy Graham's mother knew all about Wheaton, the long-established college with high academic reputation and strong

---

[1] By a nice coincidence, sixteen years later Baird's son-in-law, Sergeant Winters, found himself assigned by the U.S. Army Air Force to be orderly to Billy Graham when he preached at the American bases in Britain at the time of the London Crusade.

Christian principles, and had prayed that he should enroll there, if the family purse allowed.

One day the Wheaton men took Billy to caddy for them on the golf course. During the round Fisher told him he was a good preacher who needed more education, and offered to pay board and lodging at Wheaton for a year. Elmer Edman threw in a year's tuition, and when the president of Wheaton next saw his mother he was commanded, "I met all the students, but one was outstanding. He wants to come to Wheaton, you'll take him won't you!" Raymond Edman recalls it "very vividly, she was so eager." And, despite contrary advice from some of his friends, so was Billy: "The more I prayed, the more I was certain that God was leading, and that I must further my education at all costs."

The Florida Bible Institute had given him a first-rate grounding in Bible knowledge. As he told the students years later, when it had become Trinity College and moved to Clearwater, it was there he "learned the importance of the Bible and came to believe with all my heart in its full inspiration. It became a rapier and a sword in my hand that I have used as a hammer as well as a sword to break open the hearts of men and to direct them to the Lord Jesus Christ."

Florida had been also an academic bridge, for had Billy Graham attempted to enter Wheaton straight from high school, he would have failed. But a Bible Institute, however efficient, did not offer the courses which gave him, on transferring, enough credits to enroll as a sophomore at an accredited institution. Billy's disappointment at being accepted only as a freshman was inevitable.

But he would enter Wheaton an ordained minister. In 1939, with his parents' approval, Billy Graham had become a Southern Baptist. He was baptized by immersion, in Silver Lake near Palatka, by Cecil Underwood on December 4, 1938, and ordained in 1939 by the St. John's Association at Peniel, Underwood's white-painted clapboard church under the cedar trees between Silver Lake and Lake Rosie. Woodrow Flynn, now a leading Southern Baptist, preached the sermon.

The Florida years ended in May 1940. At graduation the class valedictorian, Vera Resue, her mind on the war and the spiritual darkness engulfing the world, and without thought of an individual, uttered words which years afterward were seen to be prophetic. At each critical epoch of the church, she said, God has "a chosen human instrument to shine forth His light in the darkness. Men like Luther, John and Charles Wesley, Moody and others who were ordinary men, but men who heard the voice of God. . . . It has been said that Luther revolutionized the world. It was not he but Christ working through him. The time is ripe for another Luther, Wesley, Moody. There is room for another name in this list."

When Billy wrote to Dr. Watson from Wheaton on September 18, 1940, "I am getting adjusted rather slowly here, as it is a new and strange place," he was typing a masterly understatement.

Wheaton was not quite his first penetration north of the Mason-Dixon line, for a month earlier he and Ponzi had rattled and punctured their way to York in Pennsylvania to conduct a mission for a pastor who regularly called for Temple Terrace students.[1]

Billy found that York barely could interpret a Carolina tongue or idiom. So at Wheaton. The Yankee accent; the harsher climate in a land without mountains or palms; the way the North cooked beans and served too much lamb and too little seasoning; the difficult drop from admired senior to insignificant freshman although almost twenty-two; and the transition from a closeknit community to a campus of about a thousand, as it then stood. He nearly fled. It is intriguing to reflect how different his life would have been had he done so.

A brown-haired, hazel-eyed girl of twenty, a second-year student at Wheaton, was in the entrance to East Blanchard Hall in the fall of 1940 when she noticed a blond fellow whom she did not know running down the steps. "He was tall and lanky and just dashed past," and she thought, "There's a young man who knows where he's going!"

The father of one of her friends had told her to keep an eye out for a young minister, a remarkable preacher called Billy Graham coming to campus, but she had not met him. Some days later she was one of a group of students meeting for prayer before going out to teach Sunday school, or for similar work. They divided into small parties in the lobby of Williston Hall and went into different rooms. "We would take turns praying, and all of a sudden I heard a voice from the next room. I had never heard anyone pray like it before. I knew that someone was talking to God. I sensed that here was a man that knew God in a very unusual way."

Billy Graham, to work his way through Wheaton (his father paid part of the second- and third-year fees, but considered he should sup-

[1] Rev. Ralph Boyer of York Gospel Center, who put out bills: "Here is youth aflame for God! Evangelist Billy Graham, Charlotte, N.C., a great Gospel preacher at 21."

port himself, and Chicago prices were high) had joined Johnny Streater, a senior who ran an aged truck which Dr. Edman says "made more racket than anything else round here." As they moved a load of old bottles or furniture, Streater announced that he was about to introduce Billy to the second nicest girl on the campus—the first, of course, being his own future wife. When he had described the virtues of Ruth Bell, "Billy was sitting on the edge of the seat." The introduction was effected in the lobby of Williston Hall outside the college cafeteria. Billy fell in love at first sight.

Ruth and Billy went together to the glee club's *Messiah* on a snowy Sunday afternoon and afterward to supper at Professor Lane's. Billy "just could not believe anyone could be so beautiful and so sweet." They stood a long time talking beside a tree near the college entrance. Billy wrote to his mother that this was the girl he would marry. Ruth had not fallen in love with Bill, as she always calls him; yet that very first Sunday night she knelt at her bedside in wordless prayer and "told the Lord that if I could spend the rest of my life serving Him with Bill, I would consider it the greatest privilege imaginable."

Ruth McCue Bell was born of Virginia parents in North China where her father, a Presbyterian surgeon, had helped build and develop a substantial missionary hospital despite civil wars and Japanese occupation. Dr. Bell describes his daughter in childhood as "an interesting mixture of deep spirituality and mischievous fun." The second of three sisters, with a younger brother, she had spent most of her life in the Orient. Her mother "always hoped we wouldn't look like the pickings from a missionary barrel," and taught her to make her own clothes but not to cook.

At Wheaton, which she entered in 1939, the ladies of the faculty thought the world of her.[1]

Ruth had many admirers. That first Sunday night, back at Professor Gerstung's home where he roomed, Billy Graham slumped in a chair and "bemoaned the fact (Gerstung recalls) that he had no chance with Ruth because he had so little to commend him."

Ruth soon thought otherwise. "There was a seriousness about him; there was a depth. He was much older in every way than the other students on the campus, not just in age. He was a mature man; he

---

[1] Her housemother, Julia Scott, wrote of her in 1943: "Very attractive, beautiful to look at and excellent taste in dress. The most beautiful Christian character of any young person I have ever known. And she has the intellectual qualities to make a success in any work she would choose to undertake. She ranks very high in the qualities of poise, forcefulness, and courtesy."

was a man who knew God; he was a man who had a purpose, a dedication in life; he knew where he was going. He wanted to please God more than any man I'd ever met." She recognized that he was a very intelligent man, though in no sense an "egghead." Her one reservation was that, though there was plenty of fun in his personality, "he was so very serious about life in general. He didn't have enough time to go to ball games. Every date we had was to a preaching service of some kind. Yet for all his terrific dedication and drive there was a winsomeness about him, and a consideration for other people, which I found very endearing."

Love grew, but there was one snag: a conflict of vocation. Ruth's ambition was to be a pioneer missionary in western China with the hope of entering Tibet, and for this she was prepared to renounce romance. Billy, though closely interested in foreign missions and ready to serve overseas, had no indication that God called him to be a missionary. He believed that Ruth was essentially a homemaker, not a pioneer, for which she had not the stamina. And he knew that when she married, it would be to him. He bided his time. The Bells returned on furlough in the spring of 1941. In the summer Ruth and Billy became engaged.

Back at Wheaton in the fall, Ruth told Billy that she was unsure after all. She feared that her desire to be his wife denied a clear missionary call, unless he too were bound for Tibet. "He went and prayed about the mission field, and he just had no leading whatsoever. Finally he said, 'Well, do you think God brought us together?' —and I had to admit I felt God had." Billy pointed out that the Bible teaches that the husband is head of the wife: "The Lord leads me and you follow." Ruth agreed, in faith.

Ruth more than anyone broadened Graham's mind. She had no need to polish his manners or graces, as D. L. Moody's were polished by his wife, but she was cultured, traveled, with a love of art and literature. She saved his seriousness from degenerating into stuffy solemnity, and preserved from extinction the light touch, the slice of small boy. Moreover Ruth and her family, loyal Presbyterians, eased Billy Graham from his unspoken conviction that a vigorous Scriptural faith could not dwell within the great denominations.

The Bells underlined the lesson of Wheaton College that any minister who was a strong evangelical should focus his vision on the entire horizon of American Christianity.

4 · *Songs in the Night*

Billy Graham expected to go on to theological seminary, and therefore chose a nontheological subject as his major at Wheaton. Anthropology was a new, exciting course under an able professor, Alexander Grigolia, and Graham had long been fascinated by the creation and antiquity of man. Anthropology would broaden his range and provide a background if, after all, he went abroad as a missionary.

Despite his indifferent early education he made good grades in the eighties.[1] He might have made the honor roll had not his life again taken an unusual turn.

Dr. Edman wished to be relieved of his part-time pastorate of the United Gospel Tabernacle of Wheaton and Glen Ellyn, a small independent church. It had been served previously by student pastors, and on his recommendation the church council in July 1941 offered it to Billy Graham, who was spending his vacation preaching in youth crusades in Florida.

The Tabernacle hired a small hall for Sunday services and a Wednesday night prayer meeting. Virtually no more than a preaching center, it was the church of many students and professors. In the words of Dr. Russell Mixter, then associate professor of zoology, Graham's delivery was "rapid, earnest, forceful, simple, a very direct approach. He had a message he wanted to get across, and it came right through without hesitation and stumbling." Undoubtedly there were extravagances, mispronunciations, a touch of Mordecai Ham and the sawdust trail. But the hall was always packed, for Ruth's memory, endorsed by that of Wheaton contemporaries, is that "you weren't impressed with his earnestness, you weren't impressed by his gestures. You were impressed that there was Someone speaking to you beside Bill. There was another voice than his."

The Tabernacle, and later his presidency of the Christian Student Council, interfered with studies. On Monday mornings he would sometimes doze in class and Professor Grigolia would murmur in his rich Russian accent, "Do not disturb dear Billy, he's tired in God's service!"

Jimmy Johnson had now entered Wheaton, for though thirty

[1] In the first article Billy Graham ever wrote for publication, submitted from Wheaton and rejected by *Moody Monthly,* he spelled "courage" as it is pronounced in North Carolina, *courge!*

years old he saw the need of the education and accredited degree which Bob Jones College had not provided: Grady Wilson had also broken with Dr. Bob and spent a year at Wheaton. Johnson and Billy were roommates for a time. Their room was a glorious muddle. The Gerstungs remember that when Billy left them, "We picked up about a washbasket of things that he had forgotten" (earliest record of a weakness known to hotels around the world). Johnson was one of the first to believe that Billy Graham had an appointment with greatness somewhere. Little things suggested it: the speed of his mind, a splendid unconcern with trivialities, and a little phrase he used if involved in argument or pointless activity, "Well, I'm going on. Over and over I've heard Billy say, 'I'm going on.' "

Graham thirsted for learning. He became one of the circle of the hospitable, wealthy Professor Mortimer Lane, a much-traveled former public servant, who combined knowledge of the Bible with a gift for imparting an understanding of politics and economics. Billy became fascinated by the American political and economic scene. As the Bells broadened Billy's understanding of the Church, so the Lanes helped him to see the Christian life in a world setting. The Lanes were Plymouth Brethren, the first Billy had met. On Sunday mornings before preaching at the Tabernacle he would go to the Lane home for the Brethren assembly and breaking of bread. He absorbed much from the Brethren.

After Pearl Harbor he offered himself as an Army chaplain. He was told to finish college, and his professors persuaded him not to volunteer for combat duty. The Army required him, after graduation, to do a year at seminary or in a pastorate to qualify as a chaplain.

Western Springs was a typical semi-rural, high middle-class suburb of Chicago: straight streets, houses with unfenced lawns, and ten or more places of worship including a well-supported Methodist center —and one mortgage-ridden Baptist church in a basement.

The chairman of the board of deacons was a vigorous, dark-haired man in his thirties, Robert Van Kampen, president of Hitchcock, the industrial publishing company. Lecturing at Wheaton College in February 1943, he noticed a student in front in a neat suit and large Lil' Abner shoes. Kampen's casual glance led in time to an invitation to Graham to be pastor immediately on graduation, at $45 a week. Since Western Springs would provide the opportunity for postgraduate work in anthropology at Chicago University as well as the year's pastorate required by the Army, Billy Graham accepted—

without consulting Ruth, to her considerable indignation, for she felt that any decision vitally affecting their lives should be discussed and prayed about together. Billy was suitably repentant.

They were married on Friday, August 13, 1943, at Montreat, the Presbyterian conference center in the mountains of North Carolina where the Bells had settled when the war prevented their return to China. The Grahams had a week's honeymoon in a room rented for $2 a day in a cottage at Blowing Rock, high in the Blue Ridge Mountains. Then they returned to Illinois and made their home in a four-room apartment in Hinsdale, a neighboring community, since they could find nowhere in Western Springs. They were one block from the main line of the Burlington Railroad, and for the first week every train sounded as if it were going straight through the living room.

Billy uncomplainingly endured Ruth's early adventures in cookery; the Grahams did not eat out as frequently as their neighbors but would save up and enjoy an occasional splurge at a restaurant. Ruth had to endure the muddle on Billy's desk and his habit (not yet cured) of treating the top of the bathroom door as a towel rack. They differed in temperament and in many ideas. "I think it is very important," Ruth commented long after, "for young couples to disagree, but to learn to disagree pleasantly and to respect one another's opinions. If you agree on everything, there's not going to be much growth for either one. . . . I don't think happy marriages are ever accidental. They are the result of good, hard work."

The biggest disagreement in those early months was over Ruth's being a Presbyterian. The church council assented to the Graham's church being called "The Village Church" with an appeal wider than to the very few Baptists of Western Springs, yet many of Billy's friends urged Ruth to be rebaptized by immersion. After studying the Scriptures she declined, despite pressure, and her refusal would in time considerably aid Graham's ability to work with men and women of different denominations.

Billy was still half a bachelor, loving to spend hours picking the brains of fellow preachers over coffee when he ought to have been home. But the Grahams' love for one another fast grew deep and abiding.

The church people enjoyed his sermons, were amused by the loud socks and ties, gratified by Ruth's poise and smartness despite a restricted wardrobe. Billy organized house-to-house calls on uncommitted residents, sought out storekeepers, especially those that other ministers preferred not to be seen with. Church membership slowly rose. With Bob Van Kampen he launched the Western Suburban Professional Men's Club, meeting over dinner seven times a winter in a charming eating place, The Spinning Wheel, to which, audaciously, Graham personally persuaded business executives of highest rank and tightest schedules to come. Soon he had more than three hundred men dining to listen to an evangelistic speaker.

He leaped to invitations to preach in distant towns, even if once by mistake he dropped in the plate his last $10 bill. When he got home Ruth told him roundly that the Lord would only give him credit for the one dollar he had intended.

Despite his activity, in the midst of a world war Western Springs seemed trivial. Graham waited impatiently for his chaplaincy commission.

And then, early in October 1943, came a telephone call from Torrey Johnson, pastor of a flourishing church, professor of New Testament Greek at Northern Baptist Seminary, and best known around Chicago for his broadcasts. Billy, almost not believing his ears, heard the suggestion that he and The Village Church take over one of Johnson's programs, *Songs in the Night*—forty-five minutes of preaching and singing carried live by one of Chicago's most powerful commercial stations from 10:15 P.M. each Sunday.

The cost would be over $100 weekly, and the station required an initial contract for thirteen weeks. The pledged income of The Village Church was $86.50 a week. The deacons were thus rather staggered. But as one of them says, Billy "had the gift of getting people to respond in faith," and in the three months before *Songs in the Night* became theirs, The Village Church people raised among themselves enough for about five broadcasts.

Billy now flew high. In Chicago lived a Canadian-born bass baritone of thirty-seven named George Beverly Shea, famous as Christian soloist and broadcaster, especially on the American Broadcasting Company's *Club Time,* a program of hymns. One of his own compositions, "I'd Rather Have Jesus," was already popular. Billy went to the radio station where Shea was a program manager and announcer and received a polite brush-off from the receptionist. Beverly Shea, modest and understanding, probably would have agreed to an appointment if asked, but Billy, thwarted, preferred the direct approach. After turning to go out he thought, "No, I've come to see him. I'm going to see him." And he walked straight in.

Beverly Shea was gracious and guarded, Billy persistent. *Songs in the Night,* with Beverly Shea, came on the air from Western Springs in January 1944.

Ruth helped with the scripts, Bev rigged up colored lights over the table where Billy sat. Young people from all over the Chicago area would hurry out after their own evening church services to see and hear Beverly Shea in person. Letters came, money came, covering not only the broadcast but enabling Billy solemnly to burn the mortgage of the church in a pie plate. Billy's Southern accent, now deliberately tamed, was an immediate hit with the Yankees. And he preached in the way that was to become specially his: against a backdrop of the latest news and world events he would proclaim the urgent relevance of Christ in such manner that the listener longed to know Him. He urged immediate decision, but did not yet sign off with his very own phrase: "May the Lord bless you real good."

In the spring of 1944, Torrey Johnson offered an even greater opportunity.

Johnson was concerned about the hundreds of servicemen who swept into Chicago every weekend, tough, cynical, sex-starved, indifferent to God and man. On the last Saturday night of April 1944 he found an answer. He was present in First Baptist Church at Minneapolis, where a thirty-year-old businessman named George M. Wilson had organized a "Youth for Christ Rally," in the belief that the Gospel could reach servicemen, and unchurched civilians too, if clean excitement was linked with an uncompromising Christian message. Johnson immediately formed "Chicagoland's Youth for Christ" and booked the Orchestra Hall, with three thousand seats, next door to the U.S.O. Center, for twenty-one Saturday nights. Most of Chicago rated him foolish: open religious rallies of such size had been unknown for years; several leading evangelists had met dismal failure in wartime Chicago; church attendance had continued to slide, and the newspapers were bored by religion.

For preacher at his opening rally Johnson chose Billy Graham. "I'll never know why," says Graham. "I was only one year out of college." The answer is simple. Johnson could have had any famous preacher from the city or afar, but wished to work with the circle of young ministers who shared his vision and had instinctive understanding of their generation. They were all Chicago men except North Carolinian Billy, but Johnson had not the slightest doubt that for an evangelistic sermon to youth, Billy Graham had no equal.

Johnson saw him "thrilled at the prospect but dreadfully afraid he might fail." On Saturday evening, May 20, 1944, they gathered in the stage room of Orchestra Hall, "waiting, hoping, praying, wanting to believe that there would be people." Billy paced up and down, biting his nails, palms sticky, throat dry, "the worst fit of stage fright of my life." They prayed together and walked onto the stage. With one consent they kept their eyes to the stalls, daring to hope that these at least would be full. They glanced higher and saw the lower balcony full too; and, to their wonder, the upper. Only the high "peanut gallery" was thin. Someone reckoned a total of 2,800, mostly service personnel, were present.

After a swift program of songs and instrumental music, community singing, Bible reading and prayer, Billy began to preach. Words came tumbling. "As my nerves relaxed, I felt I was merely a mouthpiece and soon became unaware of the audience." At the invitation to commit their lives, Billy marveled to see forty-two people come forward, a high number for the times.

All were spoken to individually, but nobody knew how to ensure their grafting into the life of local churches, civil or military.

For their twenty-first rally Youth for Christ took a stadium seating 20,000 and then began a new series in the largest Chicago church. Torrey Johnson renewed touch with George Wilson in Minneapolis, contacted Jack Wyrtzen's Word of Life in New York, and started or fostered Saturday night rallies in city after city. Billy Graham made his first airplane journey, to Detroit, as substitute for Johnson.

In October Graham was commissioned a second lieutenant in the United States Army, with orders to await entry to a chaplains' training course at Harvard Divinity School. Then, to his embarrassment as a commissioned officer aged twenty-two, he developed mumps.

Had it not been for mumps, Billy Graham would have disappeared into the Army. The mumps took the most virulent and painful form, his temperature raged and one night, as he became delirious, Ruth thought him dying. He was in bed six weeks, emerging thin as a lath, and thankful for a gift, from a listener, of $100 to go to Florida.

Torrey Johnson was in Florida too. At Miami, out in a fishing boat under the Florida sun which Billy so loved, Torrey outlined in detail a plan they had already discussed tentatively: the coordinating of Saturday night rallies, present and future, to capture and inspire American youth as no previous evangelistic movement had done. Johnson saw it as a spearhead of return to a forthright Christianity —in America, Canada, the world.

Until Billy's mumps Johnson had been uncertain how to proceed, for he himself lacked time. As the Chaplain Corps would relegate a convalescent to a desk, he proposed that Billy resign his commission and his church, and with such funds as Johnson could raise, become the first full-time organizer and evangelist of Youth for Christ. To ask for a discharge before serving a day, in wartime, was a serious step. But a desk almost certainly would be Graham's fate, whereas in the Saturday rallies he had been ministering to hundreds of servicemen. He was persuaded he could do more for America and for the war effort through Youth for Christ.

5 · *Geared to the Times*

The importance in American church history of the swift, nationwide rise of Youth for Christ at the close of the Second World War has not yet been adequately recognized. Clergy feared that it might divert their youth from regular church life, resented its vigor, mistrusted its methods, many of which in the end they adopted or adapted unacknowledged.

The Saturday night rallies had to be bright. They were not meant to be like Sunday morning services. "Saturday night," writes George Wilson, "of necessity had bright soloists, choirs, ensembles, bands, music, spotlights." In Minneapolis George Wilson even organized a sonata for no less than one hundred pianos, crashing away in four parts in a packed auditorium after weeks of practice, and followed by a plain, direct sermon from Billy Sunday's old song leader, Homer Rodeheaver. Youth for Christ leaders, Billy included, wore loud hand-painted ties and bright suits, that all the world might know Christianity to be no dreary faith. Clothes and excitements were essentially contemporary American, a counterpart to the organized cheers and chants of American college football, the marching bands and baton-twirlings at half-time.

The motto was "Geared to the Times, Anchored to the Rock." At a time when denominational leaders were convinced that the great Christian doctrines no longer might be preached with emphasis, Youth for Christ demonstrated the contrary. Young men and women responded to the unashamed proclamation of a Christ who worked miracles, shed His blood on the Cross, rose bodily from the dead, and would transform the lives of any who accepted Him. The Bible became again, not a document to be mutilated or a set of propositions to be defended, but a living Word.

Torrey Johnson believed in the combination of efficient organization and daring faith. He planned big, did not doubt that God would "undertake in miraculous ways regarding weather, money, crowds, regarding the help you need to get the job done." He was prepared to act when consequences were obscure, and could keep his head when flooded by success. Graham was equally a pioneer. In 1945 and 1946 he traveled nearly every state of the Union and every province of Canada. The Graham purse did not permit Ruth to come. Furthermore they were expecting their first child, Virginia, always known by the Chinese name of Gigi ("Sister"), who arrived on September 21, 1945. They now lived with the Bells at Montreat.

During his absences Billy and Ruth missed each other terribly. It was in truth far harder on the wife left behind. But a missionary childhood had prepared her for frequent goodbyes, and if the husband often extended his schedule when the wife expected him home, Ruth understood and encouraged.

Rally organizers soon learned to cut back on the noise and the glamor and the lights if Billy Graham were the preacher. Leighton Ford, then a high-school student at Chatham, Ontario, and director of the local Youth for Christ, and now Billy's brother-in-law and on the Graham Team, brought in musical groups from miles around. Billy said the choice must be made: a long musical program meant a short sermon, "and if I preach short we're not going to do the job of winning souls."

"We had a big crowd on an icy night," recalls Leighton, "and Billy preached with power, so we expected a great response from the young people. But it was very small. Only one or two people came forward, and I was brokenhearted. Billy put his hand on my shoulder, and he said, 'Leighton, God always blesses a man who has a burden for souls. He's given you a burden, and He's going to bless you in it.'"

At the end of the war Torrey Johnson invited Graham to join him on a whirlwind tour to launch Youth for Christ in Europe. With them would go three others: Stratton Shufelt, the Chicago singer; Charles Templeton, a former newspaper cartoonist and the Toronto director of Youth for Christ.) An artist to his finger tips, with an impressive personality, Templeton's formal education had been indifferent but he was thoroughly alert intellectually. "Charles Templeton," Graham says, "helped me tremendously to broaden my whole vision.")

The third was Wesley Hartzell, a journalist on William Randolph Hearst's *Chicago's American* (and now editor of the Sunday edition). Hearst had become interested in Youth for Christ, which flourished exceedingly in his home city of Los Angeles, and promoted it by several editorials in his national chain of newspapers, not for religious reasons but because it provided moral standards for youth and was an answer to the growing problem of juvenile delinquency. Hearst approved that Hartzell's Articles on the European tour should be handled by International News Service, which reached into nearly all American cities and large towns.

The Youth for Christ team decided, adventurously for 1945, to fly. Visas and passages were so scarce it was not until March 18, 1946, that they left, after a farewell rally at Olympia Stadium, Detroit. The stadium holds 16,000 and was full. Billy Graham was the preacher. The audience was his largest until then—a remarkable turnout for the times.

The first episode of the overseas tour proved to be pure comic opera.

The DC4 was diverted by bad weather to the American Air Force base of Stevensville in Newfoundland, where the social director for the base gladly agreed to announce a late night show, since the sight of men and women passengers convinced her that Johnson led a vaudeville troupe. Johnson did not disabuse her (the opportunity for preaching was too good), nor warn the others of possible misunderstanding. A packed theater at 11 P.M. whistled and cheered and roared at Templeton's stories, and liked Shufelt's Negro spiritual. The next item, Johnson, brought shouts of "Where are the girls?" "Show us the legs!" The audience booed and hooted when Shufelt sang again, until Chuck Templeton "knew I had to go back on, tell some more stories and call on Billy to give a brief speech. . . . We had a brief prayer together, because I was throwing Billy to the wolves."

Billy's apology and testimony calmed them slightly. The base commander, in a rage, nearly put the four in the cells, and they were only rescued from grounding next day, to await formal inquiry, by Hartzell's intervention. Billy and Chuck went for a walk in the night "and talked about what fools we sometimes were in our zeal."

In London Tom Rees, a layman who before hearing of Torrey Johnson had started rallies under the slogan, "Britain's Youth for

Christ," had persuaded some sixty clergy and laymen to a dinner of welcome at the Bonnington Hotel in Bloomsbury.

Bad luck dogged them still. Fog diverted the plane to Scotland. The team reached London by train after the dinner had been eaten, and at the station they saw one solitary Anglican vicar advance smiling toward them: Tom Livermore, who had been told by a former parishioner now in Toronto that London's youth needed a man called Billy Graham. Rees introduced the team to the patient dinner guests. Afterward he admired Billy's hand-painted tie. "You like it, *Dr. Rees? It's yours!*" cried Billy, and ripped it off his neck in front of the already overwhelmed English.

The first public meeting took place on March 24 in half-devastated Manchester,[1] where the medium-sized Houldsworth Hall was filled. Billy preached for more than one hour. Of the fifty young people who filed onto the platform after the invitation, a soldier said, "It was the first time I went to a religious meeting voluntarily. When I was at Dunkirk I prayed hard, but forgot religion afterwards."

The Americans' blend of seriousness and boyishness as they rushed through England, Scotland and Ireland in three weeks left hosts rather at a loss. A younger nonconformist and a veteran Anglican, both now warm friends of Billy Graham, recall the immediate impression: "If they had realized," says the nonconformist, "what the war had meant in Britain they wouldn't have come with that happy, cheer-us-up idea. It needed something more solid." And the Anglican: "Though we all loved their keenness and enthusiasm, we were not a bit prepared to follow their very extravagant manner of conducting their services." To some extent they were innocents abroad. British heads shook at a rumor of staying in expensive hotels. The truth was that Templeton and Graham, frozen in their cheap hotel, had hailed a taxi and asked to be taken to a better one. The taxi driver drove them to Park Lane and dropped them at the Dorchester![2] The prices seemed reasonable by American standards. When Torrey Johnson returned to London he wrathfully dragged them away.

Billy was not generally regarded as showing the greatest potential in the team. He preached pell-mell, and the content of his sermons

[1] Their arrival at the railway station was rather a muddle because the committee of local businessmen, in dark suits, looked for clerical collars and black. The Americans, expecting businessmen, looked for light grays and blues. At length in an emptied station "We discovered the businessmen looking like clergy, and they discovered the clergy looking like businessmen!" (Torrey Johnson)

[2] Equivalent of the Waldorf-Astoria.

seemed thin by British standards. He endeared himself as "a man of much courtesy and Christian gentlemanliness," in his informal American way; and whereas the others were considered a trifle blasé and know-all Americans, Billy was soaking up the British scene. As in Florida, Wheaton and across America, "Learning was an insatiable desire with me. I burned to learn, and I felt my limitations of schooling and background so terribly that I determined to try to do all I could through conversations, picking everything I could from everybody." He went to Hyde Park to study the soap-box orators at "Speakers' Corner," and listened frequently to Donald Soper, the Methodist social preacher, and other speakers. Then Billy got a soap box himself. His hearers might be few, but he particularly delighted in engaging with hecklers; as in the jail at Tampa, it sharpened his mind.

Billy Graham fell in love with Britain and longed to see a revival of religion across the land. He had begun with a tendency to dismiss the majority of the clergy as neither geared to the times nor anchored to the Rock, but knew now that a genuine revival must come through the mainstream denominations. Graham determined to work with the ministers; the Southerner who had scarcely met an Episcopalian began even to grasp the peculiar significance of the Church of England.

At Maranatha Bible Conference in Michigan, in early summer of 1946, a man named Clarence Benware heard Graham speak on the British situation and gave him $100, saying, "You must go back." Graham began to think about it and knew whom he would take as a singer.

One year previously he had gone to Ben Lippen Bible Conference in the North Carolina mountains to address a youth night. The conference song leader had left. Graham was offered an athletic Californian, twenty-two years old and on his honeymoon, named Cliff Barrows. He accepted him dubiously under the impression that this was a newly graduated, unknown college kid. Doubts were instantly dispersed when Cliff Barrows' skill and sunny disposition, aided by a fine voice, a trombone, and the piano playing of his wife, Billie, extracted every ounce of song from a delighted audience.

Barrows, son of a farmer in the San Joaquin Valley, had studied sacred music at college. Ordained a Baptist minister in California, Barrows spent nearly a year as an assistant pastor in St. Paul, Minnesota, with special responsibility for song leading and youth. After meeting Billy at Ben Lippen, Cliff worked as song leader for another evangelist.

Cliff and Billie Barrows formed Billy Graham's team for his return to the British Isles. With them for the first six weeks traveled the energetic, shrewd and exuberant George M. Wilson, leaving his Christian bookshop in Minneapolis and his part-time duties as business manager of Northwestern Schools, to complete the advance details of the itinerary, which, like that of the earlier visit, had been arranged by a Scottish Plymouth Brother and evangelist, Gavin Hamilton, who was with them all their time in Britain.

Graham had raised money which seemed enough for six months in Britain, provided they were frugal. Their target was not correspondingly modest: "We are asking God for a thousand souls a month, and a thousand young people to respond to the challenge of the mission field." Graham, this year of 1946, had very nearly gone as a missionary himself, with Dr. N. A. Jepson's China Native Evangelistic Crusade, after coming under the influence of a young man from China named McRoberts. The whole matter of overseas service was thought over and prayed through once again, proof that Billy in 1946 by no means knew yet that his vocation was to be in mass evangelism.

Soon after arriving in England in October, the team visited Tom Rees at Hildenborough Hall for the last night of a young people's conference at which the speaker was Stephen Olford, whose father was English and mother American. Olford was eight months older than Graham, but his British maturity led both to assume the age gap greater. His address on "Be not drunk with wine—but be filled with the Spirit," made Graham walk up to him afterward with, Olford recalls, "that resolute look in his eyes—that determined thrust of the jaw," and ask to know more. They were unable to talk further at the time because the Americans were leaving for London.

The Graham-Barrows meetings began shortly afterward in an obscure small Welsh town called Gorseinon. (George Wilson and Billy were guests of a mining family, the two in one bed, and so cold because of the national fuel rationing that, "We would go to bed right after the meeting with our clothes on." Breakfast every morning was a tomato stuffed with bread. For a whole week they never saw meat.) They worked next in Swansea, then in the mining town of Pontypridd in Taff Vale, only eleven miles from Stephen Olford's home.

Billy was "seeking for more of God with all my heart; and I felt that here was a man that could help me. I could sense that Stephen had something in his life I wanted to capture—he had a dynamic, a

International News Photos

ABOVE. *First picture of Billy Graham, age six months, with his mother, in 1919.* TOP LEFT. *Graduation picture, Sharon High School, Charlotte, North Carolina, 1936.* BOTTOM LEFT. *A junior at Wheaton College, Wheaton, Illinois, 1940.* BELOW. *The wedding day, August 13, 1943.*

ABOVE LEFT. *Billy Graham making a Youth for Christ broadcast with a colleague, Ted Engstrom, later president of Youth for Christ International, now with World Vision.*

ABOVE. *Los Angeles '49. "It was like an immense divine service. The people came because Graham preached with authority — and preached to the times."*

BELOW LEFT. *Billy Graham speaks at a Youth for Christ rally in State Fair Hippodrome, St. Paul, Minnesota.*

RIGHT. *Billy Graham with his parents, William Franklin, Sr., and Morrow Graham, at the Columbia, South Carolina, Crusade, 1950.*

An early photograph of the Team. Standing from left: Grady Wilson, Cliff Barrows, Billy Graham, Bev Shea, George Wilson. Second row: Willis Haymaker, Jerry Beavan, Paul Mickelson, Tedd Smith, Dawson Trotman, Lorne Sanny.

George Beverly Shea, today known as "America's beloved Gospel singer."

Song leader Cliff Barrows (he put away his trombone in 1958).

ABOVE. *From left: the Right Reverend Hugh Gough, Bishop of Barking (now Archbishop of Sydney and Primate of Australia), the late John Foster Dulles and Billy Graham, in London, 1954.* BELOW. *Part of the crowd at Waterloo Station to welcome Billy Graham to London, February 1954. Helping him through the crowd is Donn Moomaw, former all-American football player at U.C.L.A.*

Umbrellas shield inquirers from the rain after invitation at crusade in Sao Paulo, Brazil.

Initial counseling procedures are the same around the world.

Typical of all but two services at Wembley Stadium, London, 1955, is this scene of more than 3,000 persons standing on the wet grass, huddled under the protection of umbrellas to record their decision for Christ.   BELOW. Wembley Stadium, London, 1954.

thrill, an exhilaration about him." For most of two days Graham and Olford were closeted at Pontypridd's hotel with their Bibles open, turning the pages as they studied passages and verses. The first day Billy learned more secrets of the "quiet time." The next, Olford expounded "the fullness of the Holy Spirit in the life of a believer who is willing to bow daily and hourly to the sovereignty of Christ and to the authority of the Word." This lesson was so new to Olford himself that it cascaded out, revealing bright glimpses of the inexhaustible power of the love of God.

His pupil drank it in so avidly that Olford scarcely realized the heights and depths that Billy's spiritual life had reached already. At the close of the second day they prayed, "like Jacob of old laying hold of God," recalls Olford, "crying, 'Lord, I will not let Thee go except Thou bless me,' until we came to a place of rest and praising." And Graham said, "This is a turning point in my life, this will revolutionize my ministry."

It was one of many turning points. Graham—and this is one of the reasons for his outstanding achievement—has never been complacent with the quality of his inner life, or with what he already knows of Christ.

Graham and the Barrows spoke in twenty-seven cities and towns of the British Isles, at 360 meetings, between October 1946 and March 1947. A David and Jonathan bond was forged. They were alike in dedication, in ability to work without stint, but Barrows was not highly strung, and no one ever saw him bite his nails. Young Cliff nursed a secret hope that he too would become an evangelist in his own right, yet consistently pushed Graham forward. The two steadily evolved methods slightly less brash and noisy, although to the British and Irish the very idea of a song leader, especially with a trombone, seemed sensational.

At Birmingham, where in 1946 over 90 per cent of the 1,000,000 citizens were said never to attend a church regularly, adverse reports of Youth for Christ's "sensationalism and showmanship" in America caused cancellation of the city hall. Anglican and nonconformist ministers snubbed the organizing committee, and the first night of a ten-day campaign drew a paltry two or three hundred persons.

Stanley Baker, one of the ministers who had refused to help, a middle-aged Baptist, heard the telephone ring and found himself, as he wrote a week or two later, "linked with a wounded spirit and a pained heart. He wasn't bitter, he didn't chide me; he hadn't one word of a lecture; he merely wondered. . . . Within an hour I sat in Billy's hotel room. . . . His was the nearest spirit to my Lord's I have ever met." Baker at once began telephoning every minister he knew, and Billy paid calls on some twenty clergymen. "I presented the challenge as best I knew how," he wrote on December 5. One by one they began to want to help. To be on the spot he had moved into the Grand Hotel instead of staying on at the home of the industrialist, Alfred Owen, in the suburbs, and several nights two or three ministers remained into the small hours praying with Billy for blessing on Birmingham.

Numbers rose nightly. Owen secured the city hall after all for a packed Saturday and Sunday, when scores came forward, young and old. The Lord Mayor hastily reissued a canceled invitation for tea and was most apologetic. The Bishop of Birmingham, the extreme liberal, Ernest Barnes, invited the twenty-eight-year-old Graham to address a diocesan gathering on "Evangelism in the Twentieth Century."

There followed a nice little bump. On the last night, a midnight train to catch, Billy could not pay a hotel bill inflated by ministerial lunches, teas and coffees. The Grand Hotel demanded cash—Lord Mayor, Bishop and favorable press reports notwithstanding. Billy "in a terrible state" rang up Alfred Owen, who hurried down with Cliff and paid the bill.[1]

The British nation as a whole remained unaware of Graham's existence. The national press ignored him. Many evangelicals remained cautious, but Tom Livermore, the clergyman who had met the train in March, arranged a Graham-Barrows youth campaign centered on his southeast London parish in February 1947. The worst winter for a hundred years combined with the national fuel crisis to produce an icy fog-bound church and darkened streets along which young and old stumbled through the snow. Billy, bounding up the pulpit looking to Londoners like a film star, says Livermore, "had a tremendous appeal to the ignorant and unlettered and the rougher element of the

---

[1] By January 1947 they were running seriously short of money. Billy (who was lying ill for two weeks in a cheap hotel on the coast near Dublin, where the sun never shone, the rain poured, and who was homesick because Ruth had gone home after her Christmas visit) wrote in fear and trembling to the Texas construction-machinery millionaire, R. G. Le Tourneau, whom he had once met in Florida days and knew to be interested in Y.F.C. Billy need not have been so scared. Le Tourneau, months before, had specifically told Alfred Owen that Billy Graham would one day be evangelist to millions, and he sent the money, via Y.F.C. headquarters in Chicago.

boys and girls." The same was true in the fog-enclosed, bomb-shattered port of Southampton, where Joe Blinco, the Methodist pastor and evangelist, felt this man "was fresh from God; his message had a freshness about it—cleanness in the sense that a mountain might be cleaned out by the wind and the rain—you felt there was no dirt, no shadow here."

Blinco, by origin and ministry a man of the people, recognized Graham's social concern, which had been fed by further visits to Speaker's Corner. This concern might be expressed naively or dogmatically, but, says Blinco, "Billy, from the very first time I remember him, spoke always against the background of the tragic situation in society." And he had so strong a world vision that Blinco discounted it as American big talk, until he came to know Graham better.

When the tour ended with a conference of two hundred and fifty leaders in youth work, gathered on Graham's initiative at Birmingham in March, for which Torrey Johnson flew over, several Britons had begun to believe that Billy Graham should some year return for a campaign not limited to youth. They had caught a gleam which could pierce war weariness and the defeatism, the little-mindedness which had settled on much of British religion.

---

6 · *Reluctant President*

Years before, at Temple Terrace, William Bell Riley remarked after listening to Billy Graham, "That young man never misses the bull's-eye." In February 1945 Dr. Riley, eighty-four years old, sat on the platform of the Youth for Christ rally which Graham addressed in the Minneapolis Auditorium. Next morning he called for George Wilson, Youth for Christ director and business manager of Riley's school, and said, "Where did you get that young man? He's a comer!"

Riley, for as long as a man could remember, had been pastor of the First Baptist Church of Minneapolis, the pleasant city of lakes and woods and nearly half a million inhabitants in the heart of the Scandinavian region of America. In 1902, to help fill empty country pulpits, he had founded the interdenominational Northwestern Bible Training Institute in a building attached to his church. In 1935 he had added a seminary and in 1944 a college of liberal arts, the whole being then known as Northwestern Schools. Riley, a Southerner, was an evangelist and expositor, a great reader, the author of many books. He was a controversialist, but a man of charity who made even his enemies to be at peace with him. He was also used to getting his way.

Riley was attracted to Graham as a magnet to iron. In 1946 he began to talk of him as the next president of Northwestern Schools. Graham when unable to sleep would imagine Northwestern as it might be: "One of the greatest Christian colleges of the nation . . . great buildings with hundreds of students—a school that stands firmly and positively for the essentials of the faith. A place whose ministry reaches the ends of the earth." He suggested Torrey Johnson as president, with himself as subordinate, loosely attached. When Johnson declined, Riley again urged Graham. At each refusal Riley grew more pressing, until in the summer of 1947 Graham agreed to visit him, now eighty-six and bedridden, at his home in Golden Valley.

The old man, obviously soon to die, lifted an emaciated hand from under the coverlet, and pointed a bony finger. As if to make it more dramatic, a thunderstorm broke and lightning flashed. "Billy, you are the man to succeed me. I've known it for a long time. You will be disobeying God if you don't!" Riley stubbed his finger at his open Bible, at the passage where the mantle of Elijah, as he goes up to heaven, drops upon Elisha. "I'm leaving this school to you as Elijah gave his mantle to Elisha. I leave you this school!"

To the comparatively confined circle in which Graham then moved, Riley was the father-figure. Billy inevitably was flattered and shaken that this man should choose him, not yet twenty-nine, but he had no conviction at all that Riley was right.

Billy walked away a troubled man. Ruth urged him to refuse because evangelism must come first, and although the president of an independent college might travel widely to promote it, his interests were bound to conflict. Billy knew too that his background scarcely fitted him to head educational administration and to formulate policy. And he was not sure he wished to be so closely identified with Midwest "Fundamentalism," because of the unfortunate connotation of the word.

Billy Graham, trusting with all his heart the living Christ, believed in the "fundamentals of the faith": the Bible as divinely inspired, and the supreme authority in religion; the Virgin Birth and the miracles; the Atonement, the bodily Resurrection, the need for every man to be born again, the certainty of Christ's second coming. But the term "fundamentalist," which only about thirty-five years earlier had been adopted by many evangelicals in the United States after the publication of a series of booklets on "The Fundamentals," had developed regrettable overtones. It had been annexed especially by those who prolonged the unnecessary nineteenth-century conflict between science and religion, who tended to mistrust scholarship, and too often could not find it in them to be charitable toward those who disagreed.

By 1947 the term "fundamentalist" held different meanings on different lips. Liberal Protestants, particularly those who gloried in being "modernists," used it to dismiss any man who held that modern science and Biblical criticism had not invalidated the "fundamentals of the faith." To Graham it meant much the same as "evangelical": a fundamentalist proclaimed a Biblical Gospel in the Reformation heritage which enfolded Luther and Calvin, Wesley and Whitefield, Spurgeon and Moody, none of whom had ever heard the term. To Riley it meant that and more—one who in debate stood up intelligently "for the verities of God's Word," but with malice toward none, with charity for all. To one or two on Riley's board of directors, however, the defense of the faith appeared more important than the propagation of the Gospel.

Graham's primary aim, to bring men everywhere to Christ, could be blunted if he were president of Northwestern Schools, which had long sounded controversial counterblasts to modernism.

Against his better judgment, drawn by the thrilling prospect of training Christian workers, and overawed by the insistence of the man he regarded as a spiritual giant, Graham in September 1947 agreed —should Riley die within the next ten months—to come at once to Minneapolis and be interim president, with the understanding that his commitments to Youth for Christ International and other evangelistic engagements be fulfilled. He would stay only until a new president was chosen.

In November 1947 Graham and Barrows, with George Beverly Shea and Grady Wilson (then a pastor in South Carolina), undertook a three-week campaign at the invitation of the local Christian businessmen's committee. It was the first campaign on which all four were together, and their first not limited to youth. In two weeks it spilled out from First Baptist Church on Tryon Street to the Armory.

On December 6 Billy Graham was with Stephen Olford at Hattiesburg, Mississippi, for a Youth for Christ rally. Late that night Graham was told on the telephone by George Wilson that Riley had just died.

In a first address of quite remarkable maturity the new president, after a notable tribute to his predecessor, left the board of directors in no doubt that he intended to govern.

In due course the "interim" dropped off the title because the board chose Graham as president and he accepted, though still unsure the appointment was in the will of God. The administration, which soon included T. W. Wilson as vice-president,[1] proceeded by that same blend of earnestness and boyishness with which Graham at that time did everything. (Who ever heard of a college president addressing his faculty in a letter, "Dear Gang"?)

The combined schools at the start of 1948 numbered 739 students, with another 200 enrolled for night courses. They had one fine new building almost ready, and a nearly empty treasury. The motto Graham gave the schools, "Knowledge on Fire," well expressed the atmosphere, and Roger Youderian, one of the five young missionaries killed by Auca Indians in Ecuador in 1956, was by no means unrepresentative of the students in Graham's day.

Graham at once began to reconstruct the program in order to create a second Wheaton, fully accredited, double-quick. Whereupon he discovered that an educational institution cannot be treated like an evangelistic campaign. One of his firmest supporters at Northwestern Schools, a trained educationalist, had to tell him: "Evangelism races, education plods. A campaign operates on a short fuse, education on a long fuse; you never know for at least four years whether a policy decision is right." Graham found this hard to swallow. His objectives were sound; the more he strove to reach them the more they proved that a zeal for education cannot offset professional inexperience as an educator. The tactics did not always work out.

He probably would have succeeded had he stayed at Northwestern most of each year, for he had a sense of generalship which was indigenous to him, a sense of doing the right thing at the right time, and an innate decisiveness which Northwestern so developed that the dean of the liberal arts college, Dr. O. E. Sanden, a Presbyterian clergyman, could write in 1951 that he "has an amazing grasp of facts and with lightning speed seizes on the thing that is essential. ... He has a marvelous capacity for recognizing the nonessential, and he—almost rudely—bypasses it." But Billy Graham was shackled by the unceasing conflict of commitments. He wanted to "get the

[1] T. W. Wilson, like Graham, was in evangelism and Youth for Christ. The very day after Riley's death Graham asked him to be vice-president, and renewed the demand by telephone eight nights in a row. It was some months before Wilson accepted.

Gospel to as many people as I possibly can." On the other hand he thrilled to "the opportunity of training young people to go out on fire for the Lord Jesus Christ."

Although he tried to give both callings the full force of a fertile mind, it soon showed clear which had priority. He would sweep into Minneapolis from an evangelistic tour or campaign to stay a few days at a nearby hotel or rooming house.[1] He would burst into the small presidential office in the new buildings on Willow Street overlooking Loring Park with its innumerable squirrels, and the hours would be packed with interviews, each nearly always including prayer. He exuded optimism, made the place hum. "Give him five minutes and he'll think up enough projects to keep many staffs busy for months," exclaimed the devoted secretary he had inherited with the position, Luverne Gustavson. Then would come a board meeting to discuss some measure, which really required research and careful scrutiny by faculty committees, but which he wished to see adopted in time for him to catch a plane. The discussion unfinished, he would look at his watch and turn to loyal T. W. Wilson. "T, you better do the rest. Goodbye," and in a few minutes his clothes would be stuffed once again higgledy-piggledy into a suitcase.

"In my memory," says Curtis Akenson, later president of Northwestern himself, "it runs as somebody having been put in an utterly impossible situation. And it is an amazing thing that he did as well as he did."

In Billy Graham's years at (or around) Northwestern, numbers rose sharply, new buildings were occupied, a two-wave radio station opened, the college magazine, *Northwestern Pilot,* achieved the considerable circulation of 35,000. Yet an educational institution cannot be run from afar. "I hope you will understand and be very patient," he wrote in 1948 to Luverne Gustavson. "When I neglect my correspondence from time to time in these campaigns, it is because I am so busy I hardly know what to do. I am speaking four or five times a day and trying to prepare all these messages and keep my body fit and my soul prepared before the Lord, and it is awfully hard to get to any of this other work, but I am trying to fill it in between the cracks."

Whatever Billy may or may not have done for the school, there is no doubt that the school did a great deal for him. Being president

[1] The Grahams continued to make their home at Montreat, where in 1948, after Anne Morrow Graham's birth in May, they bought (on a mortgage, for $4,000) a small house opposite the Bells. Graham never drew his salary as president of Northwestern.

aided Billy Graham's development. It gave him invaluable training in finance, promotion and administration, helped teach him the delegation of responsibility, the importance of tapping the right sources of advice, the molding of a team. He brought in new blood, and several who were later to work together on a wider field met him through Northwestern.

Graham inherited unhappy divisions which were none of his making, and there were those who were jealous. "Northwestern had been a cosy little affair," is one board member's recollection, "where everybody knew everybody. And all of a sudden there are strangers who don't know anything. And worse than this, they aren't professional educators! And worse than this, *they're kids!*" The jealousy induced constant thwartings which neither Graham's winsomeness in private, nor his occasional peremptory, if charmingly expressed, bulldozing of dissent at board meetings, could push aside. For the first time he tasted failure. Billy Graham had been opposed often, but in establishing a rally or launching a campaign he would either see the difficulties overcome and the opposition melt, as at Birmingham in 1946, or the campaign would end and he could forget it all. At Northwestern the constant gap between intention and achievement, and the disapproval of a few powerful figures would not melt and could not be forgotten.

Northwestern's difficulties put into Graham's spirit the steel without which no man comes to greatness.

---

7 · *"Hath God Said?"*

For six days in August 1948 Youth for Christ International gathered four hundred delegates from twenty-seven countries to Beatenberg in Switzerland. As Billy Graham listened to Christians from Asia, Africa, Europe and Latin America, his world vision was further enlarged.

Understanding of his task was deepened too. One of the principal speakers was Dawson Trotman of Los Angeles. Before the Second World War Trotman had started a scheme, originally among West Coast sailors, of evangelism through individual contact. "The Navigators" depended on each convert amassing such detailed knowledge of the Bible by memory-training that he could win another who would repeat the process with a third. The system was redeemed from the mechanical by insistence upon disciplined devotion and transparent character. "The Navigators" thus came to stand pre-eminently for the shepherding and training of converts, which Trotman called the "follow-up."

Graham had first met him when Trotman spoke at Wheaton in 1941. Billy was also at a conference in the Trotman home in 1946 when Youth for Christ leaders were almost brutally faced by the question: How many of those scores or hundreds who had come forward in utter sincerity to make a decision for Christ at the rallies had grown to be active, informed, growing Christians? At Beatenberg, after Dawson Trotman's address on "The Miracle of Propagation —or Producing a Producer," Billy took him, Bob Evans and Hubert Mitchell for a long afternoon on a mountainside. Their discussion and prayer was to lead three years later to the close link between Navigators and the Billy Graham crusades.

From Beatenberg Graham went to the formation assembly of the World Council of Churches at Amsterdam, as an observer.

At a time when most conservative evangelicals were highly suspicious of the ecumenical movement, would not be seen near it, or attended in order to become more convinced of its iniquity, Billy Graham found the Amsterdam assembly "one of the most thrilling experiences of my life up to that moment." He knew that one of the first springs of the movement had been in the mass evangelism of D. L. Moody, his Northfield conferences and the Student Volunteers; and that one of the founders, the aged John R. Mott, Moody's friend and (indirectly) his convert, had been primarily an evangelist. Graham saw the dangers in the ecumenical movement's apparent hankering for "the coming Great Church." He regretted that theological liberalism dominated much of its thinking, but recognized that evangelicals were partly to blame. The Edinburgh Conference of 1910, of which the 1948 assembly was the fruition, had been primarily an evangelical missionary conference. When the ecumenical movement after the First World War grew increasingly liberal in theology, the conservative evangelicals began to boycott and mistrust it.

Billy Graham shared in the expectancy of that formative assembly of 1948, but was not swept into becoming a blindly ardent ecumenist; he would not trim his convictions to popular winds. On the other hand, by refusing to dismiss or despise the ecumenical movement, as did many of his friends and older evangelical leaders, he showed that he would not hesitate to break the taboos of his circle in order to further the Gospel.

In North America Graham still traveled for Youth for Christ [1] but his deepest interest now lay in opportunities with Cliff Barrows, Bev Shea and Grady Wilson for "city-wide campaigns." The phrase carried more potential than accuracy until, at Augusta, Georgia, in October 1948, they worked for the first time at the invitation of the entire ministerial association and had the full support of the churches.

Outside evangelical circles, Billy Graham was unknown to the nation. And wherever he preached he became increasingly aware that mass evangelism had lost the nation's respect.

Since the death in 1899 of D. L. Moody, whose character, message and international achievements had won the goodwill and affection of America, the work of an evangelist who drew crowds to a tent or auditorium had lost its standing as a valued and proper ministry. The dynamic, athletic Billy Sunday had been nationally known, his doings widely reported in the press; he had brought countless men and women to faith and had held campaigns in most principal cities. (When he came to Charlotte in 1924 Frank Graham had taken an apprehensive little Billy Frank, warning him not to move lest he be called down by the preacher.) But Sunday's reputation declined with his years. Although in the nineteen-thirties and forties there were many honorable evangelists, none had the ear of the nation.

Billy Graham and Cliff Barrows had often discussed the causes, apart from theological issues, of the ill-repute of evangelists in general. In November 1948 a Graham-Barrows campaign (as it was then known) was held in Modesto, California, close to Cliff's home at Ceres. The response was discouraging. As they prayed about the weaknesses of their own ministry, the issue again arose of mass evangelism's bad odor.

Billy told the others to go to their rooms in the old-fashioned Hotel Modesto and list the most frequent criticisms. An hour later Cliff, Bev Shea and Grady Wilson rejoined Billy, who recalls, "There were ten or fifteen things that we wrote down as needing correction."

Each listed Finance first. Many evangelists spent too long in their

---

[1] It was at this period he nearly lost his life in a plane landing during a snowstorm at Lethbridge, Alberta. A shaken Billy had to share a room with a stranger. Then the police came and Billy was arrested! The airline pilot and the hotel manager had difficulty persuading the police that their wanted man was not Billy but the stranger.

meetings extracting contributions for campaign (or "revival") expenses. Furthermore, before leaving a place they would ask or permit the local chairman to beg in strongest terms for a handsome "love offering," presented on the spot, and accountable neither to the committee nor, as tax law then stood, to the internal revenue. All this repelled Graham, though since no one knew another way to secure itinerant evangelists their livelihood, he accepted love-offerings once he had resigned from the staff of Youth for Christ; previously every dime had been turned in to Y.F.C. He never laid down terms and, always the most generous of men, split his offering fifty-fifty with Barrows. But he wished that preaching and its remuneration could be divorced.

Other points of criticism were listed quickly: sensationalism, over-emotionalism; a tendency to digress on prophecy and to enter controversy; anti-intellectualism. Then they reached the more basic failures of mass evangelism: "First, there's no follow-up. We want to do something about that. Secondly, the evangelists have become anti-church. . . ."

On this last point Graham's attitude was the reverse. "I have always made it a plan, a purpose and an objective," he wrote at this time, "to build goodwill among the churches, to encourage the people in church attendance and church cooperation." He deplored the attitude of evangelists who won easy popularity by "skinning the hide" off local clergy, attacking modernism, pillorying clerics rather than proclaiming Christ, and thus leaving church people in a state of shock, disappointment and turmoil. Graham spent hours visiting clergy. In Cliff Barrows' words: "He genuinely loves them, and has sought to learn all he can from them; instead of criticizing their ministry he tries to be sympathetic with the problems they face and contribute what he can to help them." After nearly twenty years of collaboration Barrows asserts categorically: "I've never once heard him publicly say one derogatory remark about any minister. In our ministers' meetings during crusades, where it's just the clergy, he's unburdened his heart to them and points out things that he felt were reasons why they were in such problems and conflicts as they were, but always in the spirit of love. He always held up the clergy in the highest esteem before the people."

In April 1949 Graham admitted ruefully to Luverne Gustavson, "I have made so many promises that I will never be able to keep them. I am asking the Lord to help me not to make any more promises to anybody for anything. And also to give me physical strength to carry out the promises I have already made."

One promise was to Los Angeles, for a three-week campaign to begin late in September 1949.

Graham viewed Los Angeles, his first major city, as a date with destiny. The committee (mainly laymen) of "Christ for Greater Los Angeles" saw Billy Graham as merely their next annual evangelist, and resisted pleas that they secure a larger tent, cooperate with all possible churches, treble the budget to the unprecedented figure of $25,000 so that plenty of publicity should ensure this be not done in a corner. When he met the committee at the end of April the project hung by a thread. "I want to see God sweep in," Graham said, "because if Los Angeles could have a great revival, the ramifications and repercussions would sweep across the entire world."

Yet when the committee accepted his conditions he was almost sorry. Billy Graham was in the thick of a spiritual battle within his own soul: "For months I had lost my peace."

Chuck Templeton had long harbored doubts about the integrity of Scripture. In 1948 he had decided to leave his Toronto independent church to enter the theological seminary at Princeton. In Montreat that summer Billy said, "I think what you're doing is right, even though everybody thinks it wrong." Believing however that Princeton was not the place for Templeton's problem and temperament, he offered then and there to join him if he would instead go to England, to Oxford. Had Charles accepted, Billy would have taken two years' leave of absence from Northwestern Schools and abandoned most of his campaigns, to read for his doctorate at Oxford.

Billy hankered for postgraduate study. He knew he was not an intellectual, but he admired intellectuals and wanted to learn from them. He highly valued earned doctorates. On the evaporation of the Oxford idea he investigated several American universities but dropped the ambition when he realized that he could not give time enough while a college president and that taking leave of absence to remain in America was not feasible. He went to see Dr. John Mackay, then president of Princeton Theological Seminary, who advised him not to go to school, saying that he had already enough intellectual understanding for the work of an evangelist, and that if he enrolled as a student he would find his time being filled in counseling other students. Mackay gave Graham suggestions for reading and told him he could pick up much knowledge as he went along. Ruth regretted at one period that he had never been to seminary; she now feels seminary might have removed the sense of inadequacy which is one of Graham's strengths.[1]

Chuck and Billy were equally dissatisfied with the superficial approach characteristic, in those days, of Youth for Christ. Billy began to widen his theological reading, including Barth and Reinhold Niebuhr's *Nature and Destiny of Man*. He subscribed to the liberal *The Christian Century*. Several times during Templeton's first year at Princeton the two friends met for hours of debate and prayer. Graham could see that Templeton's "doubts concerning the authority of Scripture were intensified. I felt that we were now moving in opposite directions." Graham believed Templeton was seeking to bolster rather than to resolve doubts; to Templeton, Graham was a surface thinker unwilling to explore the implications of his position. Once in a New York hotel, when Templeton rejected a Biblical doctrine as intellectually untenable, Graham replied that wiser men had not solved the inherent difficulty and he had not the intellect to do so, but that when he took the Bible as God's Word and used it, his preaching had power. Already he had seen men and women weighted by cares or morally bankrupt made alive and radiant. Templeton could not accept such a pragmatic argument.

As he debated and read more, Graham grew confused. Could he continue to accept the authority of the Bible, in face of problems too hard to resolve? In the middle of the twentieth century could he, with the Apostle Paul, "declare unto you the gospel . . . how that Christ died for our sins according to the scriptures; and that He was buried, and that He rose again according to the scriptures?" It was as if the Adversary, having failed to deflect him by a desk at Northwestern, now sought to silence him by the primeval insinuation: "Hath God said?" This was not loss of faith but loss of balance; not a dark night of the soul. Yet the "terrific pain at the base of my skull," which plagued him in the spring of 1949 and puzzled the doctors, was probably induced, as Graham suggested at the time, by extreme nervous tension and exhaustion.

In June the team held a ten-day campaign at the railroad city of Altoona in the heart of the Allegheny Mountains in Pennsylvania, which Grady Wilson calls "the greatest flop we've ever had any-

[1] In 1948 Billy Graham received his first honorary doctorate, a D.D. from The King's College, Briarcliff, N.Y. About twenty honorary degrees have been bestowed on him since, and others he has declined. Because none have been earned he prefers to be addressed as *Mr.* Graham, or simply Billy.

where." Local preparation had been scanty, the ministers were at each other's throats. Billy believed the cause of the failure lay in himself, his nagging uncertainty lest perhaps, after all, Templeton was right to insist, "Billy, your faith is too simple. You'll have to get a new jargon if you want to communicate to this generation." Billy felt he must soon decide once and for all either to spend his life studying whether or not God had spoken, or to spend it as God's ambassador, bringing a message which he might not fully comprehend in all details until after death. Must an intellectually honest man know everything about the Bible's origins before he could use it? Were theological professors the only ones qualified to speak of religion, or might a simple American, or an ignorant jungle villager, or even a child, lead another to Christ?

Graham believed his special gift lay in "the invitation" to receive Christ: he was a "doorkeeper in the house of my God," helping people to enter; once entered they would be aided by others to appreciate the treasures of the house and learn more fully to serve. At a Bible conference in Michigan in July 1949 he was talking with his old Florida friend, Roy Gustafson, and became "very, very serious. He looked at me with those piercing eyes and he said, 'Roy, when I come to my invitation I sense God come on me, and I feel a power at that invitation that's peculiar.' " And now might he be preaching a doubtful Gospel derived from a not wholly trustworthy Bible?

At the same conference Gustafson and Franklin Logsden, then pastor of Moody Church, were with Billy when a display of aurora borealis lit up the sky. They began talking of the Second Advent of Christ, and suddenly Billy said, "Oh, if somehow the Lord could use me a little bit." They decided to have their prayer time under the stars and northern lights. Roy knelt on his handkerchief to keep off the dew, but in a few moments heard a strange, muffled voice. Billy lay full-length in the wet grass with his face into the ground, and the others heard, "Lord, trust me to do something for You before You come!"

In the last days of August Billy went to California as a faculty member of a student conference at Forest Home, the center founded five thousand feet high in the pine-laden air of the San Bernardino Mountains behind Los Angeles by Henrietta Mears, the colorful Presbyterian educator of Hollywood whose large hats, hearty voice, humor and skill as Bible teacher made her a unique personality on the West Coast. Her expositions, the talks by Edwin Orr (the Irish-American whose addresses on "Full Surrender" at Northwestern the previous May had led to a spontaneous, day-long prayer meeting), and a conversation with Orr strengthened and encouraged Billy as he faced the imminent Los Angeles campaign and his unpreparedness. But he questioned Orr's insistence on public confession by the students. Charles Templeton was there too, and Billy was concerned by the theological direction in which Templeton moved. Billy loved Orr, loved Charles Templeton, "and so this brought about a real conflict within me."

One evening in serious discussion with Billy, a mutual friend mentioned a remark which he said had been made by Templeton an hour or two earlier. The remark had been seriously garbled, for Templeton says he had certainly not used the words quoted. He was wrongly reported to have said: "Poor Billy. If he goes on the way he's going he'll never do anything for God. He'll be circumscribed to a small little narrow interpretation of the Bible, and his ministry will be curtailed. As for me, I'm taking a different road."

Billy was deeply disturbed and hurt. After supper, instead of attending evening service, he retired to his log cabin and read again the Bible passage concerning its authority. He recalled someone saying that the prophets used such phrases as "the Word of the Lord came" or "thus saith the Lord" more than two thousand times. He meditated on the attitude of Christ, who fulfilled the law of the prophets: "He loved the Scriptures, quoted from them constantly, and never once intimated that they might be wrong."

Billy went out in the forest and wandered up the mountain, praying as he walked, "Lord, what shall I do? What shall be the direction of my life?" He knew he had reached what he believed to be a crisis.

He saw that intellect alone could not resolve the question of authority. He must go beyond intellect. He thought of the faith used constantly in daily life: he did not know how a train or a plane or a car worked, but he rode them. He did not know why a brown cow could eat green grass and yield white milk, but he drank milk. Was it only in things of the Spirit that such faith was wrong?

"So I went back and I got my Bible, and I went out in the moonlight. And I got to a stump and put the Bible on the stump, and I knelt down, and I said, 'Oh, God; I cannot prove certain things. I cannot answer some of the questions Chuck is raising and some of the other people are raising, but I accept this Book by faith as the Word of God.' "

II

Mid-Century Meteor
1949-1953

---

8 · Los Angeles '49

"We are having by far the largest evangelistic campaign of our entire ministry," wrote the thirty-year-old Billy Graham from Los Angeles during his third and presumably final week in the "Canvas Cathedral" at the corner of Washington Boulevard and Hill Street, on the edge of the skyscraper district. "You would have thrilled," he told the North-western staff through Luverne Gustavson, "if you could have seen the great tent packed yesterday afternoon with 6,100 people and several hundred turned away, and seen the scores of people walking down the aisles from every direction accepting Christ as personal Savior when the invitation was given. . . . There is some agitation that the campaign continue for several more weeks."

The "Christ for Greater Los Angeles" committee, all early hesitations having vanished, had worked hard. Never before did so much prayer precede and enfold a Graham campaign: a ministers' prayer conference, prayer groups in churches, "prayer-chains" of men and women who divided up entire days of twenty-four hours, all-night meetings in the smaller adjoining tent. Armin Gesswein, a Los Angeles Lutheran minister who had shared in the 1937 religious revival in Norway, could remind Graham, "Whenever God is going to do any kind of work, He always begins by prayer." Yet the prayer-chains were arranged only when Grady Wilson arrived with the Team.

As the campaign moved to its scheduled close, several of the committee were ready to stop, well satisfied even if most of the millions who lived in the fast-moving, thrusting city and county of Los Angeles, from Hollywood to Chinatown, had not been aware of the big tent or Billy Graham. Other committeemen urged continuance, citing the rising interest and attendance. The question was referred to a subcommittee of three, who left it to Billy. Right up to the Sunday afternoon he hesitated. He had never previously extended a campaign. As he and Cliff prayed they decided to announce a short extension and meanwhile to "seek a sign." In the Book of Judges the young, obscure Gideon, to test whether God had really called him to leadership, put a fleece of wool on the ground overnight, praying, "If the dew be on the fleece only, and it be dry on all the earth beside, then shall I know that thou wilt save Israel by mine hand." Next morning Gideon found a soaking wet fleece on dry ground, "and God did so that night."

Billy Graham "put out a fleece"—watched for a sign. The sign came by way of a telephone call in the small hours.

Stuart Hamblen, a massive Texas cowboy in his late thirties, was already a legend on the West Coast.

He had won a Pacific rodeo, and had a daily program on radio, which had not yet lost supremacy to television. He sang in an inimitable cowboy manner, composed songs such as "I won't go huntin' with yuh, Jake, but I'll go chasin' women," was a dance band leader on Saturdays. He was a great hunter too, a successful race horse owner and gambler, a heavy drinker. And, as he later said, "a hypocrite." His father was a Methodist preacher in Texas. Although when Stuart came West he "left it all behind," for some years he ran a "Cowboy Church of the Air," in which he was engagingly frank. "Do as I say," he would tell the children, "but don't do as I do!"

His tiny wife, Suzy, had a warm faith and had prayed for him for sixteen years. When Henrietta Mears, Edwin Orr and others started the informal Hollywood Christian Group for actors and actresses, Stuart occasionally and reluctantly accompanied Suzy, even eavesdropping on their prayers for his own conversion. In September 1949 he promised to attend when Billy Graham, whom he had not met, was to speak at Miss Mears' home, shortly before the opening of the tent campaign.

Early that evening Hamblen shied. "Baby, you just drop me off at

Brittingham's Bar and go on out to the meeting and pick me up on your way home."

Suzy flared, saying she had told everybody he was bringing her.

Stuart replied: "If that's the way you feel about it, let's get going! Get on your mule right now!"

They drove to Westwood. Unexpectedly Billy arrived an hour early too. "Stuart was rough, strong, loud and at times uncouth, but I was attracted to him. And because I was a Southerner he sort of took to me. And he said, 'Come and be on my radio show. I can fill your tent down there for you.' "

"That," Stuart comments, "was before I began hating the man."

Billy duly attended Warner Brothers' studio for a live interview on KFWB. Hamblen then urged his audience to go to the tent, and to Billy's surprise blurted out, "I'll be there too."

The Hamblens sat in the front row, Stuart enjoying his patronage. "When the plate was passed I would put in three bucks—or maybe ten if I was sure someone of the Team was watching me." Ruth Graham had come West for the first days and Stuart took the Team out, to Chinatown to watch Ruth's skill at chopsticks, or elsewhere for southern fried chicken.

In the second week at the big tent Hamblen grew angry. Billy's long finger seemed right at him: "There is somebody in this tent who is leading a double life." Hamblen genuinely believed such remarks were deliberately aimed. After one more night he fled to the Sierras on a hunting trip, not returning until midnight on the supposed final Sunday, October 16.

With ill grace Hamblen was beside Suzy in the front row on Monday night. "When Billy Graham got up and preached a terrific sermon, I said, O that is a lot of malarky, he is lying. When they took up the collection, I said, That is a racket! When they sang some wonderful hymns, I said, That singing is lousy." The long finger pointed again. "There is a person here tonight who is a phoney." Stuart Hamblen rose from the seat in a fury, shook his fist at Billy and stormed out in the middle of the sermon.

"I went first to one bar and then to another, but I couldn't stand the taste of the drinks they poured me. Besides, their bands were hitting sour notes. At last I gave up and started home, and on the way Christ spoke to me." Hamblen fought back. "I was still fighting when I got home and woke my wife up, and I didn't wake her up gently. I stormed into the upper bedroom where she was asleep and I said, 'Woman, get out of that bed.' She jumped out of the bed with those brown eyes all wide and aflash and said, 'What is the matter with you?' I said, 'Let's pray.' We prayed, but I still couldn't make connections."

About 2 A.M. Stuart said that since Billy was the man who had upset him they would wake him up. Billy answered the telephone, could hear that Stuart had been both drinking and crying, and told him to "come right on down" to the apartment hotel where the Grahams and the Grady Wilsons shared an efficiency suite.

Stuart, with Suzy trailing behind, banged on the apartment door. It was opened by Billy in slacks and sweater. Stuart roared, "I want you to pray for me."

Billy replied, "No, I'm not going to do it." Stuart nearly knocked him down.

"Come in, Stuart," Billy said, "and I'll tell you why."

Billy knew that Stuart Hamblen was like the Rich Young Ruler and refused to help him to a selfish, easy faith. At one point in their talk Billy even said, "Go on back home. If you're not going to go all the way and let Jesus Christ be the actual Lord of every area of your life, don't ask me to pray with you, and don't waste anybody else's time."

At last, about 5 A.M., Stuart "promised I would give up all that was mean and wicked in my heart. We started praying and we weren't whispering. Billy prayed, Grady Wilson prayed, Suzy prayed, I prayed. And as I knelt by that chair I felt I was kneeling at the feet of my Jesus. 'Lord,' I prayed, 'you're hearing a new voice this morning.' "

When they got from their knees they all talked at once for joy. Stuart called his mother long-distance in Texas and heard her weep and shout at the news. Then they had breakfast, cooked by Grady, and therefore featured grits, a Southern dish that Stuart had always detested. But now he ate two helpings with relish, and when he asked for a third, Grady exclaimed, "Boy, you've been really converted!"

That very day Stuart Hamblen told his radio audience that he had given his life to Christ. "I've quit smoking and I've quit drinking." He would sell all his race horses except one, which he would never race again. "Tonight at the end of Billy's invitation, I'm going to hit the sawdust trail."

The sensation was enormous. Hundreds of newcomers flocked to the big tent. On the next Sunday, and again the following week, Hamblen went on the platform to say, "I didn't know what it was like to be a real Christian. Do you know the thrill of it all? I like to talk about it. Boy, I talk about it everywhere"—including the bars he had most frequented. He learned that, quite seriously, the betting in "Gower Gulch" and along Hollywood Boulevard that Hamblen "wouldn't keep it up," dropped from 100–1 to 20–1; after his second testimony, to 10–1.

Stuart Hamblen's conversion was Billy Graham's "fleece." The campaign was extended.

At the end of that week Billy, Cliff and Bev Shea put out another "Gideon's fleece," praying for a clear sign whether to extend once again.

The night on which they had to make up their minds to close or extend, Billy arrived at the tent to find the place swarming with reporters and photographers—a new, overwhelming and distracting experience. Flashbulbs exploded everywhere. Billy in the middle of the sermon had to ask a man to climb down from a stepladder he had placed right in front of the platform. All sorts of questions were flung at him afterward, and next day the Los Angeles *Examiner* and *Herald Express* carried banner headlines. Someone told Graham, "You've been kissed by William Randolph Hearst." The dispatch was featured in the other Hearst papers across the country, and was picked up by Associated Press.

Jim Vaus, driving back from a conference with his gangster boss on Saturday, November 5, tuned the car radio to station KFWB. He had been amused by the front page stories about Hamblen at the big tent—"What that guy won't do for publicity!" he thought—and now wanted some cowboy singing to soothe his nerves.

Vaus, who had been in prison twice, was the son of a prominent Los Angeles minister. After expulsion from a Bible school, entered to please his parents, Jim Vaus had drifted to crime. By 1949 he made good money as an electronics expert for the notorious Mickey Cohen, "Czar of the Los Angeles Underworld," whom the police had not yet prosecuted successfully. Vaus was key man also for a gangster syndicate defrauding bookmakers by an ingenious system of split-second wiretapping which enabled their agents to place bets after a race had been won. He had just clinched his biggest and most dangerous deal, and next week would leave for St. Louis to carry it out. His wife, Alice, knew nothing. He had even hidden from her the fact that he had served time before their marriage.

On the car radio Vaus was astonished to hear Hamblen give a most unusual commercial: "Folks! Smoking won't do you any good at all! In fact you might as well quit! But if you've already got the habit, smoke ——s," naming his sponsor. The more Vaus listened the more he sensed Hamblen's sincerity. He knew, from his own rejected background, what it involved. Next day, on an idle Sunday afternoon drive with Alice, on the spur of the moment Vaus took her to the big tent to "see what this fellow Graham is like."

They managed to squeeze on the edge of a bench. Vaus despised the crowd, rated Cliff Barrows and his trombone enthusiastic but amateurish. "Then Billy Graham stepped to the center of the platform and I couldn't find anything wrong with him. . . . Something about the ease with which he moved, the flash in his eyes, the conviction in his voice, gripped me. His message wasn't new, I had heard it lots of times. What amazed me was there weren't any jokes. It was all Bible. And I knew he was telling the truth."

Billy, one day short of his thirty-first birthday, moved rapidly back and forth on the platform, facing one block of seats, then another; he walked an estimated mile during fifty minutes. Every word of his machine-gun-like delivery was audible throughout the entire tent because he wore, on his tie, a microphone attached to a long cable, controlled by Cliff Barrows. Jim Vaus, as he listened, wrestled with his conscience. The companies he had swindled, the equipment stolen, the money he would make by the St. Louis deal, persuaded him not to believe.

When Graham began the invitation Vaus clenched his fists.

An elderly personal worker (they were not yet known as counselors) gripped his arm and would have been knocked into the sawdust had he not begun praying with bowed head. For counselors to accost strangers and urge them forward would be most unlikely in later Graham crusades, but in the spontaneous atmosphere of Los Angeles 1949 it did not seem wrong. Waiting for Uncle Billy Scholfield to stop praying, before throwing him to flee, Vaus heard Billy, who had no idea of his existence, say: "There's a man in this audience who has heard this story many times before, and who knows this is the decision he should make. Yet again he's saying 'No' to God. He is hardening his heart, stiffening his neck, and he's going out of this place without Christ. And yet this may be the last opportunity God will give him to decide for Christ."

Vaus fought in his mind.

Graham said again, far away up at the platform, his voice coming clear through the amplifiers: "The only time a man can decide for Christ is when the Holy Spirit of God has brought conviction to his heart. If God is bringing conviction to your heart you dare not say 'No.' This is your moment of decision."

Jim Vaus muttered, "I'll go."

In the smaller tent he was oblivious of his counselor, of the others around, of Alice kneeling beside him making her own commitment. Vaus himself was "busy talking to God. . . . I prayed: 'Lord, I believe; this time from the bottom of my heart. . . . It's going to be almost impossible to straighten out this bewildered, tangled life of mine. But if You'll straighten it out, I'll turn it over to You, all of it.'"

As the Vauses left the tent a news photographer ran up. "Hey, Vaus. You've had your picture in the paper for everything else. How about letting us shoot a couple more and tell what happened here to-night?" His first reaction was to flee publicity, the second that it was the best way to make known his break with crime.

"WIRETAPPER VAUS HITS SAWDUST TRAIL." The news flashed throughout America.

Armin Gesswein, on a train from Minneapolis to Chicago, was walking through a parlor car while the radio transmitted a news bulletin. The announcer was excited about something that was happening in Los Angeles. Gesswein stopped in his tracks. It was unheard of for a religious revival to make the news bulletins. As soon as he reached Chicago, Gesswein rushed to the Youth for Christ office. Bob Cook at that moment was on the line to Billy Graham. He handed the receiver to Gesswein.

"Armin," said Billy, "you had better get on out here fast. Something's happened and I don't know what it is. It's way beyond me."

---

9 · *New Year Miracle*

The crowds pressed to the big tent in such numbers that despite enlargement it could not contain them. On the seventh Sunday it was full at midday for a 2:30 P.M. service and the street blocked by those unable to get in.

The campaign was the topic of all Los Angeles. "The cabbies would start talking to you about Billy Graham, and waitresses and shop girls and most anyone," recalls Ben Weiss, then principal of the Metropolitan High School. In the final week alcoholics and prostitutes and broken bits of humanity, too shy to enter the tent, would ask for personal workers. Before each service church people stood shoulder to shoulder on every inch of the prayer tent, the leader's desk piled so high with written requests that many could not be mentioned. "A tremendous spirit of prayer," Armin Gesswein described it on his return.

The atmosphere in the big tent, despite the medley of musicians which Barrows brought in to support Bev Shea, had nothing of the supposed emotion of a revivalist meeting. It was like an immense divine service. The people came because Graham preached with authority—and preached to the times.

In 1949 the United States was forging ahead economically, yet lay shadowed by fear. The Cold War was at its height. Russia's atomic bomb test demolished American nuclear security; the swift victory of communism in China, and the belief which history would substantiate, that Stalin was preparing to expand his empire by military means and subversion, made the future uncertain and drove the more thoughtful, whatever their politics, to question themselves about the true foundations of the American way of life. Graham brought world affairs right into the "Canvas Cathedral." He preached in the shadow of international crisis, and he preached straight from the Bible.

He had stopped trying to prove that the Bible was true, and just proclaimed its message. "I found that I could take a simple outline and put a number of pertinent Scripture quotations under each point, and God would use this mightily to cause men to make full commitment to Christ. . . . I found they were desperately hungry to hear what God had to say through His Holy Word." This message was not hurled thoughtlessly. An Episcopal rector thought Graham's message not only "very simple and clear and without equivocation," it was also "very provocative, and made many people think and brought them to a decision."

The numbers who came forward reached totals of two or three hundred a night—a figure which in those days seemed fantastic. For every person prayed with, ten or twenty had to be addressed in a group because of the lack of workers. For the first time Graham began to hear of divorced couples being reunited in the counseling tent. One committeeman said it was "as if the heavens had opened and God was now running the meetings."

The press naturally highlighted notable converts. *Time* and *Newsweek* both described the "new evangelist," and when a testimony was given by the converted track star, Louis Zamperini, the headlines screamed again. (That converts should be invited to speak a day or two after coming forward seemed neither unwise nor peculiar in 1949.)

Zamperini, son of poor Italian Roman Catholic immigrants, after a wild youth had become the youngest long-distance runner in the Berlin Olympics of 1936, gaining additional if curious fame by pulling down the Reichstag's swastika. During the war he had survived forty-seven days on a raft in the Pacific and a brutal captivity in Japan, which left him bitter and prey to nightmares. Listed killed, his return brought a blaze of publicity and an insurance windfall, but in four years he had sunk to poverty through his own fault.

His young and ill-used wife, Cynthia, had attended the Graham meetings in her desperate unhappiness and had gone forward. She told Louis, "For the first time in my life I have peace in my heart." Zamperini was scornful. He says that had he not been penniless, destitute, drinking heavily—"lost my car, the last thing I had, the day before"—he would never have agreed when she pressed him to accompany her. He was at once attracted to Graham, "more like an athlete than a man of God," and his emphatic, forceful manner; but Graham's matter cut too near the bone, and Zamperini, like Hamblen, left angry. When at length he returned several nights later he rebelled to the last, but like Vaus, yielded after deciding to leave.

None of the three who hit the headlines had easy growth as Christians. Zamperini suffered doubts and despondency during the rebuilding of his life. Vaus had the hardship of restitution. Hamblen was fired from his $1,000-a-week program because he refused to advertise beer. Every opening then closed, until his friend, actor John Wayne, hearing he had not taken a drink in thirty days, said: "Tell me truthfully, Stuart, have you wanted one?"

"No, John. It is no secret what God can do."

When Wayne suggested, "You ought to write a song about 'It is no secret what God can do,'" Stuart Hamblen found his new vocation.

Jim Vaus and Louis Zamperini both found theirs among delinquent boys, Vaus in New York, Zamperini in California. These three, each of such wide influence since 1949, were representative of some 4,000 men, women and children who came forward, and additional hundreds whose decisions for Christ were not recorded. As a matter of record Hamblen and Vaus had Christian backgrounds, while Zamperini long had lost contact with formal religion.

By mid-November the campaign looked everlasting. Indeed, one committeeman tried to make it so by planning a permanent evangelistic center on the site of the big tent, even as Los Angeles' famous independent Church of the Open Door arose out of R. A. Torrey's mission. Graham, with a sure instinct, threatened to walk off the platform if the project were announced. He would found no new church or sect.

The campaign had extended from three weeks to eight. Northwestern Schools, thrilled by its president's fame and achievement, wondered when he would return. As for Graham, he wrote that in a campaign like this, "all I can think about is preaching. Morning, noon and night I am thinking about sermons, preparing sermons, and more preaching. I forget the world, my own personal affairs and everything."

He had quite run out of sermons. When Ruth came West she found him "really digging into the Scriptures," begging outlines from preacher friends, and reading every recommended book he could borrow or buy. "I remember his desperate straits in Los Angeles, probably the best thing that ever happened to him—this suddenly having to get down and study, especially the Bible. He was thrown back on simple, straight *Biblical* preaching." He was now exhausted and could not sleep properly, but he had discovered that "the weaker I become physically, the stronger I become spiritually."

He set Sunday November 20 as closing day. The big tent, the seating enlarged to 9,000, overflowed. No one could estimate the audience, almost certainly the largest of its kind since Billy Sunday's New York campaign of 1917. And no one could have believed that fourteen years later the attendance would be multiplied by fifteen, when the turnstiles of the Los Angeles Coliseum clicked up 134,254, with 20,000 more outside the gates, to hear Billy Graham on the last night of the Los Angeles Crusade of 1963.

On Monday Ruth and Billy took the train for Minneapolis. The conductor treated them as celebrities. At Kansas City reporters boarded the train, at Minneapolis several prominent clergy joined with the Northwestern faculty members and the local press to provide a hero's welcome. The Grahams at last realized that Billy had been catapulted into fame. They were bewildered, frightened lest they fail their Lord in these new opportunities, uncertain whether this were a climax or a beginning, yet tremendously encouraged. "I feel so undeserving of all the Spirit has done," wrote Billy, "because the work has been God's and not man's. I want no credit or glory. I want the Lord Jesus to have it all."

"Billy nearly killed himself in the Los Angeles campaign," T. W. Wilson wrote on December 3. "It was glorious, but, boy, it cost him a tremendous price. He is now under doctor's orders to rest for a month."

The next scheduled engagement was for Boston. It seemed cruel coincidence that as far back as 1947 Billy Graham had agreed to bring his Team for the New Year of 1950, for no city in America was more sure to snuff out the fire lit at Los Angeles than Boston: predominantly Roman Catholic, with large minorities of Unitarians and Christian Scientists; reserved, proud and confident of its intellectual supremacy. Moreover the Evangelical Ministerial Association was not fully behind Graham. Except, therefore, for a united service at old Mechanics Hall held on New Year's Eve, the visit to Boston was to be held solely in historic Park Street Congregational Church, at "Brimstone Corner" where the powder had been stored during the Revolution. The Team had been invited by its pastor, Dr. Harold Ockenga, an intellectual, rather formal man in his early forties, who since 1947 had been sure that Billy Graham was the evangelist for Boston.

A month at home in the mountains sent Billy to Boston with "vim, vigor and vitality," in T. W. Wilson's phrase. The preliminary Friday night at Park Street was not unordinary. New Year's Eve saw Mechanics Hall full, 6,000 people coming in the expectancy generated by Los Angeles.

None expected the outcome: no less than 175 people came forward at the invitation, "the first time," Ockenga comments, "they had ever had any kind of a break like this in Boston for a long, long time." Ockenga himself was so moved that he leaned across to the chairman and suggested booking the hall for the Sunday afternoon. It was announced on the spot, drew nearly as many and proportionately more coming forward. That night Park Street Church had people standing in the aisles, its two subsidiary halls full and hundreds turned away. Monday January 2 being celebrated as New Year's Day, a big audience was not anticipated, but the church overflowed again, the police estimated 7,000 turned away, and in pouring rain over a thousand stood in the street singing hymns.

To continue in Park Street was absurd. Ockenga secured Mechanics Hall for a week before it was taken over by a poultry show, and, with difficulty, the Opera House for four days beyond, certain that the high rent would be covered by offerings. The Boston newspapers were now running front page stories, providing immense free publicity. Reporters and editors were astonished at the crowd. They were amazed too—since Aimee Semple McPherson and discolored memories of Billy Sunday had conditioned their ideas on religious revivals—by the reverence of the service and the calmness and dignity of those who walked forward at the invitation. (At the Opera House these had to go out on the street to reach the counseling area on the stage.)

The Bellevue Hotel switchboard was jammed, the girl operator in tears, the manager wringing his hands, swamped by long-distance calls for Billy Graham—enthusiastic friends, pastors begging him visit their town, strangers wanting spiritual counsel. Upstairs in Billy's room, Grady pecked at a borrowed typewriter, trying to answer the insistent questions of the press. "Billy would give him a little word," remembers Bev Shea, "and the rest of us would add a word, and he would say, 'Now fellows, go slower.' Here he was, a preacher all of a sudden called upon to be a pressman." And in a corner Bob Van Kampen from Chicago helped by answering scores of letters.

It was all unbelievable, frightening, yet wonderful because spontaneous: no counselor training, no careful buildup, no advertising except for New Year's Eve. Billy called at Park Street and heard strange sounds from Ockenga's study. He peered round the door and saw Ockenga full length in prayer, sobbing. "He had carried a burden for the spiritual and moral needs of New England so long that he was now finding an emotional release—though he is not an emotional man."

"It is our firm conviction," wrote Cliff Barrows to a friend on January 13, "that New England is in the midst of a great awakening, and revival fires seem to be spreading not only throughout the city but in many other sections across this area."

It might have spread like forest fire had large enough halls been available. When the Opera House [1] reverted to opera the Team returned to Mechanics Hall, cleared of poultry. On Friday January 13 the crowd surged in until the building could hold no more. The people outside pounded on the doors; to Ockenga on the platform, it sounded just like thunder. This time Mechanics Hall was free for three days only. Ockenga had found no other place when the editor of the Boston *Post* (now defunct), a devout Roman Catholic, telephoned out of the blue to suggest Boston Garden, Boston's largest

[1] Opera House, Mechanics Hall and Bellevue Hotel have all since been demolished.

indoor arena, where ice hockey games, other sports and spectacles were held. Ockenga said he had been told it was booked for weeks.

When the editor offered to secure it, Ockenga had a moment's doubt; the Boston Garden had over 13,000 seats, with ice for hockey laid over the floor. But the editor prophesied that 10,000 would be turned away.

His influence got them the Garden. When Billy, Cliff and Grady called to express thanks for his action and for the reporting, the editor said, "I don't know why I'm giving you this kind of coverage, but somehow I feel compelled to do it." In Grady's words, "We knew the answer. We knew the Lord was working. It was the sovereignty of God in answer to the prayers of all these people."

On Monday January 16 Boston Garden was indeed as the editor prophesied: 16,000 squeezed in, leaving so many outside that Billy had to deliver an unscheduled address from the steps. Newspapermen said Franklin D. Roosevelt himself had never drawn such numbers in Boston. That night, with Ruth beside him, Billy (as he recalls) "felt as great a power in preaching as any other time in my ministry up till then. And when the appeal was given, more than a thousand people responded to receive Christ."

Ockenga had announced from the platform, amid cheers, that although the meetings must stop through lack of auditoriums, Billy Graham and his Team would return in the spring, to swing rapidly through New England cities with a climax for four days in Boston Garden. After the service the Grahams immediately took a train for Canada, where he had an engagement in Toronto. Speeding west across Massachusetts Billy felt a compulsion to get off at Worcester and again at Springfield, to telephone Boston that he would stay in New England. Again and again the feeling came to him that now was the hour. Invitations had poured in; from universities, schools, cities. Any town of New England would book its largest hall to hear Billy Graham. The press would carry his words across the nation. If the Team stayed in New England six months, he felt, God might light a fire in America that never would be put out.

Graham was used to acting on impulse, to sacrificing engagements to greater opportunities. But to return would mean abandoning a long-prepared campaign in the South. Furthermore he was desperately tired, and he was frightened—frightened of the press. "Whatever I said was being quoted. I knew that I was not qualified, I didn't have the experience to say the right things. And I was afraid that I was going to say something that would bring disrepute on the name of Christ."

Ruth and he prayed, then slept. They stayed a day and a night at Niagara Falls, which was beautiful in winter dress. Here the press underlined his fears, though bringing the Grahams a laugh: at Boston Garden he had mentioned in an illustration his contacts with a bank robber (meaning Vaus); the famous Brinks bank robbery had now occurred, and a Boston reporter was on the line, soon to be followed by the arrival of local police—both asking him to tell what he knew about the robbery!

At Niagara Billy again "felt tremendously impelled to call back to Boston and say we should continue." He let it pass.

He now believes that "unwittingly I disobeyed the voice of God."

---

10 · South and North

Columbia, capital of South Carolina, a typical city of the Deep South and the "Bible belt," had scores of churches, their influence weakened by denominational suspicions.

A Wheaton friend of Graham's, Don Hoke, then on the staff of Columbia Bible College, had gone dove hunting on a rainy day with J. Pou Taylor, a state solicitor (now a judge). Taylor was a Methodist. His dramatic conversion a few years earlier made him particularly open to Hoke's suggestion, as they drank coffee in a cabin with the rain beating down, that Graham be invited for a city-wide campaign. Hoke and Taylor decided to work through the Laymen's Evangelistic Club. The ministers followed lamely, their suspicions muted by the fact that Graham was Carolina born and—since these preliminaries took place before Los Angeles—virtually unknown and therefore not on any denomination's black list.

Preparations would have remained sluggish had not the committee secured the full-time service for six months of the secretary of the Laymen's Evangelistic Clubs of North Carolina, Willis Haymaker.

A fifty-four-year-old Presbyterian who had known Billy Graham since boyhood, Haymaker had organized campaigns for Gypsy Smith, Bob Jones and many other evangelists of the nineteen-twenties and thirties, except for Billy Sunday. Haymaker, who stayed with the Graham Team from Columbia onward, had an immeasurable part in their development, for he taught them the basic facts of organization.

"Haymaker" in American boxing jargon means a "knock-out wallop," but Willis Haymaker was a peaceable man, warm, encouraging and friendly, never downcast, immensely patient. Dawson Trotman, who had opportunity to study him at work, left a vivid description: "He goes into a city where there is antagonism, fear, jealousy and disinterest on the part of pastors and people alike. He gets committees together, sets up publicity, gets the men working together and vast numbers of people praying." Graham says, "Willis Haymaker taught us and urged us to put prayer before everything. He has a marvelous way of organizing people to pray." Haymaker believes that repentance and prayer forms "God's blueprint for a crusade or great spiritual awakening." He covered Columbia with home prayer meetings for a month before the opening of the Great Columbia Evangelistic Crusade in February 1950. Thus, as Haymaker says, "Billy stepped right into a revival. It had been 'prayed down.' "

Haymaker introduced the term "Crusade." "A crusade is a continuing thing; a campaign is more just a part of a crusade. A crusade goes on and on and is world wide in its ramifications." Billy Graham was soon speaking of "our crusade to bring America to her knees in repentance of sin and faith toward God."

The Columbia crusade began on Sunday February 19, 1950, at the Township Auditorium, which could just be made to hold about 4,000 persons, standing room included. The coachloads pouring in from upstate proved the immediate need for a bigger hall than Columbia possessed. On Monday Haymaker suggested throwing up a timber "tabernacle," such as he had built for Gypsy Smith, and extending the crusade two weeks.

Plans and estimates were hurriedly drawn, endorsed with enthusiasm by a meeting of ministers only to have them vetoed by the crusade committee. When the treasurer made a baleful speech against the "wooden cathedral," as Billy preferred to call it, Billy arose (remembers Bev) "like the voice of a prophet, and pointed, eyes blazing. 'O ye of little faith,' he said. 'Here you are, a man older than the rest of us. You've walked with God all these years and yet you've come to the place where you refuse to believe God can do something.' " The man sat white-faced. Afterward Shea saw Billy go over and put his arm round him.

The crusade had two great advantages over Los Angeles and Boston.

The governor, a Baptist, endorsed and supported the Team, brought prominent Carolinians to the services, arranged for all city high schools to attend a special crusade rally, and invited Billy to stay at the executive mansion for the later part of his visit. Thus instead of beginning in a tent on wasteground, or as the effort of a single church, the Columbia crusade was held in high honor.

It was also news from the start. The city's two papers, *The State* in morning and the evening Columbia *Record,* had among their assistant editors a former Columbia Bible College student, Tom McMahan. *The State* printed a front-page story daily and the entire sermon verbatim inside. Such coverage, circulating throughout South Carolina, made all districts eager to share in the crusade, thus confirming the discovery Graham had stumbled upon at Los Angeles: the secular press of its own volition will, in effect, promote the Gospel when evangelism is on such a big scale that it is news.

This discovery now led him into temptation.

On March 1 Billy Graham addressed a joint meeting of the state legislature, a remarkable honor for a preacher of thirty-one. He diagnosed the uneasiness of modern life and spoke of what was much on his mind—that America lay under judgment. The threat imposed by the atomic bomb, Graham said, would become a reality unless the moral bases of the nation were renewed, for the times were analogous to those of Isaiah, who was sent to warn a backsliding people to repent or God would use an external enemy to destroy them. But, Graham affirmed, "our nation is awakening and is turning to Christ. How can we speed up this revival?"

Graham's address was read at home by the late Bernard Baruch, the aging Jewish financier, confidant of Churchill and former colleague of F. D. Roosevelt. Baruch drew it to the attention of Henry R. Luce, his house guest at Yeamans Hall near Georgetown. On the morning of Thursday March 9 Billy Graham learned that Luce would stay that night at the executive mansion and would attend the crusade.

Few men in America could be more important to Billy Graham at that juncture than the founder-proprietor of *Time* and *Life* magazines. If those weeklies, with their international circulation, featured his crusades favorably, the press would indeed promote the Gospel, in the United States and many parts of the world. But, of all his sermons, Billy had announced for that Thursday the one almost surely distasteful to such a sophisticated man—the sermon on Judgment and Hell, which would be described in graphic detail.

"The temptation came to me very strongly" to switch to another subject. When, by his usual custom, Billy locked himself into his room at midafternoon to prepare, he seriously considered doing so. Like any perceptive speaker he adapted approach to audience, but his subject had been announced! "And the Lord seemed to say to me, 'Now you are going to change because of the fear of man.' " Billy turned to a familiar passage, God's words to Jeremiah (1:17): "Thou therefore gird up thy loins, and arise, and speak unto them all that I command thee: be not dismayed at their faces, lest I confound thee before them." The verse hit him hard. "God said, as it were, 'If you pull your punches, I'll confound you before them.' In other words, 'Don't. If you compromise, then I'm going to confound you and make you look like a fool in front of them.' "

As he lay down for his hour's rest and shut his eyes, the verse ran in his mind. Preacher after preacher had faced the issue, whether to seek favor of a powerful man, or to maintain integrity.

While he relaxed perspiring in his very hot bath ("It gets poison out, it clears the mind"), Billy made his decision. As he sipped the light soup or the tea which was all he would take before preaching, he knew he had decided rightly. He left the mansion before Luce's arrival, and during the sermon on Judgment and Hell forgot him, though subconscious awareness was probably the reason why it seemed an exceptionally difficult delivery, a preaching without liberty. Then 256 people came forward to be counseled. Billy realized that "there is a great difference between liberty and power. . . . Sometimes when I have the greatest difficulty in speaking God does His greatest work in the audience."

That night Henry Luce and Billy Graham sat talking into the small hours at the executive mansion. An enduring friendship was born.

Next day Luce ordered a team from *Life* to Columbia. For the crusade committee had been persuaded to make the closing Sunday, March 12, a "gigantic step of faith" by booking the outdoor stadium of the state university, which held 35,000.

The weather forecast was poor.

PROCLAMATION. *Whereas* The Greater Columbia Evangelistic Crusade, a God-inspired, Christ-centered, Spirit-led movement, being conducted by the Rev. Billy Graham and his party, now in its third week, is having a profound impact on the people not only of the Columbia area but throughout the great State of South Carolina, and

Whereas there are evidences that a genuine spiritual awakening is sweeping our state as well as our nation, and

Whereas the mighty crusade in our capital city will come to a climax with a state-wide rally in the Carolina Stadium on Sunday March 12,

Now therefore, I, J. Strom Thurmond, governor of the state of South Carolina, do hereby proclaim Sunday March 12 as *South Carolina Revival Rally Day.* ...

Billy, with his farmer's nose, believed the day would be sunny despite the forecast. But he hardly slept the previous night, awed by thought of tier upon tier; burdened by the sermon; concerned lest the fame and publicity were turning South Carolina more Graham-conscious than Christ-conscious, and lest by inadvertent word or action tomorrow he should besmirch the name of Christ. Again and again, leaving Ruth sleeping, he knelt in prayer beside the bed.

The day had a touch of Southern spring putting the temperature into the seventies, but with a strong wind blowing. A crowd of 40,000, including solid blocks of students and of Negroes, packed the stadium. Billy hardly believed he would ever preach to a bigger audience though the police estimated that a further 10,000 had been turned away. On the platform, with many South Carolina notables, sat Billy's parents.

Nothing marred the reverence, not even Cliff Barrows' trombone waving. No offering was taken, for crusade expenses had been met days earlier. The great crowd joined Cliff in "All Hail the power of Jesus' Name" and "What a Friend we have in Jesus," and listened to Bev Shea singing "Roll, Jordan, Roll" and his own "I'd rather have Jesus." And they stood for the prayer. During Scripture reading Billy sat tense, biting his nails, praying. He felt the quiet expectancy in the stadium, "a deep longing and hunger on the part of thousands for a personal encounter with God."

He preached on Noah and the flood as a picture of judgment. The wind blew Billy's hair into his eyes, giving him in the *Life* photographs a rather demagogic look. The day grew overcast, and the wind stronger. It may have been because the sky looked ominous that Billy cried suddenly, "I wonder how many people there are here today who will say, 'Right where I sit I want Jesus to come into my heart. I want to make sure right now'?" Hundreds of hands went up. Billy stopped abruptly. He gave the invitation to come forward. A moment later, as the choir began to sing "Just as I am," *The State* reporters saw trickles of persons. "Then some of the aisles down the great sides of the stadium got full. Some of the entrances onto the playing field became a living stream of people flocking to crown Jesus Christ Lord of all their lives."

As Billy Graham left for a hurriedly arranged two-week preaching tour of South Carolina, using auditoriums or, when available, outdoor stadiums, he told Columbia's ministers that the torch had been passed to them: "You face the greatest opportunity of your lives." A month later he heard that "the churches over Columbia have experienced a wonderful growth since the crusade," for although many of those who had signed cards (more in three weeks than in eight at Los Angeles) had been hitherto nominal, indifferent or self-satisfied churchmen, there were scores who were unchurched. One of these was the state amateur golf champion, Emory Harper, who as a result went to church for the first time in fifteen years.

Some years later Billy Graham was greeted by the famous golfer Johnny Spence, the "professionals' professional," with the words, "Hello there, Grand-daddy!" Billy asked what he meant, and Spence replied, "I'm your grandson in the Lord. You won Emory Harper to Christ, and Emory Harper won me to Christ." Both Harper, once a gambler and heavy drinker, and Spence are lay preachers.

Exactly six weeks after the Carolina Stadium rally a great "Peace Rally" on Boston Common was proof indeed that "We seem to be on the verge of a great national awakening."

The pace since South Carolina had been grueling. One week's rest and the Team whirled through twenty New England towns from Rhode Island to Maine. A corps of national pressmen had attached itself. At nearly every place Billy had to deliver a second talk to the overflow crowd in the street, often in the rain, and at Houlton, Maine, on the Canadian border the only auditorium large enough was the airport hangar. At Fall River, Massachusetts, Billy was sick and Grady Wilson preached. Grady's assurance to reporters that Billy could continue the itinerary emerged in the Boston papers as "In Spite of Death Peril, Graham Carries On," which led to much intra-Team kidding. Yet Billy really had been close to abandoning the tour through exhaustion; alone in a hotel room he kneeled on the floor in prayer, and before he finished he could feel strength returning to his body.

The Team returned to Boston for four nights, Wednesday to Saturday. Boston Garden was not quite full the first three.

Billy had addressed Brown University, in Providence. Back in Boston, at the Massachusetts Institute of Technology, the Rockwell Cage gymnasium was filled with students evidently intending, on a rainy afternoon, some mild amusement with an ignorant, hillbilly preacher. Beer bottles were waved from the front row, and a prank had been planned: a fellow on crutches would hobble down the aisle in the middle of the address, yell "I'm cured!" and throw the crutches in the air.

Billy, who was not biting his nails for once, whispered to Ockenga, "Harold, give me the most intellectual introduction you have ever given anybody." Ockenga spoke at length, tying up the Institute's recent centennial addresses on science with the present opportunity, until the audience was sobered and alert. Then Billy followed with "a terrific address," says Ockenga, and the result was "as quiet and restrained and beautiful a service as you would want."

Sunday April 23, the day for the Boston Peace Rally, broke damp and rainy. At midday a reporter telephoned to ask the location of the alternative indoor site; but Billy had prayed and was sure that the sun would shine by three o'clock. Not only the reporter but Grady too reckoned his serenity unfounded. It was cold and drizzling when the great congregation gathered around Monument Hill. The Boston *Post,* basing their headline on the police estimate, put the crowd at 50,000. Billy's own estimate was no more than 25,000. The crowd was far smaller than the one that gathered there during his Boston crusade of 1964, but it seemed unbelievably huge for 1950. The rain stopped but the clouds were black throughout the preliminaries. As Billy rose to walk to the pulpit the sun peeped through.

Not even an incredibly tactless aerial advertiser for motor oil, circling hopefully overhead, could distract the audience as Billy preached on "Peace in Our Time," nine weeks precisely before the sudden Communist invasion of South Korea. He urged that President Truman call a national Repentance Day, and he offered a five-point plan for peace. The first three points called for the United States to maintain strong military, internal and economic security. *"Fourth,* we must continue confidence in each other—race with race, creed with creed, color with color, remembering we are all Americans. . . . *Fifth,* we must have a moral and spiritual regeneration, through repentance, individual faith in Christ, national humility, united prayer for peace."

For Billy Graham an abiding memory of Boston was of a little incident the day before.

He had become close friends with John Bolten, the German-born millionaire head of Standard International Corporation, who had re-dedicated his life to Christ during the January meetings. On the Saturday afternoon Billy wanted to pray on the Common. He took Bolten, Bev Shea and one or two others, and they strolled up Monument Hill where the platform was still being constructed. As they prayed, John Bolten had such inward conviction that afterward he took Billy for a walk alone. "Billy," he said, "I believe God's telling me you are going to preach in the great stadiums of every capital city of the world the Gospel of our crucified Lord. I believe the world is ripe and ready to listen."

---

11 · The Team Together

The early months of 1950 brought the Billy Graham Team two new members.

Gerald Beavan, a young Baptist minister, tall and gaunt, had joined Northwestern's faculty shortly before Riley's death. Graham promoted him to the job of registrar. They did not yet know each other well, but after Los Angeles Jerry Beavan said casually he would give anything to go to Boston. "I might be able to handle the press," he suggested. Following Columbia Graham sent for him.

New England at once proved the value of the choice. A press secretary was a necessity, for at that time any unscrupulous reporter could make Graham give an opinion on any or every subject, regardless of his competence or the construction which could be put upon the answer. Beavan learned quickly how to work with the press, and a few months later was also named executive secretary and public relations director for the Team. He was well read theologically, had a marked flair for organizing, and could assess a situation rapidly. With Grady Wilson and Willis Haymaker he took the unceasing telephone calls which would have left Billy no time to prepare his sermons. Among them they handled complaints, sorted muddles, smoothed ruffled feelings when plans changed, and protected Billy from those who would exploit him. They extricated him from commitments when Billy's friendliness and desire to aid had overridden his capacity or wisdom.

Jerry Beavan had an artist's temperament, backed by a Northerner's hustle which could irritate inhabitants of more placid climes. His sense of urgency sometimes made him brusque. His delight was in a man who would roll up his sleeves and work as hard as he; Billy discovered him at one crusade site cleaning out an unkempt men's latrine.

Tedd Smith, a Canadian, joined as pianist. Now only twenty-two, he had won his first gold medal for music at age nine. A graduate of the Royal Conservatory of Music at Toronto, Smith could have made a career as a concert pianist. Just as Billy Graham does not preach without study and sermon preparation, so Tedd Smith practices Bach or Beethoven daily, even in periods when the music required of him is simply revival hymns.

Like Barrows and Shea, Smith believes that crusade singing should not attempt merely to reproduce the conditions of a formal worship service. The three of them helped, with Paul Mickelson, who was Team organist 1950–1957 and now is succeeded by Don Hustad, to give the Billy Graham crusades their distinctive blend of informality and warmth with reverence.

The Billy Graham Team was forming without any idea that one day it would be much larger. No one recruited a big group and then set out to do a job. It was the other way around: the opportunities, as they came, made necessary the expansion of the Team.

In 1950 the Team was predominantly young, strengthened by the older wisdom of Willis Haymaker and of Colonel Paul Maddox, who as Chaplain to the European Command had given Graham early opportunities of addressing troops, and on retirement had become his deputy at Northwestern, and then his personal assistant. They all discussed everything together, prayed together, took decisions as they came. Even the two secretaries, Luverne Gustavson and Betty Lowry, both from Northwestern, were active in policy deliberations. Luverne could understand and anticipate Graham's mind, and she took in stride endless traveling and long, irregular hours. She had organizing ability, helped him arrange press articles and, later, his books. "Her advice and her counsel in the early days," says Graham, "were indispensable."

The world addressed him as "Billy," Luverne as "Mr. Graham," though she also had a habit of referring to him as "my Boss," which Billy disliked. "We're all working for the Lord," he would say. "My 'Boss' certainly has the most sincere and humble spirit completely yielded to Christ that I have ever seen," she wrote home, "and it's no wonder that people flock to hear him when they sense the power of God in his life."

The Team worked informally and did not always conserve their energies. The men would enjoy late night "fellowship dinners" with crusade committees or sit around either jawing and kidding, or planning and praying. Grady once stayed up most of a night exchanging fishing yarns after a weekly rest-day expedition out of town. Bev Shea would go to bed, "but he would hear us talking, and he was afraid he would miss something. He'd get out of bed and come back downstairs." When they returned to town they found Billy sick and Grady must preach. "I was totally unfit physically. I just had to fall back on the energy that the Lord gave me." That taught them all a lesson.

There could also be eruptions of boyish immaturity, the most blatant example being when Billy Graham was invited, on July 14, 1950, to meet President Truman at the White House—an indication of the increasing importance of Graham as a religious figure.

At Graham's request Barrows, Grady Wilson and Beavan were invited too. They all bought white summer suits and white buckskin shoes because "this is the way he dresses." At the end of a cordial twenty minutes Mr. Truman stood up. Billy asked if they might have prayer. The President cleared his throat and said, "Well, I don't suppose any harm could be done by that."

When Billy prayed, Cliff "kept muttering under his breath, 'Amen,' " Billy recalls, "and when I prayed for the President, Cliff said, 'Do it, Lord!' "

On leaving Mr. Truman they were immediately surrounded by pressmen, who shoved and yelled and extracted from Billy more of the presidential conversation than protocol permitted. When they heard he had prayed with the President, they persuaded Billy foolishly to pray on the White House lawn, the four friends kneeling while cameras clicked.

Mr. Truman was not amused. And Billy learned another valuable lesson: never quote the private words of the famous.

However much the crusades, from the start, were the work of a team, nevertheless each member was different. Cliff Barrows: boyish, gay, effervescent yet unruffled by excitement and publicity, happy leading a choir whose personnel might change every night, or in the counseling room, or acting Bible stories with verve at the vast children's rallies which were then a Saturday feature of crusades. Bev Shea: calm, mature, shy and self-effacing, already acquiring the title, "America's Beloved Gospel Singer." Graham wrote in 1949: "His depth, sincerity, dignity and personal spiritual life make a great impact upon the people to whom he ministers in song. Beverly Shea sings with deep spiritual dignity the grand old hymns of the church."

Shea generally sings twice at each meeting, once just before Billy Graham preaches. In this spot, particularly, he exhibits his special gift for singing in such a way that the audience, however vast, is brought to a quiet expectancy, their minds already on Christ.

Grady Wilson preached as Graham's substitute when needed, and at subsidiary meetings and on local radio during a crusade. His most vital contribution lay behind the scenes. In his company Billy could relax. Beneath jollity and buffoonery Grady hides a rapier mind, and if his gift of seeing the absurd could relieve tensions induced by awkward committees or sudden adversity, he could also, as Billy's closest friend, help him retain his balance. "If the Lord keeps Billy anointed, I'll keep him humble."

Billy himself had three inbuilt antidotes to losing his head or letting it swell as he shot from obscurity to fame. The first was his sense of humor, which bubbled in private and in spontaneous public comments which often disarmed a hostile audience and were generally far funnier than the rehearsed stories he told. Next was his insatiable appetite for information and knowledge, which in conversation made him genuinely sure the other man knew more than he. Billy would pick any brain, read any book, explore any situation. He seized on the offer of a friendly police sergeant to take the Team on midnight crime patrols, and in another Southern city prevailed on a distinguished minister to conduct him (disguised in dark glasses!) through the streets of its specially notorious red light district.

The third antidote to pride was a continuing sense of inadequacy: "The Lord has always arranged my life that I have had to keep dependent on Him. I just had to stay dependent on God because I have severe limitations. . . . Over and over again I went to my knees and asked the Spirit of Wisdom for guidance and direction. There were times when I was tempted to flee from problems and pressures and my inability to cope with them; but somehow, even in moments of confusion and indecision, it seemed I could trace the steady hand of God's sovereignty leading me on."

But beyond any other human factors helping him to keep his poise and maintain the pace were his mountain home at Montreat and the inestimable contribution of Ruth.

Their six-room gray stone house stood in a small shrub garden on Assembly Drive, the main road which led to the artificial lake and the buildings of Montreat-Anderson College. Immediately across a side road were the Nelson Bells. Dr. Bell practiced as a surgeon in Asheville, eighteen miles to the west, and was founder and co-editor of the

Presbyterian Journal. The side road ran steeply up to the wooded hills which enclose on three sides the saucerlike valley and are Billy Graham's delight because he enjoys hiking. On the fourth side, where the valley joins the narrow plain at Black Mountain, is a small golf course.

The Graham's third daughter, "Bunny," Ruth Bell Graham, was born in December 1950, and their elder son, William Franklin, in July 1952. Ruth loved to join Billy at least part of each crusade, but the Grahams remembered the tears of another evangelist's widow who told them she had been on the road so much that none of the family grew up in sympathy with their ministry. Ruth says, "A mother, like the Lord, needs to be a very present help in times of trouble. A mother has to be with the children. Personally I love it." Occasionally she would be wistful because Billy was away so much. "I'd wish we could be more normal. But God never asks us to give up one thing without giving so much in return that you wind up almost ashamed of yourself."

Ruth found it a little hard at first when her husband began to be treated as public property, but their unanimity of aim, her thrill at the unbelievable spiritual opportunities now opening, and her basic qualities enabled her to adjust quickly. Cliff, Grady, and Bev, like Billy, know that they never could have continued without the sacrifice and understanding of their wives, but as a former member of the Team, Larry Love, puts it, with Billy Graham "it would have been literally impossible. . . . Ruth is a remarkable person. She has a warmth and vitality about her and a depth that one does not often see. She's utterly unconscious as far as one can tell of her own personal attractiveness. . . . She is a perfect hostess and you can't help but feel at home."

She is also eminently practical whereas her husband cannot drive a straight nail—though Ruth says he could if he tried!

12 · An Hour of Decision

In the summer of 1950 Billy Graham reached one of his formative moments—which he did not immediately recognize.

During the first Boston visit he had heard of the sudden death of Walter A. Maier, founder and weekly radio preacher of Lutheran Hour, *Bringing Christ to the Nations.* Dr. Maier had had the ear of

America, preaching a clear evangelical Gospel in the context of the social, political and moral state of the nation. Billy and the Team immediately prayed together that someone be raised to take Maier's place.

That summer, while attending a conference at Ocean City on the New Jersey shore, Billy and Cliff drove over the bridge across the bay to play golf on a morning. That same morning a Philadelphia clergyman, Dr. Theodore Elsner of Calvary Memorial Church, happened to wake up late at the family cottage in Ocean City, which he and his son-in-law Fred Dienert, an advertising agent in Philadelphia, had rented for the summer. Elsner was president of the National Religious Broadcasters. As Elsner shaved he prayed for Billy Graham, whom he knew was at the nearby conference. As he prayed, a definite sense came to him that Billy Graham was the man to fill the gap left by Maier. For although the Lutheran Hour was continuing (and is still one of the world's most widely heard religious broadcasts) the approach no longer had Maier's topicality and his distinctive punch.

Alone in the cottage—having come down to open it for the season —Elsner at noon drove off to find a lunch counter. "A strange impression came upon me," he says, to cross the bridge, although he could easily get a sandwich in Ocean City. "But the impression became so strong, and I've learned to obey." On the mainland at Somers Point he saw a roadside diner and walked in. There sat Billy, Cliff, and a third golfer. Elsner ordered a sandwich but barely touched it for exhorting Billy, until Billy in enthusiasm began to pace up and down the diner. "How am I going to get on radio," he asked. "Who's going to help me?"

Elsner told him of his son-in-law, Fred Dienert, whose senior partner, Walter F. Bennett of Chicago, had promoted and helped arrange the great Lutheran Hour rally there and had handled many religious programs.

On subsequent reflection, Billy rejected the idea; a national weekly program could be almost a full-time occupation. When next month, at a conference in northern Michigan, two well-dressed strangers introduced themselves as Walter Bennett and Fred Dienert of the Walter Bennett Advertising Company, Billy charmingly sent them away. They reappeared at Montreat, and told him that a peak Sunday afternoon time would shortly be available coast-to-coast on the American Broadcasting Company's network, for an initial thirteen week contract at a total of $92,000, a sum which to Graham appeared astronomical.

Shortly afterward Graham began a six weeks' crusade at Portland, Oregon, where an aluminum temporary auditorium had been specially erected by the crusade committee. Bennett and Dienert pursued him by telephone and telegram to explain that the program cost about $7,000 a week; if he raised $25,000 he could go on the air, for after three weeks the gifts of listeners would certainly maintain it. None of his staff had ever seen Billy Graham lose his temper, but he now became irritated with these most persistent partners and refused to see them when they came to Portland. Ten days later they were back again. He used the rear elevator and even the fire escape to avoid them in the hotel lobby. They waited a week, received an appointment at last, only to find that Billy had escaped to Mount Hood for his rest-day, a Monday.

On Tuesday morning at Mount Hood Billy and Grady were breakfasting when a call came from Texas, from Howard Butt, a friend of their own age, heir to a great grocery chain. Butt said that if it were true Billy might go on radio, he and their mutual friend, Bill Mead, head of a bakery business, wanted to give $1,000 each to start a fund.

When Billy returned with Grady to the Multnomah Hotel at Portland on Tuesday afternoon, he avoided Bennett and Dienert and retired for his usual rest. Grady walked in with a message that the partners had booked a flight home that evening.

Billy told Grady to send for them.

Bennett and Dienert found him pacing back and forth, dressed in his pajamas and the golf cap he always wore to keep his hair straight when he rested. He told them he was undecided, but reported the offer of $2,000 and supposed he might contact other wealthy men if only his time permitted.

"Billy," said Fred Dienert, "I don't think the money is going to come from a lot of big people." Bennett and Dienert suggested telling the Portland audience about the opportunity.

At length Billy said, "Boys, let's pray."

He knelt by a chair. Walter and Fred lowered themselves to the bedside, and "Billy really poured out his heart to God." They had never heard a prayer of such childlike directness. As at Los Angeles, when uncertain whether to extend the campaign, Billy again sought a sign of God's will by putting out a "Gideon's fleece." But Walter and Fred were astonished when they heard what it was.

"Lord, You know I'm doing all that I can," is Fred Dienert's memory of the words of Billy's prayer. "You know I don't have any money, but I believe we ought to do this. You know, Lord, I have a mortgage on that little house in Montreat. Lord, I'll put another mortgage on; I'll take the little I have and put another mortgage on.

"Lord, I don't know where the money is, and if I did know where it is, I'm too busy to go out and get it.

"I feel the burden for it, but it's up to you, and if You want this, I want You to give me a sign. And I'm going to put out the fleece. And the fleece is for the $25,000, by *midnight.*"

Walter and Fred stole away. In the taxi to the airport they agreed, in awe, "You could feel the Presence of God there. You could feel a state of expectancy. God was listening to Billy. Something is going to happen." At the airport, therefore, they turned around and drove to the crusade, seating themselves unrecognized at the back. A huge crowd had come, which they appraised with satisfaction at about 20,000; when the plates were passed the amount ought to be raised.

The moment came for the offering toward crusade expenses; Billy said not a word about radio. The partners were disappointed.

The offering taken, Billy spoke of the radio opportunity. He said he felt he should take this available time for God rather than let it go to a tobacco company or such like; that he had no money nor the time to raise it. "But if any of you folks would like to have a part, I'll be in the office back here at the close of the service tonight." When he mentioned $25,000, Billy heard a ripple or two of laughter.

Bob Pierce, founder of World Vision and fresh from the Korean battlefront, gave the address that night, reporting much about the hand of God in relief work. To the anxious partners he seemed overlong. Billy followed with the basic points of the Gospel, gave the invitation and followed his normal custom: "Shall we pray. Every head bowed, every eye closed. . . . You come, as everybody in this place prays for you. You come . . . you hundreds of you come. . . ."

People had far to move from the ends of the building and the overflow seats outside. The time passed slowly. Billy stood at the podium, saying a word or two at intervals: "That's it. That's it, come on. . . . There are others coming. . . . Give your heart to Christ tonight . . . I beg of you to come. . . . That's it. . . . Many are coming, you come. . . . Sing it again softly as others come. . . ."

Bob Pierce then rose to address the hundreds who had come forward. Walter looked at Fred. Neither thought many of the audience would wait to see Billy at such a late hour. Fred murmured, "But God is faithful. Whatever He starts, He finishes."

At last the audience was released. Soon a long queue formed near the back office, where Grady held an old shoe box. Scribbled pledges and dollar notes were thrust in. A lumberman from Idaho left a $2,500 pledge. An old lady in a worn black dress produced a $5 bill, saying it was all she had. A couple of youths asking, "Dr. Graham, is chicken feed acceptable?" threw in a handful of change and a dollar, and Billy said, "God bless you. Thank you." A businessman said he was a Lutheran who had been one of Dr. Maier's most ardent supporters, that Graham should certainly pick up Maier's torch. The man pledged $1000, with the promise of more. Graham caught sight of Walter Bennett and introduced the two Lutherans.

Grady gave the box to the crusade chairman, Frank Phillips, and the Team went to their favorite eating place, Louie's-on-the-Alley, for oyster stew. Billy loved a late night meal after preaching. Bennett and Dienert joined them, and Frank Phillips entered excitedly saying that the tally, including the promised $2,000 from Texas, was just $23,500.

They all looked at Billy. "It's a miracle. You're as good as on the air!" Billy, almost in tears at the generosity and trust of the people, firmly said, No; the fleece was for $25,000 before midnight, $25,000 it must be. The devil might have sent the lesser sum to tempt him. When the two partners offered the balance, Billy refused them.

A subdued Team returned to the Multnomah Hotel shortly before midnight. Billy went to his room, Grady to the mail desk, where he was given three envelopes delivered by hand.

In each was a pledge from somebody unable to wait in the queue: one for $1,000, two for $250. Together they made up to $25,000.

Grady Wilson kept the shoe box in his shirt drawer overnight. Next morning he was told by the bank that if, however temporarily, he entered cash and checks under his name he would be liable for income tax, nor could it go tax-free under "Billy Graham Radio Fund" unless this were a properly constituted body. He put the money temporarily into the account of the Portland crusade, and Billy called George Wilson at Minneapolis.

Wilson flew West, bringing articles of incorporation which he had had drawn up the previous year against some such eventuality, and Billy, Ruth, Cliff and the two unrelated Wilsons signed them to form The Billy Graham Evangelistic Association. The others firmly overrode Billy's strong opposition to the trumpeting of his name. The name would identify, and the name was trusted. Periodically since 1950 Billy Graham has attempted to remove it, saying it puts the emphasis in the wrong place. The Board of Directors has always voted him down.

As for a title of the radio program, Ruth vetoed "The Billy Graham Hour." She saw that whereas the name of Billy Graham would rightly endorse the Association, it would be "the height of poor taste" on a program primarily designed for millions without definite faith in Christ, to whom it might imply the building of a personal following for a preacher. It was she who suggested *Hour of Decision,* an apt choice. Billy's emphasis was on *Deciding for Christ.* A "decision" might not be the moment of conversion, which God alone knew, but when sincere it was an act of will in response to the call of God, as the preacher set forth the issues of sin and salvation, of repentance and faith.

Meanwhile, unknown to the Grahams, the program had been killed. Bennett arrived at the American Broadcasting Company's Chicago office to sign the contract on Friday afternoon, as arranged by telephone, only to be told that the New York headquarters had changed their minds and would not sell time to Billy Graham. "They further informed me," writes Bennett, "that the decision was final; they had spent hours discussing it and had taken a unanimous vote on this action."

Bennett and Dienert flew to New York that night. Although ABC's executive offices were always empty on a Saturday, they went round next morning. A vice-president entered unexpectedly. He had missed the board meeting which had refused the contract but had learned of it by memorandum. "After a lengthy discussion he agreed that we were entitled to a review. He even contacted one of the top executives on the golf course to set up a meeting for Monday morning. The network deliberated for two days and on Wednesday announced the program's acceptance."

At Minneapolis George Wilson set up a one-room office in Harmon Place, a few yards across Loring Park from Northwestern Schools, and hired one secretary. That seemed enough, for they might not get many gifts or spiritual inquiries.

"Billy always hoped for the best and planned for the worst in an operation like that," says Wilson.

As for the program, Billy's friends urged him to speak quietly and slowly on radio, in contrast to his preaching. He rejected the advice. In a careful study of radio newscasters, commentators and radio preachers he detected that those who spoke fast won the largest audience; he modeled himself on Walter Winchell and Drew Pearson, both subsequently his personal friends. He would cover as much ground as he could, touching social and international issues, packing in illustrations and Bible quotations, each message to be "straight evangelism calculated to stir the Christian and win the person outside the church to Christ. . . . Fast, hard-hitting." [1]

The *Hour of Decision* (a half hour of time, the word "Hour" in the title following the normal custom of American radio) went out over 150 stations on ABC network on Sunday November 5, 1950, from Georgia, where Willis Haymaker had set up the Atlanta crusade in a specially constructed tabernacle on the baseball field of the Atlanta Crackers at Ponce de Leon Park. Cliff Barrows introduced and led the crusade choir and audience. Jerry Beavan gave news. At first there had been no role for Grady Wilson, whom Billy was determined not to leave out. They decided to have a Scripture reading, and Grady Wilson reading the Bible became one of the *Hour of Decision's* most appreciated features.

Bev Shea sang. Then Billy Graham stepped to the microphone. Three days previously the Chinese had massively intervened in the Korean War and were about to inflict a heavy defeat on United Nations forces.

"An Associated Press dispatch from Hong Kong in an Atlanta paper this morning"—Graham rattled out the words—"states that observers in that British colony have a bad case of war jitters, and many feel that the third World War is just around the corner. Certainly this is the most tragic and fateful hour in world history."

He spoke of those who blamed Christianity for the world's ills. "What a wicked, wanton lie! . . . You cannot say that Christ is responsible for this war! He pleads for peace, not bloodshed. And if all men would follow His counsel, no more battles would be fought. . . ." Graham turned, the thoughts and illustrations pouring out, to the early Apostles, and demonstrated their revolutionary intervention in the affairs of their day: "By their message Paul and Silas, as all true ministers of the Gospel, were restoring right and truth and justice. Every time they pointed their hearers to the Cross, the shackles of

[1] Armin Gesswein's young daughter, listening to one of the first *Hour of Decision* programs, said, "Is that the great Billy Graham? He doesn't let you get your breath, does he!"

ignorance, superstition, tyranny, the bonds of sin, vice and hatred were loosened. Their simple direct sermons pointed the end to cruel slavery, the end of polygamy, the end of fearful vices. . . .

"Today, Christianity must likewise be revolutionary. Our world has been directed utterly wrong. Race has been pitted against race, Communist against capitalist, employee against employer, 'haves' against the 'have nots'. . . ." He quoted in contrast Christ's plea: "A new commandment I give unto you, that ye love one another, as I have loved you."

Graham spoke of the reported possibility of a hydrogen bomb, and, again emphasizing the urgency of the hour, pleaded for a nation-wide movement of prayer: "Faith, more than fighting, can change the course of events today. United, believing, self-humbling, God-exalting prayer now can change the course of history."

Only right at the close of the address did he sound a direct evangelistic call, ending: "A crucified and a risen Christ will forgive sins, lift burdens, solve problems and give assurance of salvation to many. This experience can be yours, whoever you are, and whatever your circumstances may be, if by faith you will open your heart to Jesus Christ. Right now you can say an eternal Yes to Christ, and you can become a partaker of eternal life."

13 · Problems and Opportunities

In five weeks the *Hour of Decision* had earned the highest audience rating ever accorded a religious program. In eighteen months it was rated higher than most news commentators in daytime Sunday listening. Within five years it was heard weekly on a total of some 850 stations across the world, paying time on 350 network stations in North America.

The *Hour of Decision* had a considerable influence on the Team. For Billy Graham's development as preacher, it could hardly have come at a more vital moment. Whereas each crusade or rally brought a different audience and sermon material could be used over and over again, the *Hour of Decision* demanded every week a fresh address of highest caliber. Each took him most of two days to prepare. The necessity disciplined him all the more to study the Bible and theology, and to observe and assess contemporary events in the nation and the world.

Cliff Barrows became a skillful producer. At first the programs were broadcast live. With the development of tape recording Cliff could build up a library of Bev Shea's solos, crusade choral singing and Grady Wilson's readings, and coordinate them with the sermon recorded by Billy Graham wherever he happened to be.

The letters which listeners wrote to Billy Graham—178,726 the first year; 362,545 in 1952, and rising steadily—made necessary an increase of staff at the Minneapolis office, which by 1954 had eighty employees. For George Wilson, being secretary-treasurer of the Billy Graham Evangelistic Association soon became a full-time job. A "stocky, square-built man with broad, friendly face and a mind quick as a guided missile," who never stops working, he has been described by Billy Graham as having "more bounce to the ounce than any Christian I know." The students at Northwestern Schools, when he was business manager, had been a little afraid of him; but they found, as one of them says, "a tremendous warmth of personality and affection behind his apparent brusqueness." Vociferous football fan and mildly impish practical joker, he is a devoted family man and a Baptist lay-preacher. George Wilson did "an astounding job of organization" (so wrote a business engineer in November 1951), "in developing the interlocking system required to handle the monumental requirements of the *Hour of Decision.*"

The *Hour of Decision,* indirectly brought to a head a problem which had long bothered the Team.

They made no direct money appeal over the air until the program was well established and trusted by the networks. Cliff Barrows, on that first broadcast from Atlanta in November 1950, described how they had "felt definitely led into this venture of faith." He ended simply, "Now, we're looking to you, our listening audience, for the encouragement your letters will bring." Instead, by arrangement with the committee of the Atlanta crusade, envelopes were distributed to the audience on the final Thursday and Friday addressed to Billy Graham, which could be handed to ushers or posted to Minneapolis with a gift for the *Hour of Decision.*

On the last night of the six weeks' crusade the treasurer took up a love offering. Graham had not asked for it and was staggered on hearing the amount: it brought him more than many American clergymen earned in a year.

Next morning the Atlanta *Constitution* placed two photographs side by side on the front page: Billy Graham, happily grinning, waving a farewell to Atlanta as he steps into a car; another of volunteer ushers, grinning from ear to ear, holding high four enormous money bags. The implication was obvious. And although the captions were not offensive they included a statement that envelopes addressed to Dr. Graham were also taken up on Thursday and Friday.

"The cynics and the lukewarm have been howling to high heaven ever since," an Atlanta editor told Graham. On leaving Atlanta Billy and Cliff were "worried night and day," recalls Cliff, "because we didn't want this image to characterize our ministry." The dilemma appeared insoluble. At Los Angeles Graham had startled the audience by announcing that he would give the whole love offering of $12,000 to "the work of evangelism in Southern California"—and some accused him of making a grand display. At Portland he gave most of an even larger amount privately to the Navigators—and heard criticisms "that I am hogging it all to myself and getting rich." He accepted Atlanta's offering "in the spirit of generosity and love with which it was given," and after distributing shares to the others to add to their honoraria (Cliff had now insisted on receiving less than Billy), and paying travel and other expenses, he held a substantial sum. Furthermore, he had received and refused three separate film offers which would have made him indeed wealthy.

Ruth and Billy decided to live on an income no higher than that of the pastor of a large city church. Billy paid off the mortgage on his home and bought some cheap woodland—about 200 acres for $3,200—on the top of the mountain behind; it would be nice for hiking and meditating, and might one day make a farm. They gave away over half of the Atlanta offering to foreign missions (in Formosa) and to the *Hour of Decision*.

But giving away money did not solve the dilemma. His colleagues knew Billy as a man of uninhibited generosity. Cliff says the attitude between them always was, "Buddy, if I've got anything you want, it's yours."

Neither self-sacrifice nor generosity would destroy the public belief that evangelism was a racket. Billy Sunday also had been extraordinarily generous, but was remembered, erroneously, as a man who made a fortune. Over the next nine months Graham consulted men of experience on what to do. His warm friend, Jesse Bader, secretary of Evangelism for the National Council of Churches, pointed out that Billy Graham was already incorporated as an evangelistic association: "Pay yourself a salary and don't take love offerings, and you can make history in evangelism. You can lift evangelism to a place of confidence and high regard in America that it has not had since D. L. Moody. Bader suggested the salary be $15,000 a year, comparable at the time to a senior denominational executive or a leading city pastor.

The last love offering was taken at Greensboro, North Carolina, in November 1951. Thereafter all public and private receipts went directly to the Association. For some months Graham allowed honoraria to be paid to the Association, and then broke through to the new principle that from the viewpoint of a crusade committee his services were given free. He too was a salaried member of the Billy Graham Evangelistic Association. Instead, a weekly offering was taken for the *Hour of Decision*.

The public quickly appreciated the new approach. Some older evangelists did not.

Graham's attitude to expenditure was fresh, too.

"If it costs a quarter of a million dollars to touch a city for Christ," he wrote in October, 1950, "I believe in spending a quarter of a million dollars." The gauge should not be the penny-pinching expenditure of religious enterprises, even in America, but what the world spent: most crusades cost less than the sum earned by a champion boxer in one big fight!

Graham considered that evangelists and those who prepared locally for their coming should be "ready to step out in faith" and to expect money to be given generously by large numbers of people. If accounts were audited and published, if care were taken not to misspend, there could be adventurous budgeting. "As long as the money is not going into our private pockets, and as long as our motives are right before God, I see no reason why we cannot spend almost any amount in order to reach a city for Christ."

And the money contributed to make possible this kind of outreach would have to be contributed in a prayerful spirit. A millionaire sought out Graham in 1952 and offered to underwrite him, "so you won't have to worry about finances." Graham instantly refused: "I can't accept it. We get about three or four thousand letters a week and in most of those letters there'll be a dollar bill, sometimes five dollars, but every letter says, 'Billy, I'm praying for you.' My work would nose-dive immediately if people knew that a rich man was underwriting me." [1]

---

[1] A further reason for Graham's refusal, of course, was his determination never to allow himself to be run or exploited by any individual or group, whether right wing, left wing, political or religious.

Although criticism of Billy Graham's finances died quickly, he was criticized plentifully on other grounds. In the rising religious interest which was sweeping America in the early nineteen-fifties (much of it genuine, but some of it mixed in motive, as when city dwellers, on moving to the suburbs, took to churchgoing as a status symbol), the role of Billy Graham was a subject of widespread debate.

The secular press viewed him with a latent sneer, as a freak, or a sudden comet that would disappear as swiftly as he had risen. His deliberate playing down of himself, his emphasis on being an unqualified country boy—"God laying His hand upon the most unlikely prospect among His servants"—obscured the steady climb upward before Los Angeles '49. He only seemed a sudden arrival from nowhere.

All public figures suffer from misquotations and quotations out of context, the trap question, and especially the reporter who takes no notes, then prints in quotation marks what he thinks he remembers was said at the interview. For Billy Graham it was worse because most of the secular press were writing about a subject beyond their competence. When he first talked with Henry Luce, that night in Columbia, he pointed out that *Time* had sent to Los Angeles an interviewer who was a secularist, ignorant and suspicious of the concept and message of evangelism. "Would you send a dress designer to cover a ball game?" asked Graham. Luce took the point. *Time* and *Life* eventually became eminently fair and objective. Some other papers did not. Editors and reporters were continually attempting to relate him to a disreputable or ridiculous norm. Harmless or sensible comments would be blown up to absurdity, and Graham still occasionally made foolish statements. He had a tendency to sound an alarmist note which, though it made sense to his listeners in the context of a complete address, could look wild as an isolated newspaper paragraph and be used to ridicule his whole message. However much in after years he might wish he could withdraw "some of the statements I made in those early days because of immaturity or a lack of knowledge and experience," they were filed, with the misquotes and misinterpretations, to be dredged up by solemn researchers like Dr. William G. McLoughlin, Jr., anxious to prove Graham's outlook derisory or dangerous.[1]

[1] Superficial students of Graham are misled by the fact that in shorter press accounts of his addresses most of the space is given to his few sentences on topical issues, the Communist menace and so on, and the spiritual teaching

By 1952 Graham was showing a marked gift for handling press conferences, but the press of America remained lynx-eyed for the fall they considered inevitable, whether by scandal or innocent but irretrievable misjudgment. Graham's life must be an open book, to the extent that he could never stay in a hotel without having a male associate able to account for every moment and movement. To Graham this end of privacy was a small sacrifice against the value of the press, whose work he honored and endeavored to aid. As he wrote a friend, "I believe it is for the glory of the Lord Jesus to keep this nationwide coverage."

All this time Billy Graham and his Team were giving a new look to evangelism. They had adopted the term "crusade" instead of "campaign" or "revival." They changed "personal worker" to "counselor," a word long used in education but never previously in religion, though Billy Graham so popularized its use that it has become a normal religious term. They kept to their determination never to work in a city without an invitation from a substantial group of representative churches, though this presented no difficulty, for Graham was swamped with invitations. The final decision on which to accept was always his personally, after full discussion with the Team.

They moved from city to city with apparently inexhaustible energy, working for four or five weeks in each. Wherever they went the Team left behind a host of friends and converts, and sometimes critics.

A comparatively small critical group objected that Graham ignored the Sacraments—a criticism which he considered misconceived, for he values them highly. A much larger group considered his theology old-fashioned. He would hear that he had set back Christianity fifty years, to which he would reply that he was disappointed: he had hoped to put it back two thousand. Liberal ministers were puzzled by his success. "They agreed," ran an account in *The Christian Century* after the Portland, Oregon, crusade, "that Graham is sincere, but deplored his theological literalism and his appeal to fear. While holding his homiletics immature, they recognize the great strength of his preaching, attributing it to his personality, his sensationalism, his publicity techniques and his burning conviction that he is indeed a latter-day prophet."

Nevertheless, one of the most significant developments of the early nineteen-fifties was the widening range of church support behind him.

which took up most of the actual address is almost or entirely ignored. Archbishop William Temple suffered from the same distortion.

Like D. L. Moody, Graham accepted gratefully the goodwill and aid of any who let him uninhibitedly preach his message. He insisted that the executives of a crusade be men in full sympathy with his objectives, but he welcomed all, whatever their theology, who would co-operate with his platform. Thus Graham, by 1952 the most widely heard preacher in America, was spearhead of a new ecumenicity, breaking down barriers raised by a generation or more of theological bitterness.

He was not surprised when attacked by men who denied the intervention of the Holy Spirit in human affairs or the contemporary relevance of the Bible. When an ill-wind blew from another quarter he was, at first, hurt. Certain conservatives such as Dr. John R. Rice and Dr. Carl McIntire pronounced him guilty of association with men of false beliefs on the Bible, the Atonement and other "fundamentals of the faith"; he should separate himself from all who were unsound—an attitude which would have condemned St. Paul for preaching in a synagogue. Billy Graham could not believe it Christ's will that he should treat every supporter of the National Council of Churches as a theological leper. Moreover he knew modernists whose beliefs and ministry had been revolutionized by taking part in an uncompromisingly evangelical crusade.

The fundamentalist critics did not seek out Billy Graham "to counsel with me, pray with me, talk with me, love me"; they wrote cold, hard, demanding letters, and articles. He was tempted to reply, but instead adopted—on a hint from V. Raymond Edman of Wheaton—the policy expressed to critics by Nehemiah: "I am doing a great work, so that I cannot come down: why should the work cease, whilst I leave it, and come down to you?"

Only occasionally did Graham reply, and Willis Haymaker says "it was always like a love letter. You couldn't take offense with it. He'd take the humble place, and be just like a son to a father—God honored that."

In 1952 two episodes, one at the start and one at the close of the year, considerably increased Billy Graham's stature in the eyes of Americans.

The Team held a five-week crusade in Washington, D.C., at the National Guard Armory near Union Station. The invitation had come from Democratic and Republican senators and representatives. President Truman did not attend, but the respect with which many national leaders listened was extraordinarily impressive to an English clergyman, Colin Kerr, a prebendary of St. Paul's Cathedral, London. He remembered Graham from 1946 and "thought all I would see and hear would repel me." Instead he found "a new Billy Graham. . . . All the extravagance had gone." Kerr was a little frightened, too, that there might be evidence of "a sort of magnetism." As he watched the inquirers file into the counseling room—clerks from the Pentagon, a congressman or two, a marine who later became a pioneer missionary in a tough area of Bolivia, Washington housewives, Negro cleaners—"the look on their faces removed any doubt. It was the work of God's Spirit and not just an overawing by a great and fascinating personality. There was a look of sincerity, of seriousness on their faces."

The cold rainy Sunday of February 3 saw a unique service on the steps of the Capitol in Washington. The Sergeant at Arms of the House of Representatives reckoned the crowd greater than at most presidential inaugurations. The Speaker of the House, Sam Rayburn, with whom had lain the final authorizing decision, said, "This country needs a revival, and I believe Billy Graham is bringing it to us." The service had been permitted by an unprecedented Act of Congress, and was carried live by radio and TV across the nation. Millions heard the thirty-three-year-old Graham read Lincoln's 1863 proclamation for a day of humiliation and prayer, and follow it with a short, stirring plea that at this time of war and corruption a new such day be proclaimed, that the nation return to God, the Bible, the Church.

The Washington Crusade brought Graham the high regard of political leaders and warm friendship with men of both parties, among them Senator Richard M. Nixon and Senator Lyndon B. Johnson. He attended the 1952 Republican and Democratic presidential conventions but declined official invitations to lead the opening prayers.

He declined also to run for senator in his home state. Writers who cannot conceive a man driven by neither political nor materialistic motives at times try to prove Graham's real, if secret, aim to be to advance the interests of one or the other party. The advice given Graham by a close, older friend in 1952, after reading an erroneous report that Graham had boasted of power to sway a presidential election, in fact accurately represented Graham's own position at the time, a position which has only once—in 1960—come close to faltering: "You have won so many people in this country because you have a spiritual message; given even the slightest intimation that there are political aspirations and this influence for righteousness will be dispelled in large measure. People of many backgrounds recognize in your ministry the thing which our nation needs more than anything else. They also have seen so many build up a following and then try to use it for other purposes, and if they become disillusioned about your motives, or your estimation of your following for other than spiritual purposes, it is bound to do harm." [1]

During the closing days at Washington Graham had been troubled by a sore on the inside of his lip which a specialist diagnosed as possibly malignant. Graham went straight to the Mayo Clinic in Rochester, Minnesota, where the sore was cleared up quickly and he got a clean bill of health. He went on to Minneapolis and on February 25, 1952, resigned the presidency of Northwestern Schools.

He had tried to resign unsuccessfully a year earlier. A small group of trustees would have been joyfully rid of him, but the majority loved him and judged the prestige of his name to be greater than the inconvenience of a reluctant, intermittent president. Ruth continued to urge concentrating on evangelism. At last, hiking the trails at Montreat that Christmas, meditating and praying, Graham reached his decision.

"God had given me an unparalleled opportunity to preach the Gospel throughout the nation. I could see people all around me in the fire of confusion, frustration and problems. I had met people everywhere whose lives were a mess." He could touch men and women at every level of society—he was being invited to clubs as well as churches—and he believed that the unparalleled opportunity would not last. Ought he not to give himself wholly to it?

He read again every Bible passage on the call to evangelism. As he walked narrow trails which only he and his family knew well enough to track through the fallen leaves, "I thought about Christ's death on the cross. Above all other motives as a spur to service and incentive to evangelism is the cross of Christ and its irrepressible compassion." One day when he had climbed the dirt track to the Reed field on his own mountain side, where the homestead now stands, he looked out across the mist-filled valley and found himself singing (no one to mind the off-key notes) the old mission hymn:

> Rescue the perishing, care for the dying,
> Snatch them in pity from sin and the grave;

[1] To this letter Graham replied, after setting the record straight: "I want and need your suggestions, counsel, advice; and any time you feel like jacking me up and kicking me in the pants, please do. I have enough people patting me on the back. I get sick of it. I need some real friends from time to time who will talk turkey to me."

Weep o'er the erring one, lift up the fallen,
Tell them of Jesus, the Mighty to save.

He knew without shadow of doubt that henceforth he must have "no other desire, no other goal, no other ambition."

At the end of the year Graham was able to carry the Gospel to the Korean battlefront.

The Korean War was in its third winter. The front line had been stabilized for more than a year, a cease-fire had come and gone. Local actions continued, and the American dead alone already totaled more than 21,000. Late in October 1952, during a short vacation in Florida after the difficult Pittsburgh crusade, Billy Graham, recalling numerous letters received, determined to spend Christmas with the troops if possible.

It nearly was not possible. Washington withheld permission. At the end of the crusade in Albuquerque, New Mexico, on November 30, Jerry Beavan rushed to Washington where, aided by Graham's friends in Congress, he at length extracted the necessary papers for Graham and Grady Wilson, in time to hand them over at Los Angeles a few hours before the scheduled departure.

Graham and Wilson were joined by Bob Pierce of World Vision, just returned from Korea. The first leg of their journey, to Hawaii, was the occasion of a practical joke of frontier rawness whose originator, of all people, was the gentle Ruth. Grady had been talking too much about the wonderful yellow sleeping pills he would use on the tedious night flight. Ruth quietly substituted capsules filled with mustard powder. Grady had a terrible time. "I took one after another, thinking 'Maybe I'm immune to them.' I got heartburn and indigestion! I thought it was the steak sauce I had poured heavily in Hollywood." Billy enjoyed a good laugh out of Grady's stunned look when he heard the truth gleefully revealed in Tokyo before an audience of missionaries!

In Japan and Korea Billy Graham found Washington's reluctance replaced by top-level welcome. With the local rank of major-general and facilities and staff similar to those given Cardinal Spellman, he held evangelistic services in many parts of Korea. Christmas Day was spent at the front, preaching to the sound of gunfire, twice to smaller groups and once, a few miles behind, to a great concourse of officers and men sitting on rough benches or standing armed in the snow.

Graham's visit, says General Mark W. Clark today, then Commander-in-Chief, "gave a great boost to the morale of our troops." It also deepened Billy Graham's ministry. As he visited the wounded, once getting on the floor to look up and talk with a soldier paralyzed by bullets in his spine, who was forced to lie face downward, Billy was faced by human suffering far beyond his previous experience. To Grady Wilson it seemed that "Billy began preaching with more compassion than ever before. I could tell a big change as soon as he got back to the states. I would put it down as one of the turning points."

The Korean episode deepened Graham's concern for Christian missions overseas. "During the past few days," he told his *Hour of Decision* listeners on December 21 from Seoul, "our hearts have been rent and torn at what we have seen, felt and heard." The poverty and war miseries of Korea, the devotion of Korean Christians, the stories of martyrdom, and all he learned in Japan, Formosa and the Philippines made him determined to promote the work of missions. He began, too, to hope that he would have opportunity himself one day to preach to great crowds in missionary lands as in the United States.

---

14 · Expanding Ministry

Returned from Korea, Graham was called to the Commodore Hotel in New York by President-elect Eisenhower a week before his inauguration in January 1953. They had met first, by the General's invitation, in Paris the previous March. At Denver, during the election campaign, Graham had given him a Bible. The General, known in the Army as a rare churchgoer but a man who openly declared his belief in God, had explained his position to Graham, adding that he would not join a church, lest this seem vote-catching, until after the election, when he would do so, "win or lose."

Now in New York in January 1953 they chatted for half an hour. The President-elect walked to a window and looked out across the city. He turned to Graham and said that perhaps one reason for his election was to help set a moral and spiritual tone to the nation; he would, he said, like to introduce a spiritual note into his inaugural address. "General," replied Graham, "you can do more to inspire the American people to a more spiritual way of life than any man alive." They talked of possible Bible passages. Graham offered Psalm 33:12 ("Blessed is the nation whose God is the Lord") and the verse from II Chronicles, which the President ultimately used. That Eisenhower

closed his speech with prayer, the first prayer offered publicly by a
President at inauguration, was as much a surprise to Graham as to
the world.

In the first year of Dwight D. Eisenhower's presidency Billy Graham made an important decision on a national matter not then in
prominence, but which was to become one of the problems of the era
—the race question.

Born and bred a Southerner, with normal Southern attitudes, Billy
Graham had, however, never lost those uncomfortable feelings which
followed upon his conversion. In Charlotte in the nineteen-thirties, a
city without formal segregation or awareness of a race problem, Negroes were assumed to form a lower order from which there could be
no rise. Each side accepted the division. Billy felt a general uneasiness about white complacency toward Negro poverty and their lack
of opportunity, but there was no indefiniteness about his feelings toward churches that did not admit Negroes to worship: "From the
time I was converted I could not understand segregation in the
church."

Back in 1952 the word "integration" was unheard. A few far-
seeing political and religious liberals, a few outspoken Negro pastors,
were the only voices raised against continuance of the traditional attitude toward Negroes. At crusades in the South the Team left the seating arrangement to the local committee: some had no segregation,
others the customary Jim Crow sections. But Graham often publicly
deplored the Jim Crow laws, and from the very earliest crusades insisted—and it occurred to no committee member to protest—that
whites and Negroes should come forward together at the invitation.
"There's no racial distinction here," Billy would say from the pulpit.
"Here are white and colored alike, standing before the cross of
Christ. The ground is level at the foot of the cross." At Houston,
Texas, in May 1952, a shady section of the stadium was put aside
for Negroes. "So often they are shoved aside," wrote Luverne
Gustavson to her family, "and Mr. Graham has been so concerned
about reaching them here in the South."

At Jackson in June a leading minister asked him if he realized that
the United States was on the verge of a racial explosion. The white
minister had been president of a Negro college. To him the conversation was casual and soon forgotten;[1] to Billy Graham it resolved his

[1] As this minister now does not believe that he made the remarks, I keep back
his name.

uneasiness. "The Negro is emerging," said the minister, and he talked of their resentment and their determination to end discrimination. With remarkable accuracy he predicted the course of events. "Human justice is on their side. Religion is, too. Billy, you've taken leadership in the field of evangelism, and this is something you're going to have to face."

Billy Graham thereupon made a thorough study of the Bible's teaching on race. He came to the firm conclusion that it allowed no grounds for practicing segregation or treating one race as inferior to another. In so doing Graham stepped clean away from the views of many evangelicals, whether in North or South.

On March 15, 1953, more than a year before the famous Supreme Court decision of May 17, 1954, began the first deliberately integrated Billy Graham crusade, at Chattanooga, Tennessee. In this Southern city below Lookout Mountain the civic officials had constructed an auditorium for the crusade. Graham told the crusade committee that Negroes must be allowed to sit anywhere; he overruled protests and ignored forecasts of trouble. To his disappointment the attendance of Negroes was sparse. Those who came tended to group together, embarrassed to mingle with the whites, despite the absense of any ugly incidents upon their entering. The city's principal newspaper did not even comment on the integrated seating.

Segregated seating reappeared at Dallas in May and June 1953; the local crusade committee refused to abolish Jim Crow sections. "I reluctantly accepted their decision. Thousands of Negroes attended but they sat in their own section, though it was agreed that none of the ushers would refuse any who wanted to sit in white sections. A number of them did come and sit in white sections, and there was no difficulty." The crusade committee, as a small concession to Graham's principles, had agreed to remove the signs which indicated where Negroes should sit.

Graham made plain his personal feelings against segregation in an incident at his hotel. He had been receiving a daily massage from a Negro with whom he became great friends. One afternoon they happened to meet in the hotel lobby just before appointment time. Graham said they would go up together. The Negro answered that he was not allowed on the elevator but would use the back stairs. "Nonsense," said Billy. "You'll come with me."

As the Negro stepped into the elevator, a bellman intervened. Graham was indignant. "Either he rides with me or I go to the back and walk up with him. You can take your choice."

The assistant manager hurried forward from his desk and hastily assured the hotel's distinguished guest that he might take his Negro friend with him.

After the Supreme Court's decision Graham could insist on integrated crusades. This he did at Nashville and New Orleans in 1954 and in all subsequent Southern cities. Meanwhile in 1953, though it lost him friends and brought him abuse, he frequently and publicly stated his conviction that the Bible did not support segregation, and that "Jesus Christ belongs neither to the colored nor the white races. He belongs to all races, and there are no color lines with Christ, as He repeatedly said that God looks upon the heart." Graham considered that the Church's attitude to race was lagging behind that of the worlds of sport and politics.

Extremists on both sides caused most of the trouble, Graham saw, and he believed that the pace could not be forced, nor could desegregation be imposed by legislation, without certainty of violence. He stated then, as often since, "There must be a process of education, and faith in Christ. Christ alone can give the love in the hearts of the two races that ultimately will ease all tensions and solve all problems in this matter." [1]

In these years of the early nineteen-fifties, although the long succession of city-wide crusades was Graham's main thrust, he was fulfilling his determination to get the Gospel to as many as he could, by every means he could.

In the last days of Los Angeles '49 Bob Pierce had introduced Graham to a thirty-two-year-old film producer, Dick Ross. Ross was a former air force navigator and prisoner of war in Germany who had been production manager for Moody Institute of Science films. Now he owned his own small company, Great Commission Films. At Graham's invitation Ross made a documentary of the Portland crusade, including a superb scene with Cliff Barrows enacting for schoolchildren the cleansing of Naaman in the River Jordan ("Seven Ducks in Muddy Water").

At the Fort Worth crusade in the Texas cattle country in February and March 1951 Ross produced a feature film, a fiction story based on the actual decision of a roughriding cowboy. For the lead parts he used two professional singers, cowboy Redd Harper and cowgirl Cyndy Walker, who were members of the Hollywood Christian Group. It needed courage for Graham to promote this first "Christian

[1] Letter to Ralph McGill, editor of the *Atlanta Constitution*, October 31, 1953.

western," *Mr. Texas;* for many evangelicals in 1951, fiction films and actors were, by definition, of the devil. But Graham believed that "if we are going to arrest the vast pagan masses of America, our methods are going to have to change while our message remains Christ and Him crucified."

Mr. Texas had songs, a rodeo scene and shots from the crusade. It cost only $25,000. The première took place at the close of the Hollywood Bowl crusade in October 1951 to an audience of 25,000 —the biggest première in Hollywood history—with Cecil B. de Mille and other film moguls present. And the projector broke down in the middle! Billy "wanted the floor of the Bowl to open up and let me fall through." He called some of the others, and on the edge of the crowd they knelt and prayed. In five minutes the projector recovered. When Billy spoke briefly at the end, nearly five hundred of the audience came forward. "This seemed to be God's seal of approval on our weak and faltering beginning in making dramatic motion pictures."

The trade paper, *Variety,* was scathing: "Off-beat, amateurish . . . Will find an audience only on the religious circuit and even there may be limited to Billy Graham converts." Its artlessness was in fact its strength, and it immediately proved to have power to draw the unchurched. When a few weeks later *Mr. Texas* was shown to two big audiences of North Carolina state prisoners, with Redd Harper in person giving the closing invitation, the director of prisons told Graham that it was "the means of more than a hundred men and women committing their lives to Christ."

Mr. Texas, however primitive its production and brash its Billy Graham, retains remarkable power, and in 1964 it ranked third in popularity of the current thirty-four Graham feature films.

World Wide Pictures was incorporated in 1951 to produce and distribute Billy Graham films. The next, *Oiltown, USA,* a more advanced and expensive production, was a story of Houston, in 1952, where the crusade broke through to the upper crust of the city. The story is based on the conversion experience of a millionaire. Billy Graham films were soon being shown in the United States and abroad at army camps, prisons, schools, at churches which would never invite an evangelist, in scattered communities. Graham had proved that "thousands of unconverted will come to a film that would never hear a preacher."

During 1951 Graham started a weekly Sunday night television *Hour of Decision* on the strength of a gift of $50,000 from two friends in Texas. By the standard of the enormous impact that the Graham Team was to make on TV after 1957, these early experiments seem unsuccessful. Contemporary experts, however, thought Graham the TV personality of their dreams. In November 1953 the National Broadcasting Company invited him to sign a five-year contract, at a very high sum,[1] to be host on a daily secular program, in which he could weave a religious theme throughout the half hour.

Whereas he could dismiss with a laugh the numerous invitations to sell the commercial value of his name for the promotion of soaps, food, clothing and other products, Nelson Bell saw him "actually frightened until he could reject the offer."

In these years also Graham broke into the printed word.

Walter Bennett and Fred Dienert could think of no way to bring Billy Graham's ministry within daily reach of millions of newspaper readers until Bennett, on a flight to New York, happened to read a problem column. It suddenly struck him that problems enough were submitted to Graham by radio listeners. On the return flight Bennett's eye caught the familiar "My Day," by Eleanor Roosevelt. Words clicked in his consciousness: "My Answer, by Billy Graham." The partners prepared a sample. Billy doubted his capacity to sustain a daily column, but suggested they pray about it and meet again.

Bennett and Dienert approached editors and were told: "We don't have space to put Jesus Christ daily. It's either once a week or not at all." At length the *Chicago Tribune–New York News* syndicate commissioned the column. "My Answer" began on a daily basis in December 1952, and by the close of 1953 ran in seventy-three papers reaching fifteen million readers. Twelve years later it was carried by one hundred and twenty-three daily newspapers in North America alone. Billy Graham soon developed a skill in dictating answers to questions on a far ranging variety of subjects, from spiritual problems and theology to sex and ethics and domestic tensions. Because of pressure on his time, he has often asked an associate to draft answers; but, as Billy can say, "I've never sent a single 'My Answer' in all these years that I didn't re-do until it became mine."

In November 1953 came the publication of *Peace with God*.

An editor of Doubleday's, attending a 1952 crusade, detected a

---

[1] NBC told him that, in their experience, the host of this program could expect to make, by his salary and the subsidiary income that would accrue, a total of one million dollars a year.

likely best seller and approached Billy Graham. Graham knew the urgent need for a book that would set forth the Gospel "in utter simplicity" for those who would read neither a brief tract nor a work of theology. But he doubted whether he was qualified to write a book for a big New York publishing company. He asked if Doubleday would provide editorial assistance. They agreed, enlisted someone whom Billy presumed was their employee but (as he did not discover for years) was a professional free-lance ghost-writer, to whom he sent an outline and a mass of sermon material. The literary skill of the ghost was not matched by spiritual perception or full understanding of Graham's thought. As the first ghosted chapters reached Graham, "I can remember yet, looking at them appalled. I chucked the whole thing in the wastebasket, and Ruth and I wrote that book, *Peace with God*. He submitted the script to several friends, wrote and rewrote, and prayed often. Apart from inevitable editorial revisions, *Peace with God* is genuine unghosted Billy Graham.

It sold 125,000 copies within three months, and millions over the years in many languages. By 1965 one and a quarter million copies had been sold in English alone. From his share of the royalties Billy Graham formed a trust fund for the education of his children.

Peace with God was the early work of a preacher turned author, and some of its phrases can be faulted under a theological microscope. For the purpose to which it was dedicated—to confront ordinary people, reared to different forms of Christianity or none, with the basic Christian claim, and to enable them to put their faith in the living Christ and take the first steps on the road to spiritual riches—it has proved matchless.

Of all the letters which reached Graham from readers in the first year, two gave him special happiness. A Californian of sixty-one, who had not been to church since he was sixteen, on a business trip fell into conversation in a Boston cemetery with an elderly gentleman who mentioned the book. "For some reason," the Californian told Billy in July 1954, "I bought your book on Monday. Went into New York City on Tuesday and over the next few nights read a few chapters. On Sunday, May 2, I'll never forget the date, I was in the hotel in Easton, Pennsylvania. That afternoon I went to my room and in a spirit of wanting help, read the rest of your book. Your words unfolded to me exactly what I was looking for, and thru the guidance you gave, as I read the last page, I closed the book and told God I was His to lead forever. God came into that room that day and I sincerely felt His presence." The man bought a Bible, his habits and ap-

Billy Graham gives Indian greeting to ladies during 1956 rally in Madras, India. BELOW. *Final meeting in Nairobi, Kenya. Speaker's stand at right.*

"He punches home the facts — the facts that he reads out from the Bible in his hand and which he asks his audience to read again and again in their Bibles."

Billy Graham visiting with students at the University of Chicago, February 1962.

Billy Graham chats with New York youth. BELOW. *Relaxing on the porch of his home.*

President and Mrs. Dwight D. Eisenhower with Mr. Graham and Dr. Edward L. R. Elson, *pastor of the National Presbyterian Church, Washington, D. C., March 1955.* LEFT. *Billy Graham with President John F. Kennedy.*

Billy Graham with President Lyndon B. Johnson.

Brandenburg Gate, Berlin, July 1960, before the wall was built. Half the choir came from East Berlin. BELOW. Broadcasting the Hour of Decision from Egypt, with the Pyramids in the background, 1960.

With his grandson, Stephan Nelson Tchividjian, at Montreat, October 1965.
BELOW: *Billy and Ruth Graham with their family in 1962: Franklin, Ned, Anne, Virginia, Ruth (Bunny).*

Billy Graham greets throng at air terminal before September 1962 crusade in Sao Paulo, Brazil.

"By the evidence of the demands for crusades, his first forty-seven years have been merely a prelude and preparation for the years ahead."

petites changed, his wife believed too. For him *Peace with God* was a new beginning, and as he wrote in October 1965, "My faith is *lasting.*"

The other letter came from St. Paul's Episcopal Church, Kansas City, written on December 30, 1953, by Father Robert Bull, a chaplain of the State prison, shortly after the execution of Carl Hall for kidnapping the Greenlease child. "Reverend and Dear Sir," it ran. "Carl Hall had three final requests. One of them concerned you. Carl read and reread your *Peace with God*. It had a great deal to do with his conversion. And he wanted me to express to you his deep appreciation. That book I now have, for he autographed and gave it to me the night he died. I shall treasure it for a dual purpose. May God bless you in your work."

---

15 · Follow-up

"Graham's equipment for getting and holding audiences was more than adequate," runs an article in *Presbyterian Life* in October 1953. "He was handsome in an odd, off-beat way that made him compelling as well as pleasing to watch. He was well dressed. He had a powerful and expressive, though not beautiful, voice. He had long, rangy limbs that made his gestures intelligible even to the backmost viewers in a crowd. He had an intensity and vigor that seemed to come from the vitality of three men. Most of all, he had an earnestness and sincerity about speaking of Christ that few have doubted. What he did not have was a way of ensuring that his hearers would persevere in the Christian life after the Billy Graham campaign moved on to the next city. Three years ago Graham and his advisers worked out a follow-up plan."

Those who had come forward at early Graham crusades had been given five simple hints: "Read your Bible every day.... Pray everywhere you go.... Witness for Christ, tell somebody else you are a Christian, and live a consistent life for Christ in home and business.... Above all, go to church. Join a church if you are not already a member. If you are, tell your pastor about your decision, and he will be glad to help you." Passing the torch to ministers as he left a city, Graham would say that he knew that of those who had come forward, some were following the whim of a temporary emotion, some did not realize what they were doing, "but scores of others meant business and were truly giving their hearts to Christ." If the pastors were alert to careful shepherding of all who made decisions, and received their names, most would grow to maturity. If as in Portland, Oregon, the committee arranged for laymen to be trained before a crusade, there could be adequate counseling. But in the very places most needing revival of church life—where their churches were weak and pastors sleepy—the harvest of a crusade would be squandered. Small wonder that Graham wrote: "I have come to the conclusion that the most important phase is the follow-up." Without proper follow-up, mass evangelism was little more than mass movement, a crowd following a crowd, a wave of religious emotion which quickly evaporated.

Billy Graham sought an answer. "When we move into a town, seemingly the Lord opens the entire city." "The entire atmosphere," wrote one Southern city's secular journal in its editorial, "is charged with a devotional upsurge that cannot be explained away as the result of simple, natural causes." Yet Graham could not properly seize the hour until every individual who came forward, in full conviction or in ephemeral emotion, whether a finder or a seeker, received the help he needed.

"At the close of the sermon," wrote one of Graham's colleagues from Northwestern Schools, visiting an early Southern crusade, "I found myself surrounded by hundreds of anxious souls, needing instruction and guidance in the Word, while the absence of personal workers was appalling. After leading six men in succession to a full surrender to Christ, I trembled at seeing scores leaving without anyone to speak to them." And he knew that he ought to have given the whole of his time to each one of the six.

Graham began to pray, "Lord, send us someone who knows something about this."

He turned to Dawson Trotman of the Navigators. Three times Trotman refused.

Trotman was not enamored of mass evangelism. All his work lay with small groups, with training the one to lead the one. Billy believed that Trotman's principles could be transferred from the group to the mass, but Trotman had no time, with the Navigators expanding rapidly in many parts of the world. He doubted too whether there would not be a clash of personalities. He was eight years older, independently minded, the unfettered boss of his enterprise. Could he work with the Graham Team, or they with him?

Billy pressed. "If you can't do it who's going to do it?" Late in 1950, says Trotman's widow, "Dawson was on a beach in Formosa. God laid on his heart to say Yes."

Dawson Trotman was relatively small, with a shock of dark brown hair, a delightful, boyish grin and a determined jaw. In his youth he had been arrested six times. He was converted at the age of twenty, after learning Bible verses. A lumberman and truck driver until his Navigators enabled him to devote himself full-time to Christian service, Trotman's education was insufficient for his genius. "A dynamic speaker, poor in rhetoric and grammar," recalls one of his staff. "He seldom finished one sentence before he started another. But he had an electric quality to his speaking that held the audience in a vice." "You could listen to him for an hour and a half and not grow weary," says another Navigator. "He was a great challenger and stimulator and exhorter." Though warmhearted, Trotman could be forthright, abrupt, a disciplinarian sweetened by an uninhibited love for God and man that drove him relentlessly.

Trotman had devoted himself to the building up of young Christians until they should be fruitful, informed, integrated in the churches and consistent in their lives.

His concern for the individual perfectly matched Graham's concern for the mass. Their coming together in 1951 may have been one of those little-known, unrecognized but decisive moments in the growth of the Christian church.

Trotman visited the Team at Fort Worth early in 1951. That crusade underlined his decision in Formosa. "I've found a man I can follow," he told Lorne Sanny, his chief lieutenant. To the next crusade, at Shreveport in April, Dawson Trotman brought a small team of Navigators. Billy, according to his custom, having selected the expert, left him free. "I have tried to tell Billy and other members of the Team that this is really a new field to me," wrote Trotman, "but they don't seem to take my word for it but just laugh. . . . The task is tremendous." The follow-up scheme collapsed because the local chairman had not prepared the counselors. Trotman had to start again, with the realization that if follow-up is to succeed it must begin with the training of counselors by his own team. He held highly successful early morning classes for Shreveport ministers and their active laymen. "Somehow," wrote Trotman a week after the close, "the stock of the Team is so high that practically anything we say is taken not only in a good spirit but as the truth, and as a challenge to be followed by new converts and older Christians."

The effect on one young Shreveport businessman was an example of the importance of the counseling classes in themselves. Dan Piatt, afterward to join the Billy Graham Team and become one of their leading trainers of counselors, had been converted two years earlier in Texas but had remained an insignificant Christian. "My life," he says, "was absolutely transformed through the Shreveport classes, and the preaching of the Word by Billy night after night. It was in the Counselor classes that we learned the A B C of the Christian life."

Soon after the crusade began, the Shreveport auditorium was crowded out. Many were staying away knowing they could not get in, when Jerry Beavan startled Billy with the suggestion that the crusade move the next night to the stadium, which they had expected to fill on the last night only. In face of doubts from Team and committee that an outdoor crusade could succeed, the move was effected and the attendance jumped from 3,000 to 17,000 in a night. Billy and Cliff, Willis Haymaker and Jerry, learned that nonchurch people will come more readily to an open air crusade. Therefore, when climate and circumstance allowed, they chose a stadium.

At Memphis (May–June 1951) Trotman found he had "learned already at least two or three times as much about this whole thing as I did in Shreveport." Here the Team established the revolutionary principle that counselors should be selected, not snapped up merely because they volunteered. Until then an evangelist was grateful for whom he could get. The idea that a worthy Christian, doctrinally impeccable, might prove unsuitable as a counselor indicated rising standards.[1]

Trotman was a creator, a brilliant strategist, but less of a tactician. He needed a calmer, more patient staff officer, and in Lorne Sanny he had one. In the history of the Billy Graham crusades, Trotman was the genius of the follow-up system, but Lorne Sanny, and another quiet man, Charlie Riggs, did most to develop and to apply the ideas. In earlier years both of them divided time, as did Trotman, between Navigators and the crusades. Eventually, as crusades in America and

[1] The Memphis crusade has another, and comic, claim to fame, as the scene of one of the best of Billy Graham's occasional unintended tongue twists. He had been asked one night to commend a road safety campaign. The city placed a neon sign on the platform behind him showing the number of days without a traffic fatality. Billy said to the stadium audience: "You see this sign back here? That 150 days? That means there have been 150 days without a *fertility*." The word came clear through the P.A. There was a stunned silence, then a roar of laughter. Poor Billy looked bewildered until Cliff shouted, *"fatality, man, fatality!"*

overseas needed longer and fuller preparation, Charlie Riggs became a full-time member and a department head in the Billy Graham Association. Riggs had been a roughneck in the oil fields and had never received higher education. Wherever he began counseling classes in the years to come, Riggs removed suspicions, radiated confidence, brought men and women of different denominations together in unity, and by clear teaching of Scripture led scores of sincere but Biblically ignorant and uncommitted churchgoers to a new depth of faith. He would work in his own simple, rugged way, pausing occasionally to bite on a mint, with a characteristic "Excuse me." A sophisticated or pretentious man would never have had ministers, doctors, lawyers and factory workers sitting at his feet.

By 1952 the chief elements of the counseling and follow-up system had been established, however primitive in form; and, as Lorne Sanny says, "Far more important than the system is the spirit, the *conviction that God can use laymen.*" Gathered together for the classes they would learn the crusade's objective, "not only to get a person forward, but to see a clear decision for Christ and the person going on with the Lord, integrated into the life of the Church as a fruitful, useful Christian." Each inquirer is an individual, with an individual problem. A counselor must be patient and a good listener, must learn how to point to Christ, and be spirtually alert.

In mass evangelism previously, any large response tended to produce chaos, with the inquirers, like casualties after a railway disaster, waiting in turn until a harassed first-aid worker could dab on spiritual iodine before rushing to the next. The Billy Graham Team evolved a new plan. Counselors were placed at strategic places throughout the auditorium or stadium. When Billy Graham gave the invitation and inquirers began coming forward, the counselor, at a sign from his section chief, would join an inquirer—a young man stepping beside a young man, an older woman beside an older woman, a well-dressed professional person allotted to someone of similar standing, so that of the crowd pressing forward to the front, half would be inquirers and half counselors wearing their badges. It was carefully planned, but the individual inquirer would not feel caught up in a system. His dominant impression would be of contact with another individual, and the finding of a sympathetic ear.

The counselor's first task is to learn the inquirer's reason for coming forward, whether to accept Christ, to rededicate himself or for restoration of a lapsed faith. A high proportion have always been "first time decisions," the acceptance of Christ, at which the counselor, using his Bible, is no more than a spiritual obstetrician. As Lorne Sanny emphasized in the training courses: "It is Christ that saves; not doctrine, not theology, not the Church. It is Christ who lifts burdens, who works in the heart. Bring them to Christ and not to some experience. . . . As you talk with a person there is that certain point where God takes over, and causes the light to shine, and a miracle takes place." The counselor should be the forgotten man in the experience of conversion. Significantly, of 14,000 Billy Graham converts who have been interviewed by one of his associates over the years, few remembered their counselor's words.

Before they part, inquirer and counselor pray together and the counselor fills in a card. (If the inquirer has no church preference the designations committee of local ministers will select one.) The inquirer is given a booklet, which for some years was called *Beginning with Christ,* and he is encouraged to start learning the first Bible verses in it that very night. Finally he is introduced to an adviser, almost always a minister. The counselor is specifically told not to say in introducing the inquirer, "This is Mr. ——who has just made his decision," but simply gives the name and withdraws. The adviser says: "What decision have you made tonight, Mr. ——?" and thus gives the inquirer his first opportunity of public confession of faith in Christ.

The counselor should follow up Mr. —— by a visit if possible, or a telephone call or letter, within forty-eight hours; he is, in Sanny's words, "a brief stop-gap until the other follow-up wheels are in motion." After that his sole part is to pray for Mr. ——.

The decision card has enabled prompt information to go to the appropriate local minister. The crusade office helps at first by correspondence and by checking back to insure that the minister has called, but the responsibility passes to the local church.

Throughout 1952 and 1953 the follow-up system was being polished. Like Billy Graham himself by 1953, it had come a long way, was by no means mature, but had vast potential for further development and improvement. At Dallas in June 1953, which astonished America by bringing together 75,000 people in the Cotton Bowl on the last night; at Detroit, the first industrial city Graham had dared to attempt, where the five weeks' crusade in the fall was notable for massive church support with the Episcopalians officially in the van; and in the other five full-length crusades of 1953, Trotman, Sanny and Riggs were seeking ways to minimize wastage.

As Billy Graham says: "There is no human way to guarantee that a convert is going to follow on. That has to be ultimately in God's hands, as is salvation. We declare the message, and then we give the people an opportunity to decide 'Yes' or 'No.' But the actual conversion must be of God.

"Salvation is of God; growth is between the person and God. The great follow-up agent is the Holy Spirit. If a person has been born of the Spirit, he is going to grow. Look at Los Angeles. We didn't have all this elaborate system that we have now, but look at the results of that little crusade."

But Graham had recognized clearly that in the New Testament and in Christian history, growth is in the environment of churches, and he was determined that crusades should feed them wherever he worked. Never before in interdenominational evangelism on a comparable scale had the converts been so fully passed to the churches.

And here lay the strongest and sometimes the weakest link of crusades in the years to come.

III

"To God Be the Glory"

1954-1955

---

16 · London Calling

Above Montreat, overlooking the valley, stands the former home of Wilbur Chapman, the early twentieth-century evangelist. During winter it is empty, and the sun porch is a perfect place for silence and prayer. In the first weeks of 1954 Billy Graham sat there often, reading and meditating to strengthen himself spiritually, then climbing higher on the trails, walking and running to harden his body. For ahead, like a mountain barrier, lay the greatest test of his ministry—the three-month Greater London Crusade timed to begin on March 1, 1954.

The invitation had been given two years earlier in March 1952 after a masterly Graham address at Church House, Westminster, which removed many British misconceptions and fears. It came in the name of a private body, the Evangelical Alliance, since the Archbishop of Canterbury, Geoffrey Fisher, viewed the prospect of a crusade with courteous caution, and the British Council of Churches declined to endorse it unless Billy Graham would first try a pilot campaign in the provinces. This he refused, for he did not believe, as he wrote in July 1952, that "we need to test God in this matter by having a campaign to see if it will work. I am confident He will honor us by stepping into the hardest and most impossible situation, and daring by faith to launch out, resting entirely upon His promise of blessing."

"This mission," he added, "should be the greatest evangelistic effort ever attempted in London. No amount of money should be spared to awaken and stimulate the consciences of London's ten millions."

During 1952 and 1953 several prominent Englishmen returned from visiting crusades in America reassured and eager, hard though it was to believe that a mission could succeed on the scale envisaged by Graham. Since the end of the Second World War the tide of evangelism had slowly risen. *Towards the Conversion of England,* a report prepared by the (Anglican) Church Assembly had called for just such a vigorous proclamation of the Gospel as Billy Graham made. The Methodist "Commando Campaigns" and the Bishop of London's Mission of 1949 had caused considerable interest. In 1953 the Coronation evoked a widespread spirit of dedication. Yet the Churches were hesitant as to the basic elements of the Christian message and its authority, and few Englishmen dared to expect that the nation would ever be shaken from indifference. Moreover in the early nineteen-fifties there remained a strong suspicion of America and a deep distaste for what was reckoned American "hot gospel" and ballyhoo.

The executive committee of the Greater London Crusade, after some difficulty, secured an auditorium: Harringay Arena in North London. Harringay was owned by the Greyhound Racing Association, and at the signing of the three-month contract the managing director said, "Gentlemen, we know that this will adversely affect our business if it succeeds, but we are concerned for the welfare of our country, and we believe it needs some such activity of this sort. We'll give you every help we can." Afterward he admitted they expected the contract to be broken in two weeks, because no speaker had filled it more than one night.

When counseling classes began in September, Trotman, Lorne Sanny and Charlie Riggs speedily disarmed prejudice; and Jerry Beavan, as associate crusade director under Roy Cattell, secretary of the Evangelical Alliance, showed genuine desire to understand and work with the British. Beavan staggered the crusade chairman, Major-General D. J. Wilson-Heffenden, an Anglican with a distinguished military record in Burma, by announcing that the publicity budget would be about £50,000. The general, with his Anglican reserve, was a little taken aback when Billy Graham's picture appeared all over London, but the committee had seen the point made by Beavan and well expressed by the publicity firm, that whereas on a bus or billboard it was impossible to explain even the elements of the great doctrines of the Church, combat lethargy and "sell" a name and a place, the one thing which could and had to be done was to "sell" the man Billy Graham and the building in the shortest message possible. This resolved itself into *Hear Billy Graham.*[1]

Some of the necessary money to mount the crusade had to be raised in America, and Graham and the Association did not find it easy. To encourage major gifts Beavan ordered a magnificent illustrated brochure about Britain's need and the crusade's objectives. It was 12 inches by 17 inches, half an inch thick. Each copy cost $12.

The first few were delivered during the Dallas crusade in June 1953. They were hand-pulled proofs, containing eight misprints of British names and a misquotation of Shakespeare. Graham and Beavan showed one to John Cordle, an English businessman and later a Conservative Member of Parliament. Cordle noticed that in describing the grievous decline of religion during and after the war the writer had used a word, *socialism,* in a sense that would convey an unintended and political meaning to Englishmen for whom socialism is almost synonymous with the Labour Party. Beavan changed the words to *secularism* and thought no more about it. Unfortunately George Wilson, not present at the conversation, returned to Minneapolis with an unaltered brochure, quite unaware that it contained a stick of dynamite.

"I feel totally inadequate and incapable," wrote Graham to Prebendary Colin Kerr in London in December. "To go to London for a campaign is indeed frightening and humbling. If anything is done for Christ, it will have to be the Lord's doing. I feel I have so little to offer." In using the word "frightening," as he was inclined to before a great crusade, Graham did not refer to physical fear, such as he had felt one night in Algiers in 1948, when he and some other Americans were surrounded by Arabs with knives, who stole his wallet and tried to cut away his watch. He meant, rather, a fear lest he should fail Christ, and an awe of the heavy responsibility. The London crusade would be the most extensive and ambitious yet attempted. An English bishop touring America had announced that Billy Graham would return with his tail between his legs. Old Dr. Bob Jones of Bob Jones University was reported saying that Graham went to Britain out of pride, and should have waited ten years. The British press, though at least occasionally noticing his existence thanks

[1] At Graham's insistence the names of Cliff Barrows and Bev Shea appeared also when space allowed.

to Jerry Beavan and the sheer size of the project, was generally rude or supercilious. Beavan himself, in letters and telephone calls, was alternately depressed and elated.

Billy went to the West Coast in January 1954, for a most encouraging tour to cities of former crusades. Back at Montreat he resumed constant study, prayer and exercise. The Grahams were making a rough swimming pool by damming a stream on their mountain. It was later completed by Graham's friend and associate, Lee Fisher, to the delight of the children. Then there was Belshazzar, the Great Pyrenees, who accompanied Billy on his walks and would march confidently into the house beside him, though never daring to enter when Billy was away. After Belshazzar had nipped the coat of a visitor Ruth once remarked, "I wish there was such a thing as getting a dog converted."

The joys of home did not lessen the burden as London drew near, though a great consolation was that Ruth would come too. No previous crusade had so weighed on him. "I'd walk for hours at a time, praying." In the spirit of Psalm 37, "Commit thy way unto the Lord; trust also in Him," he would commit the crusade, "and it would be committed, but six or seven hours later it would be back. One side of me seemed to be committed totally, and I knew it was in God's hands; the other side had this concern, I would rather call it a burden than a worry."

In London preparations were proceeding with British thoroughness. "In all the campaigns we've had in America," wrote Trotman, "we have had none that have had the preparation, the number of counselors, the publicity that the London campaign has." The prayer meetings in homes were organized in five days. Jerry Beavan reported three thousand starting on February 1. Billy had called the millions of *Hour of Decision* listeners and viewers to prayer, and all over the world people prayed for London. Korea alone had hundreds of special prayer meetings.

Most of the Team, which numbered over twenty (each, from Billy downward, accepting a salary drop of $50 a week for the duration of the crusade) had converged on London by early February. In Washington Billy Graham was received by President Eisenhower, who assured him he would be praying. The President agreed that Senator Frank Carlson should be his representative at the opening night, but the Senator's duties prevented his leaving Washington. Senators Stuart Symington (Democrat) and Styles Bridges (Republican), who would be visiting Europe on official business, promised to attend. The

American Ambassador in London had already sent assurances of aid.

On the way through New York, Billy called on Henry R. Luce at the Time-Life offices. "If you can get an article in the *Daily Mirror*," Luce said, "or one of the newspapers with mass circulation, it will probably help." As Billy commented long afterward, "Little did we dream what was in store for us from the British Press."

One of the six friends who sailed with the Grahams on the *United States* was Dr. Paul Rees of Minneapolis, who had taken leave of absence from his church (First Covenant) in order to hold ministers' meetings during the crusade. Walking the deck together, Graham told Rees that some Americans urged he should hammer away in London as he did anywhere else. Graham said he doubted the wisdom of this advice, especially in view of the difference of accent. Rees agreed. "I told him the pace at which he spoke might well be slowed down for the London audience, and that he would be well advised not to be as dramatic, and not to shout quite so loudly at the top of his voice." Rees begged him not to rob himself of liberty, yet use discipline. Graham said, "The more I think about it, and pray about it, the more I feel that you are right."

Graham was convinced, as Dr. Rees recalls, that he moved "in the line of God's providence, and that therefore he had every right to expect God to confirm the guidance that he felt had come in accepting the invitation. There were times when he seemed relaxed and very gay. And then the seriousness of this whole thing—the massiveness of it—the unpredictability of it seemed to come over him, and he would gather us for a season of prayer and waiting on the Lord."

On Monday February 22, one day short of Southampton, the first steward tapped on the Grahams' door and handed Billy a radio news sheet. Near the bottom of the page, following the weather report and a story about Indo-China, Graham was stunned to read, datelined London: "A Labour Member of Parliament announced today that he would challenge in Commons the admission of Billy Graham to England on the grounds the American evangelist was interfering in British politics under the guise of religion."

The Captain deleted the item before mimeographing and distributing the news sheet to the passengers, and the Grahams were grateful —and completely mystified until Jerry Beavan in London came through on the radio telephone.

It appeared that Hannen Swaffer, the columnist on the left-wing

Daily Herald, who in January had complained that Billy Graham by taking Harringay would deprive the people of three months of ice hockey, had discovered a prayer calendar prepared by the Association in Minneapolis; and there, under a picture of London, appeared, unaltered, the sentence which had been changed in the lavish brochure at Dallas: "What Hitler's bombs could not do, socialism with its accompanying evils shortly accomplished." Deftly touching up the small letter *s* to a capital, Hannen Swaffer under a headline, "Apologize—or stay away!" had written a blistering article pillorying Billy Graham as a political adventurer in disguise, who had "more gravely libeled us than anyone has dared to do since the war," by attacking the former Socialist government and the Labour Party's 14 million supporters. Taking their cue from Swaffer's "disclosure," the London press was in uproar, hot for Billy Graham's scalp.

In the perspective of years it seems unbelievable that so small a matter should have caused such violent reaction.

Graham did not even recall the details of the brochure and had never seen the calendar. At Minneapolis George Wilson immediately took responsibility for having used in ignorance the original brochure, with *socialism* unchanged to *secularism,* as "copy" for the back page of his calendar. Beavan sent an explanation to the press, Graham and Wilson wired apologies to the Member of Parliament, Mr. Geoffrey de Freitas, who intended to raise the matter. Swaffer, who was a Spiritualist, was not mollified and followed up with an attack on Hugh Gough, Bishop of Barking (now Archbishop of Sydney), Graham's foremost Anglican sponsor, and on "the wild fanaticism of Billy Graham's evangelism."

Momentarily, Billy was engulfed by certainty that all was over, and by the injustice of the accusations. Then, swiftly and instinctively, as Paul Rees saw, "he turned to the Word for something fresh from God to meet the situation." He remembered that opposition was inevitable; he knew that Christ must triumph; and when they reached Le Havre it was no effort to send by the *Daily Herald's* reporter a friendly greeting to Hannen Swaffer.

Coming up Southampton Water the ship was boarded by a tugful of pressmen and photographers. They ignored a film star to crowd round the Grahams, who realized later that the "socialism" furor had been a blessing in disguise by making Billy front-page news. The reporters were hostile. "Who invited you over here, anyway?" "What do you plan to do about Russia?" "Do you think you can save Britain?" and, to Ruth: "Is it true your husband carries around his own special jug of water for baptism?" After submitting to newsreel cameras and a TV interview on the dockside the Grahams entered the customs shed. As Billy opened his suitcase (badly packed as usual) the customs officer said, "Welcome to England and good luck, sir. We need you." Billy was eternally grateful for that encouragement, swiftly followed by a dockworker's "God bless you, sir. I'm praying for you."

Next day, Wednesday February 24, in the train to London the Americans gathered in the Grahams' compartment for Bible reading and for prayer about the serious situation: the press still in full cry, lukewarm supporters in retreat, friendly clergy being scorned or criticized. After prayer came a temporary drop from the sublime to the ridiculous. At that time British evangelicals rated lipstick worldly, and Billy wanted to please them. And thus (as Ruth wrote in her diary), "Bill stooped from being a man of God to become a meddlesome husband and ordered my lipstick off. There was a lively argument—then I wiped it off. He got so busy getting the bags together I managed to put more on without notice. Then we were at Waterloo. Stepped into a sea of happy singing people. . . ."

Londoners had converged on Waterloo Station until the platform ticket machines gave out, post-office vans and taxis were held up, and a harassed official exclaimed, "If these are Christians it's time we let out the lions!" A happy milling concourse sang "What a Friend we have in Jesus." The hymn stopped abruptly when the loudspeaker announced a last-minute change of platform. Luverne Gustavson commented feelingly, "It didn't seem possible that the same crowd that sang so beautifully could push so hard!" It was the greatest crowd at Waterloo since the arrival of Mary Pickford and Douglas Fairbanks in 1924.

Billy Graham and the reception committee barely made their way to the limousines, and they left the station to the sound of two thousand voices singing Wesley's hymn, "And can it be that I should gain / An interest in the Savior's blood?"

During the following days, in addition to the dedication service at Harringay, Graham went twice to the House of Commons, once to apologize to the Labour Member, who showed him over the chamber, and again to speak at a big dinner for Members and their guests. He addressed also a banquet of titled and social leaders at Claridges, presided over by Lord Luke and paid for anonymously by a tough, gruff, high-living Texas millionaire, the late Syd Richardson.[1]

[1] Swaffer ridiculed the fact that at a dinner for an evangelist guests wore white

More important, Graham held a press conference (wearing a black doublebreasted jacket, gray trousers, white shirt with a tie of red, yellow and green blobs on navy blue!), and the resulting articles in the papers were the pressmen's attempts to reconcile editorial orders to "debunk Graham," (as one of the reporters told Luverne) with their surprise at his genuineness, kindness, and skill in answering trick or hostile questions.

He said that he had not come to "save Britain," but, at the invitation of British churchmen, to preach the Gospel. "I am going to present a God who matters, and who makes claims on the human race. He is a God of love, grace and mercy, but also a God of judgment. When we break His moral laws we suffer; when we keep them, we have inward peace and joy. I am going to insist that honesty and integrity pay in individual lives. The revival I am calling for is not a foaming-at-the-mouth revival, with people screaming and shouting. I am calling for a revival that will cause men and women to return to their offices and shops to live out the teaching of Christ in their daily relationships. I am going to preach a gospel not of despair but of hope—hope for the individual, for society and for the world."

Graham also spoke to a luncheon of 937 clergy. Billy's old friend Stephen Olford, then minister of Duke Street Baptist Church, Richmond, wrote in his church journal: "Without doubt, nothing like this has happened before in this generation. Dr. Graham . . . addressed the assemblage in a most moving manner. I should say that he won his audience almost to a man."

Nevertheless on Sunday February 28, the day before the crusade was to begin, *The People* newspaper hurled abuse at "Silly Billy." "Must we be turned into better citizens and kinder husbands by the antics of Billy Graham's American hot gospel circus? . . . Being bulldozed into loving God by ecstatic young men who talk about him with easy familiarity is something which makes the biggest British sinner shudder. When the cheer leader of the troups turns out to be as ignorant of current British history as Billy Graham, we are entitled to protest. He would have done more good for his cause by staying away and sending over the money that would have been saved on the fares to buy candy for our poor kids."

The opening day, Monday March 1, broke cold and cheerless.

Billy spent most of it preparing and at prayer, in his study filled with books which Jerry Beavan had secured, ranging from devotional

---

ties and decorations; but when the invitations were sent, President Eisenhower's personal representative (Senator Carlson) was expected to be present.

volumes to a complete set of *Encyclopaedia Britannica.* The Team had chosen a small hotel near Oxford Circus out of deference to British prickles about American "luxury," but it had the advantage, rare in England of 1954, of adequate central heating. (The Americans all suffered much from London cold. One Team wife was found the evening after her arrival sitting on a radiator at Harringay.)

The weather worsened. Billy, his nerves taut, developed a splitting headache. As Olford recalls: "If ever man was stripped of any confidence in himself it was dear Billy. He was shaking from head to foot." At 3:30 P.M. a message came from one of the two American Senators whose intention to attend the crusade had been announced in the press, to say that they could not come after all. The ostensible reason was a dinner engagement, but the Senator who telephoned murmured something about political implications. Billy believed that the Ambassador, who had washed hands of him at the "socialism" dispute, had urged them to stay away. Billy "had a terrible sinking feeling. I dropped immediately to my knees in prayer and committed the entire matter to the Lord."

One hour before the meeting was timed to begin, Ruth was writing up her diary. Billy came in from the other room with news that—as she recorded it—"Jerry just called to say there aren't more than 2,000 people at Harringay, [which seated 11,400] and around 200 or 300 newspaper men, television cameras, newsreels, and so on. And some of them are getting discouraged. Bill looked sort of stunned when he told me, and I thought I heard him praying in the other room just now."

Their fears arose from a garbled message. Jerry had further commented on the telephone to a Team associate in the hotel, quite cheerfully, that it was early yet, and the sleet might be making people late. The relaying associate had misunderstood and changed Jerry's casual comment into a message of woe for Billy.

The Grahams prayed together and thought of the thousands praying for London all over the world. They entered the car lent by Ford of Dagenham at the suggestion of Ford in Detroit. Behind the broad, reassuring back of the Ford company driver, William McCloud, they held hands in silence. "Our hearts were prepared for whatever God had planned."

17 · *Harringay*

The forecourt of Harringay Arena was empty. The Grahams could, however, see crowds streaming toward the Greyhound stadium beyond. Billy said to Ruth, "Let's go face it and believe that God has a purpose in it."

Willis Haymaker came toward the car. "The arena is jammed! It is full and running over, and thousands are on the other side!" Billy, a little dazed, walked through the door to his special room, to a great sound of hymns from the arena. There stood two smiling Senators, saying, "Billy, we just couldn't let you down!" One of them said they had hurried from a meeting with the Prime Minister and would shortly have to leave for a formal dinner which the American Ambassador was giving for the Foreign Secretary, but they were determined to speak on Billy's behalf.

Squads of pressmen and roving photographers did not make for an atmosphere of worship. (The London dailies had sent an extraordinary array, including theater and literary critics, foreign and industrial correspondents.) From the moment the choir burst into a verse of "Blessed assurance, Jesus is mine," followed by the stately cadences of the opening hymn, "Praise to the Lord, the Almighty," the service had a genuineness and reverence which puzzled the press, still attempting to relate Graham to "snake-handling fundamentalists" and hysterical demagogues.

He preached on John 3:16: "God so loved the world, that He gave His only begotten Son, that whosoever believeth in Him should not perish, but have everlasting life." With his microphone looking like an oversize tie pin he darted back and forth. He tried to keep Paul Rees' advice, but for English ears on that first evening he talked too fast and seemed inclined to shout, so that his voice became expressionless and less effective. But its impact remained unspoiled. "I believe there is a world-wide hunger for God. I believe this great crowd is evidence of that hunger for God in London, and," he went on, daringly as it seemed to his audience, "before three months have passed I believe we are going to see a mighty revival in London and throughout Great Britain."

At the last moment before preaching, Billy had hesitated whether to give an invitation on this first, press-distracted night. Bishop Gough said, "Give it." To the surprise and gratitude of the London executive, 178 people, "mostly young but scarcely to be described as of one distinct type," moved quietly forward, some of them weeping, to be joined by counselors and to stand before the flower-decked rostrum, for a few short words from Graham before they entered the counseling tent adjoining the arena.

The second night the weather was a blend of snow flurries and rain. Numbers were slightly down. After that, there was never an empty place throughout three months, despite rearrangement to accommodate more than 12,000. On the first Saturday afternoon Harringay was filling so fast for the evening service that Jerry Beavan and Roy Cattell sent for Billy Graham to take an unannounced meeting in the arena for the first 5,000, who then left. "Full up" notices in the subway stations did not deter Londoners pouring toward Harringay. They would not disperse. At 9:15 the arena was emptied again and Billy preached a third sermon.

By the end of that first week the counseling room had already been enlarged three times, for London was bringing forward inquirers in numbers that America had produced only at the climax of a crusade. "The British are thrilled, the Team are thrilled," Dawson Trotman had written home on March 5. "People just didn't believe it could happen here, and yet it's passing all records in practically every field." The extraordinary influence of the crusade, from the beginning, humbled and heartened all concerned.

Billy Graham had released Britons from their reticence; it suddenly became easy to talk about religion. Tongue-tied English Christians had the opportunity of their lives, clergymen visiting in their parishes found that small talk vanished quickly. Billy Graham was the topic in homes, as in factories, clubs and public houses. From the first night, too, came the singing in the subway. "From the seemingly endless queues waiting at the station for tickets one hears wave after wave of song rolling back toward the street," ran a letter in the *Daily Telegraph*. "The tube trains are packed with these singing multitudes, and there is a smile on every face. This quite spontaneous demonstration of Christian joy is most impressive, and one cannot fail to observe the effect it has on the passengers who board the trains at subsequent stations. After the first surprise many smile sympathetically and often enter into conversation; others begin with disapproving looks but soften considerably during the journey. I noticed one young girl with a very hard and scornful expression on her pretty face as the hymns of praise and faith rose around her; but before she left the train I saw tears in her eyes, and at the last moment she too smiled at us."

They sang the great hymns of the Church. They sang "Blessed Assurance" with its chorus, which Cliff had made the signature tune of the crusade. One song caught on right across London: "To God be the glory, great things He hath done." Words and tune are nineteenth-century American (by Fanny Crosby and W. H. Doane), yet until London they had not been known to the Team, who now adopted the hymn as their own for its apt expression of their message, experience and aim.

The intensity of the early press attacks on Graham had brought out the British sense of fair play for the underdog. Londoners wanted to give him a chance, wanted to hear and see him. While associates fanned out to factories and churches, and Paul Rees began his memorable talks for ministers at Westminster Chapel, Billy Graham received numerous invitations not normally sent to clergymen.

He was asked to give a fifteen-minute talk at the London School of Economics. The presiding professor told the packed theater that this was the first time a minister had been on their platform. When he remarked that their school was "founded on secularism," the students cheered. There were boos when Graham stood. He told three funny stories in a row (he always enjoys joking to a British audience because they start laughing before the punch line), and had just turned his listeners serious when a crash of glass brought a student through an upper window, who stood scratching like an ape while the audience roared. Graham's own laughter was genuine; he could not have stopped had he tried. Then, off the cuff, he said, "He reminds me of my ancestors." Everyone laughed. "Of course, all my ancestors came from Britain." That brought down the house. When the laughter subsided he gave his vigorous, uncompromised message, in total silence.

At the opposite end of the scale, Billy and Ruth were guests for luncheon with the officers of the Queen's Guard at St. James's Palace, the invitation being brought round by hand of a Coldstream Guardsman resplendent in scarlet uniform. The Captain of the Guard, Richard Carr-Gomm, and his lieutenant and ensign, invited their commanding officer and his wife and a few other friends, "and we had a most successful and happy party." Billy surprised them by chatting about pheasant shooting in Korea and never mentioned religion until they drew him out. Each of the party visited Harringay, where Major Carr-Gomm found Billy "tremendous but a different man. He stormed and shouted and gesticulated. But it was good, full of the Bible. For fifty minutes he spoke and I never moved. Later I went forward in rededication and never regretted it." Richard Carr-Gomm afterward founded the Abbeyfield Bermondsey homes for the aged.

The guardsman servant who waited on Billy at the luncheon was so taken that he too, unknown to the officers, went to Harringay, writes Carr-Gomm, "and was converted. He told me that he felt hot and cold all over as Billy was speaking, and then found himself standing with the converts at the ringside in uniform. He felt confused but was glad later, and eventually I attended his adult baptism."

By the third week of March opposition had melted. The press had turned from vociferous suspicion to a respect which soon became admiration and support, though Hennen Swaffer remained obdurate if subdued. The only voice still loud in protest was that of Dr. Donald Soper (now Lord Soper, and that year president of the Methodist Conference) because Graham did not see Christianity in terms of socialism and pacifism. Soper, contemptuous of Graham's whole theology, declined suggestions that he should meet Graham, but Graham, anxious to learn from his critics, went and heard Soper preach in Hyde Park, just as in the nineteen-forties—only this time Billy had to wear dark glasses and pull his hat over his eyes, for if recognized he would have inadvertently cost Soper his audience!

From London and all southern England the crowds flocked to Harringay, from curiosity, conviction, or by invitation of churches or friends. Many of those who came forward to accept Christ had an early, lost background of religion, like Joan Winmill, the successful young actress who had played the juvenile lead in *The Chiltern Hundreds*. She had built herself a brittle façade of gaiety which hid "terrible unhappiness inside," until she was on the verge of suicide. For others Harringay was a turning point in a spiritual pilgrimage or the end of superficial religion, as it was for Ernest Shippam, head of the famous meat and fish-paste firm. "At that time," he said in a BBC *Lift up Your Hearts* broadcast in 1960, "there were shameful things in my life, which I seemed powerless to eradicate. My home was unhappy; our business was my god; my church-going was merely in the pattern of my social life. Events led me to hear Billy Graham at Harringay. All I can actually remember him saying was this, 'If Christ could carry His Cross to Calvary for you, can't you trust Him with everything you have got?' The Holy Spirit made me realize my need. In a flash I saw what my life was like—and it was pretty rotten; and at that moment seeing the tremendous love of Christ for me, He also filled my heart with such love and trust for Him that I committed all to Him. It was an act of absolute and complete yielding to Christ."

On their decision cards more than half of the converts described themselves as of no *regular* church connection, and by deduction it would seem that in every Harringay audience many had never been to a religious service other than a wedding or a funeral. Or they were like the pickpocket who said to the stranger beside him as they started for the front, "Now I must give you back your wallet I took a few minutes ago!" (These two strangers had been overheard earlier discovering a mutual dislike of Americans, sermons, and American evangelists in particular.)

A large percentage of those who made decisions were between the ages of fifteen and twenty-five, the younger ones often being members of church youth groups whose leaders had prayed and worked for their decisions. In all age groups were found inquirers who had come to the crusade because of the change in their workmates and friends. When a typist saw a colleague suddenly stop being disgruntled and cross, when a store manager was handed back stolen goods by a contrite customer, they wanted to know why. The crusade organizers frequently heard of such chain reactions. "I confess I was practically dragged to Harringay," wrote a nursery teacher. "I was cynical and eager to denounce God. . . . Amongst the staff more than half have been converted and we now find we can work together as never before, and have greater understanding of our deprived children."

For very many of his British audience Billy Graham was the first man to take the Bible and preach it in simplicity, with clarity and urgency.

"He has no magic, no magnetism," wrote the *Daily Mail*, "he makes no appeal to the emotions. His power—and power he has—is in his indivisible conviction that he knows the right way of life, in his unassailable belief that the 'Spirit of Christ' must drive away all unhappiness from the heart of the individual and break down the evil that seeks to destroy the world. . . . He punches home the *facts*—the facts that he reads out from the Bible in his hand, and which he asks his audience to read again and again in their Bibles."

Behind the preaching lay Graham's character: his sincerity, love, growing maturity of judgment; his buoyancy and enjoyment of living, his regular devotional habits. "The more you get to know him the more he rings true," was the experience of Geoffrey King, the prominent London Baptist. Behind, too, lay prayer from all over the world, and in London several unforgettable all-night prayer meetings.

Personal goodness and widespread prayer alone would not have made Harringay.

The crusade, as Bishop Gough said at the great ministers' meeting for 2,400 ministers at the close, was "a tremendous demonstration of the preaching of the Word of God with authority and conviction . . . that Old Testament emphasis, 'Thus saith the Lord God'; the authority which our Lord Himself used and which so impressed the people of His day, a Man speaking with authority."

"There is authority," Graham told the clergy, "when this Book is quoted. And the more Scripture I quote the greater number of people come and respond to the invitation; I found that out night after night. The Word of God, even though the hearer doesn't understand all about it, somehow becomes a hammer and a sword that hurts and cuts and convicts and washes and cleanses—the quoted Word of God."

Whenever he could steal a moment from the grueling round of interviews and addresses, Graham filled himself from the Bible. The Ford chauffeur, William McCloud, remembers, "He carried it everywhere, reading passages again and again through long drives," when they traveled in later parts of the crusade to universities, U.S. air bases and other preaching engagements.

Graham ran short of fresh sermon material. Canon Livermore, his old friend of Youth for Christ days, presented him with a copy of an old Puritan treatise, Robert Watson's *A Body of Divinity* (1661), reissued by Charles Haddon Spurgeon and carrying Spurgeon's signature. Billy dug out of it the basis for his three weeks of sermons on the Ten Commandments. Yet the theme was always the Gospel. A retired Anglican clergyman who attended all the meetings remarked, "You preached the same sermon every night!" Those who supposed Graham's phrase, "The *Bible* says," meant that he wrenched texts out of contexts to buttress personal views were convinced on hearing him that, whether they liked it or not, his sermons expounded the basic New Testament message as it stands. He offered no easy salvation. It was not mass persuasion. Frequently converts would say, "I felt as though I was the only person in the arena, and that every word was meant for me."

"I am sure," said Graham in the closing days, "that all of you that have been to Harringay have become aware that the atmosphere has been charged with the power of the Holy Spirit. . . . I felt like a spectator standing on the side watching God at work, and I wanted to get out of it as much as I could and let Him take over." "It didn't seem to depend very much on what was said," recalls a committee member. "The power of God was in it. Billy would stop at the most unlikely place; still they would come forward."

As the weeks wore on, Billy Graham put less and less force into his closing invitation; there was no need to press when so many were waiting to accept Christ as soon as he stopped preaching. He would move to the front of the rostrum, and they came. Worldly, sophisticated Malcom Muggeridge described it on BBC *Panorama:* "One or two at first, and then the movement gathering momentum, as the choir sings quietly. I looked at their faces, so varied, so serious, and for me this was far and away the most moving part of the proceedings. . . . This movement . . . gave every indication of being spontaneous and sincere, and the faces of the people gathered under the platform were touching in their sincerity and intentness."

Leslie Weatherhead, the minister of the (Methodist) City Temple, renowned as pastor, preacher and psychologist, told his people that "I could not find anything in the whole service that was psychologically unsound." In retrospect he wondered whether the singing, as the inquirers walked forward, of "Just as I am without one plea," to a "sultry and exotic tune, repeating in a whisper, 'I come, I come,' " was not bound to engender immense emotion. Years later in certain crusades Graham eliminated this singing, and nothing would be heard but footfalls; yet in the confined space of a covered arena silence can create more intensity than song.

On Monday, March 29, the Greater London crusade extended itself by a totally original means—post-office landline relays.

Bob Benninghof, the American Broadcasting Company's engineer traveling with the Team to supervise *Hour of Decision* broadcasts, hit on the idea of hiring long-distance telephone lines. The BBC used them for outside broadcasts; long ago a speech by David Lloyd George had been relayed from a hall in London to a hall in the provinces. After some hesitation the post office took up Benninghof's idea and offered terms.

The first relay was laid to a movie theater just across the Thames. The next night 2000 people in Glasgow heard Billy Graham in London. Thereafter the applications mounted, until by early May the post office had more than they could manage. Harringay thus became a nationwide crusade. The services were often clearer to the ear of a relay audience than in the arena with its echoing amplifiers, and the message came in stark simplicity unaided by atmosphere or the personality of the preacher. In hired theaters, concert halls, city auditoriums and churches, Britons heard Billy Graham. The very originality of the idea had captured their imagination.

The relays were a prominent feature of the English spring of 1954, while in London the crusade went from strength to strength. On Saturday afternoon, April 3, Trafalgar Square was packed as it had not been since VE day. On Good Friday, April 16, sunny and warm, an open-air rally in Hyde Park, at which the police estimated more than 40,000 present, covered half a square mile. Graham spoke on "God forbid that I should glory, save in the cross of our Lord Jesus Christ."

The crusade chairman, General Wilson-Haffenden, felt that at this great meeting Billy found fresh spiritual strength: "There seemed to be an even greater depth than before." Physically he lost weight rapidly. Holy Week had been designated a rest period without meetings, but Graham and the Team sensed that it would be an error to break the momentum of the crusade. Even Sundays were filled. Rest was impossible. On Sunday April 25 he preached at Cambridge in the packed University Church, with the service relayed in two neighboring churches. On another Sunday he preached in Bryan Green's church in Birmingham at the annual service of the British Industries Fair. Almost every day he met leading men in church and state, individually or in groups at which, Roy Cattell says, "he always had a strategic message which had a profound influence upon those who heard it."

The strain of so packed a schedule was immense. Each week Billy looked thinner, and the rings under his eyes blacker. A distinguished physician prescribed vitamin pills; they had such big effect and looked so small that Billy, prescribed one a day, took four!

If London exhausted him physically (and a man much over thirty-five could scarcely have stood the strain), the Greater London crusade gave Billy Graham new stature.

America had followed his troubles and read of his triumphs with such avid interest that he now became a household name to his countrymen. And the experiences of Harringay lastingly influenced his ministry. He learned to speak more slowly and quietly; in dress, he abandoned the loud ties which had suggested superficial showmanship. Similarly, Cliff Barrows stopped using his trombone to stir the singing. All of the Team were steadied and matured by working with British Christians, and were encouraged to find themselves reaching not only a capital but a nation.

The crusade already had drawn a million and a half (the final attendance figures topped two million) when it was announced that the closing service, for the evening of Saturday May 22, would be held in London's largest outdoor stadium, Wembley, where the soccer league's Cup Final is played. The bookings became so heavy, even before the posters were out, that the smaller White City stadium, a few miles south, was taken for an additional service earlier the same afternoon.

The Lord Mayor would be present at Wembley, the Archbishop of Canterbury would give the benediction.

In the last week of the crusade Billy Graham again met the press. "My, what a difference between this conference and the first one," wrote Stephen Olford. "Then there was cynicism, censoriousness and a cold indifference. Today the atmosphere was completely changed. I have never seen newsmen more subdued, convinced, respectful!" The next day the *Daily Mirror* carried Cassandra's scintillating account of his famous meeting with Billy in a public house, the Baptist's Head. ("A teetotaler and abstainer able to make himself completely at his ease in the spit and sawdust department; which is, in my view, a very difficult thing to do.") They became firm friends and correspondents. Cassandra (William Connor) told his readers: "I never thought that friendliness had such a sharp cutting edge. I never thought that simplicity could cudgel us sinners so damned hard."

At the final ministers' meeting in Central Hall, Westminster, the Bishop of Barking said: "A new flame of hope has been lit in our hearts, new courage and new faith. A fire has been lit which will continue, please God, if we are willing to obey the guidance of God's Holy Spirit in the days and years to come. May the church of Christ in this great area be united in spirit more and more in the days to come, and let us go forward together in faith with recognition of the glorious possibilities these coming years hold for us."

"It's harvest time in England," Billy Graham said in the course of his address that morning. "This is the hour of the church in England."

Next day a greatly loved national figure, unable to be at Wembley, sent Billy Graham a private message which very beautifully expressed the widespread feeling in England as the crusade drew to its close: "The immediate response to your addresses, and the increasing number of those who are anxious to hear them, testify both to your own sincerity and to the eagerness with which a great host of the people of this country welcome the opportunity to fortify their religious belief and to reaffirm the principles which you proclaim." The letter paid tribute to "the spiritual rekindling you have brought to numberless Englishmen and women whose faith has been made to glow anew by your addresses."

18 · Wembley, Winston Churchill—and After

The last day of the Greater London crusade, May 22, 1954, brought weather as unpropitious as the first. Nothing else was the same for Billy as he awoke, weary. The previous evening Harringay had filled so early that two and a half hours before the service the BBC broadcast police warnings that without a ticket one should stay home. And the morning news was of special trains and coaches converging on London, and even of people camping out, despite the cold and wet, to make sure of places at White City or Wembley. Billy Graham, as he looked at the rain, had a sinking feeling that one or other stadium would be half empty.

Chauffeur "Mac" drove the Grahams to White City, which holds 67,000 persons. They found that an overflow crowd had been accommodated in the nearby Queen's Park football ground, where Roy Cattell and Jerry Beavan had swiftly set up loudspeakers.

Billy preached on "Choose you this day whom ye will serve." "It was absolutely thrilling," wrote Trotman, "to see how the counselors and inquirers were placed together—just as smoothly as the running of the engine of a big ship." Some 2,000 inquirers walked out of the stands and crossed the running track toward the platform, to stand in the drizzle.

The police said the roads round Wembley were chaotic with traffic. Too late to hire a helicopter (Beavan tried!) the Team moved across by a bus under police escort, to reach Wembley in time for the tea given by the stadium directors for the Archbishop, Lord Mayor, Members of Parliament and other distinguished guests who were to sit on the platform or in the royal box. As Billy, who says he "just did not know where I was going to find the strength for the sermon," looked out of the window, amazed to see every seat in the enormous oval already filled, the gates were opened and an overflow was allowed to swarm onto the precious turf. That cold wet evening witnessed the greatest religious congregation, 120,000, ever seen until then in the British Isles.[1]

On the platform during the first half hour, which was being broadcast, Billy glanced at the Archbishop and other great men near him and was suddenly tempted to switch from his simple message to "something impressive in an intellectual framework." He rejected the temptation and preached again in simplicity, without trace of his weariness, ending: "You can go back to the shop, the office, the factory, with a greater joy and peace than you have ever known. But before that can happen you must commit yourselves to Jesus Christ. You must make your personal decision for Him. And you can do that now. Choose this day whom ye will serve!"

The *News of the World* described the scene that followed: "There was no emotional hysteria, no tension . . . only a very deep reverence. . . . Within minutes thousands of men, women and teenagers were moving to the track. They were of all ages, of all classes of society. Husbands and wives were hand in hand with their children, young men walked forward alone." To the newspaper it looked like 10,000; in fact 2,000, with their counselors, stood before the platform. The Archbishop stepped to the microphones and prayed, "simply, clearly, movingly," wrote Ruth.

Grady Wilson was so overcome by the whole experience that, as they descended the stairs and the Archbishop made a remark, he threw his arm round Dr. Fisher's shoulders and called him "Brother Archbishop."

The press surged about Billy. He told them it was too early to assess results. "But I leave Britain for the time being with the belief that she is on the verge of the greatest spiritual awakening in her history."

As the Team's bus inched slowly through the crowds waving goodbye and singing, "To God be the glory," Billy stood up. "I want all of us to bow our heads right now and give thanks to God for all He has done and is doing. This is His doing, and let none fail to give Him credit."

When Billy had prayed, Bev Shea, the whole Team joining, began to sing softly, "Praise God from Whom all blessings flow."

[1] The figure is the official turnstile record given by Wembley Stadium. Attendance figures for Graham crusades are normally from stadium sources. The vast figure for, *e.g.*, the final meeting of Los Angeles (134,254) in 1963 was a turnstile figure, though officials at the Los Angeles Coliseum reported that they let in additional, uncounted people through the gates to relieve pressure. The Graham Team insists on accuracy to forestall press exaggerations.

On the day after Wembley Billy Graham went to Oxford University to address a packed congregation of undergraduates and dons. On the Monday, lying in bed in his London hotel, which he was to leave that night for a holiday in Scotland, he was summoned at short notice to 10 Downing Street by Sir Winston Churchill.

Billy had written inviting the Prime Minister to Wembley. Papers concerning Harringay were placed before Churchill, and he consulted his party's Chief Whip before deciding not to attend. One of his principal private secretaries, John Colville, had met Billy at a luncheon. Colville asked the Prime Minister if he would see him, but Churchill said No. However the reports of Wembley so impressed him that when John Colville returned to the subject Sir Winston agreed to give Graham five minutes, intending merely to be civil. As the hour approached, Sir Winston paced back and forth, saying he was nervous about the encounter: "What do you talk to an American evangelist about?"

At the stroke of noon on Monday, May 24, Billy Graham was shown into the Cabinet Room. Sir Winston stood at the center of the long Cabinet table, an unlighted cigar in his hand. Billy was surprised to see how short a man he was. Sir Winston motioned Billy to be seated and said he had been reading about him and was most happy to have him come, "because we need this emphasis." Then he said, "Do you have any hope? What hope do you have for the world?"

Billy was naturally overwhelmed at meeting privately the greatest man of the age, but did not forget why he had been allowed the privilege. He took out his little New Testament and answered, "Mr. Prime Minister, I am filled with hope."

Sir Winston pointed at the early editions of three London evening papers lying on the empty table, and commented that they were filled with rapes, murders and hate. When he was a boy it was different. If there was a murder it was talked about for fifty years. Everything was so changed now, so noisy and violent. And the Communist menace grew all the time. "I am an old man," he said, and repeated the phrase at different points in the conversation nine times. Several times he added, "without hope for the world."

Billy said again that he was filled with hope. "Life is very exciting even if there's a war, because I know what is going to happen in the future." Then he spoke about Jesus Christ, and began right at the beginning, turning from place to place in the New Testament and explaining, just as he would to an insignificant inquirer in his hotel room, the meaning of Christ's birth, His death, His resurrection and ascension, and how a man is born again. He moved quickly, inwardly agitated lest he should not put across the essentials in the short time granted him.

Billy got the impression that Churchill was very receptive. He made little comment but listened closely—a different attitude from that which Churchill is reported to have shown to ecclesiastical dignitaries. Perhaps Graham evoked in Sir Winston memories of the nanny of his boyhood, Mrs. Everest, who must have talked about the matters Billy was explaining; at any rate beneath Churchill's indifference to church affairs was that respect for the Bible which occasionally emerged in his writings, and his profound faith in a guiding Providence which he had expressed vigorously to the nation in the worst moments of the war.

Billy went on to speak of the Second Coming of Christ, the belief publicly recited so glibly in the Apostles' Creed, "He shall come again," which to Billy Graham was a vital, future certainty. The Prime Minister continued intent. The five minutes which he had scheduled for Graham had long flown, the clock showed twelve-thirty, and Sir Winston was sitting well forward in his chair, drinking in every word.

The interview lasted forty minutes. At last Sir Winston said: "I do not see much hope for the future unless it is the hope you are talking about, young man. We must have a return to God."

As he stood up and shook Billy's hand, Sir Winston said, "Our conversation is private, isn't it?" Billy, who had long ago learned the lesson of not revealing confidences, assured him he would not divulge it, nor did he during Sir Winston's lifetime, except for a phrase or two. Nor did Sir Winston reveal to his staff what they talked about. But his private secretaries recall his comments, that he had been "terribly impressed," had found Billy Graham "most interesting and agreeable."

All Billy said to the press as he left Downing Street was: "I felt like I had shaken hands with Mr. History."

More than 38,000 people had come forward in the Greater London crusade.

They came day by day in unexpectedly high numbers, as it seemed then, though numbers were small by comparison with those in Australia in 1959 and in American crusades of the nineteen-sixties. The follow-up system was swamped. Qualified counselors were in short supply. Some cases of unfortunate counseling occurred. The Team had not learned yet how to expand the administrative side of the follow-up program to keep abreast of inquirers however numerous, and cards reached clergy days late.

Ministers and churches were indeed presented with a pastoral opportunity unparalleled in the first half of the twentieth century. A small handful blatantly rejected the offer, tearing up or returning cards. Others never bothered to call, or allowed the cards to sink into the bottomless mire of a parson's desk. One parson, receiving seven cards, dispatched notes which stated certain rules of life and gave a time when he would be available. Lorne Sanny tried to impress on the man that "these people were sheep. They would not come knocking; someone needed to go out after them." A provincial businessman had given the name of his vicar and was told he would shortly hear from him. "I waited about a week. I saw him in the village and it appeared to me that he took avoiding action. About a week later I countered what was obviously an avoiding action and asked him if he had heard anything from the Billy Graham people about me. He said, 'Oh yes, and we must have a talk about it sometime,' and left in a great hurry."

At length the businessman called on the vicar and told him of his decision (which already had resolved deep personal and family problems). "He assured me I had been emotionally upset, but everything would be quite all right in a few weeks' time, and if I came back in a couple of months, he felt that he might be able to be of some help." The vicar brushed aside a plea for aid in Bible reading and when asked "if he could help me in my prayer life said that he could not —he had great difficulty himself—but suggested I start by saying grace at meals."

In contrast the churches which put most into the crusade received most benefit, not only in new members but by the stimulus given to old members to pray, witness and evangelize. At All Souls, Langham Place, the Anglican church next door to the BBC, the training school for laity doubled its numbers in the year following Harringay. As the crusade continued, churches hitherto lukewarm had begun to cooperate, to receive new members, find new opportunities. Life and hope streamed in to replace decay and despair.

Numerous clergy and ministers gratefully accepted the cards (nearly 80 per cent of London churches cooperated) but did not know what to do with the converts and the seekers. Billy Graham did not claim that all the thousands of inquirers were born again, but "their interest has been aroused and their conscience has been pricked." They were open hearts, waiting for spiritual help. Those who had been born again needed to grow, within the church. Their growth could not be Graham's responsibility. He was not founding a sect. Nor would he allow Team members to organize a "class system" such as John Wesley had been forced to use in the eighteenth century. The Graham Team served the churches, but as Billy frankly told the clergy: "I disavow any responsibility if the follow-up program cannot be handled by the ministers and the churches."

But many London clergy in 1954 were not ready. Too few understood what was happening. They could not welcome converts eagerly, lovingly, effectively because they themselves had only just become sharply aware again, through the crusade, of the authority of the Bible and of the power of the Holy Spirit. Yet they were willing to learn—and learn from Billy Graham. The Archbishop of Canterbury had spoken and written warmly of Graham; hundreds of English parsons now trusted this young American.

To the British nation in the early summer of 1954 Billy Graham was the man who understood them and could help them know God.

When Billy preached on Monday June 7, at Cliff College in Yorkshire, 60,000 stood in the rain and mud. At hotels on his journey people gathered in the streets outside, hoping to see him. When he went to Glasgow for three days of discussions with Scottish church leaders about a crusade for 1955, the police had to hold back the crowds at the station.

Graham was alarmed and confused.

The expectancy was prodigious. He had invitations to all the major cities of Britain. He wondered what he ought to do. Should he abandon his imminent preaching tour in continental Europe, abandon the Nashville and New Orleans crusades scheduled for August and October? Should he, instead, take a rest, and then return to Britain in the late summer and autumn of 1954, for as long as Britain needed him?

It would be difficult to cancel crusades. Weighing on him even more was a fear lest "there was too much interest in me as a person. . . . There might be a Billy Graham sect forming, and I might do something to hurt the church in Britain."

Back in London he laid his fears before the Archbishop of Canterbury. Dr. Fisher agreed, and advised Graham to wait a year.

A committee had been formed to launch a week's crusade in Wembley Stadium itself, following the 1955 Glasgow crusade. There was a discussion about a provincial tour later that year, and those whom Graham consulted were divided on the wisdom of returning so soon as the immediate autumn of 1954. Why not let the 1955 plans develop? Besides it would be difficult to book auditoriums on short notice, and English weather makes outdoor stadiums risky.

By the time of these discussions Billy Graham was weary and now believes that fatigue affected his judgment. Looking back, with the hindsight of more than a decade, Graham is certain he should have stayed.

"What would have happened?" mused sharp-tongued David Frost, star of "That Was the Week That Was," in the *Daily Mail* of May 18, 1963, after learning this history from Billy Graham. "Would we have become a nation as dull and narrow-minded as some of his followers? Or a nation as vibrantly and flagrantly Christian as Dr. Graham himself? Or what? I wish he'd stayed."

---

19 · All Scotland

In the second week of June 1954, Billy Graham and a nucleus of the Team sailed for Scandinavia.

In Helsinki, Stockholm and Copenhagen the one-day meetings planned by Billy's old friend Bob Evans, founder of the Greater Europe Mission, were each changed into an enormous stadium rally, so great had been the interest generated in the press by the London crusade.

They were before 40,000 at Amsterdam on June 22, and the local Navigator "crew" had 800 decision cards to follow up. Two days later, after a side trip to the American forces in Frankfurt, they came to rebuilt Düsseldorf. Bob Hopkins of the Navigators had been unsuccessful in his efforts to enroll and train counselors; the local German pastors "wouldn't hear of it because nothing was going to happen." Since all Protestants, save a fraction, were nominally members of the Evangelical Church (the union of Lutherans and Reformed), with its tendency to equate membership with full Christian discipleship, the prejudice against mass evangelism lay deep. Only at the last moment was the meeting moved to a large enough stadium. When 700 people came forward the muddle would have been total had not Hopkins hurriedly recruited twenty American Christian G.I.s as counselors.

That night in his cramped hotel room Billy woke with a searing pain in the small of his back—a pain that wracked and stabbed until, believing it poison, he thought himself dying. Jerry Beavan, finding him on the floor of the bathroom at 2 A.M., managed to rouse a doctor who gave him pain-killing shots. The Team had been joined by Billy's old friend John Bolten of Boston, born ten miles from Düsseldorf and a Ruhr industrialist in pre-Nazi days, who had often begged Billy to preach in Germany. In the morning Bolten took him to a specialist who x-rayed and diagnosed kidney stone.

Against the specialist's advice Billy and the Team flew next day, Saturday, to Berlin, where the Olympic Stadium had been taken for Sunday June 27. Much depended on the meeting. The East Berlin press was playing it up as a new form of American imperialism. Cartoons showed Billy flying over Berlin with a Bible in one hand, the atom bomb in the other, and Secretary of State Dulles cheering in the background. Dulles had lately failed in his attempt to create a European Defense Community—known in Germany as EVG (*Europaische Verteidigungs Gemeinschaft*). By calling Graham's activity EVGelism they "exposed" him as a mischievous substitute for Dulles. And all Saturday night the Russian guns beyond the Eastern sector fired practice rounds.

There was no Berlin Wall in 1954. Billy had already been visited by East German pastors who told him of grievous conditions in the Russian Zone. Thousands of East Berliners would cross the line to hear him.

At seven o'clock on Sunday morning Billy's pain returned. Bolten called the American military hospital. Billy refused the offer of an ambulance, and military regulations forbade a visit at the hotel. Bolten found a German doctor who gave him a stronger pain-killing drug for Billy, but when Billy was told it would make him sleepy, he would not take it; he must preach that afternoon.

Billy looked at John Bolten, sitting at his bedside. "John, why is God doing this to me? I can't understand it."

After a pause he continued: "I know what it is," he said. "I have just had a wonderful crusade in England. God has blessed me beyond imagination, and now I'm going to preach in Hitler's stadium before 100,000 people. And I would have probably talked to them in my own strength. God is humbling me. He is not going to divide His honor with anybody. He is telling me to lay everything at His feet and ask Him to fill the empty Billy with His own strength."

Bolten helped him dress. Billy had eaten nothing but tea and toast. They drove in a long motorcade down Hitler's route. Bolten, who had known Hitler personally and had broken with him in 1928, reflected how "a young Timothy with a very different message now went the same road to the same place." Instead of Nazi songs the hymns of the Reformation echoed round the stadium. Where the swastika had stood Graham and Bolten saw the text: "I am the Way, the Truth and the Life."

As so often in that wet European summer of 1954 it was raining. Because the service was broadcast, many stayed away and numbers were down to 80,000. As he preached, none could have told that Billy was ill.

Since the stadium refused to permit movement on the turf, Billy could not ask inquirers forward; they must stand in their seats in open witness. Billy Graham preaches easily through an interpreter, for he uses short, simple sentences. But that afternoon when he reached the end of his address and cried, "Those who want to *decide for* Christ, stand up," the interpreter used words that to the Germans (who anyway were chary of such demonstration ever since Goebbels, in that same stadium, yelled "Do you want total war? and they roared back Yes!") implied, "Do you want to *confess* Christ?" Tens of thousands stood: every deacon, every pastor, every layman who believed himself a disciple. Billy said, "No, no, you misunderstood." He explained again the meaning of repentance, faith, a first-time decision for Christ, the new birth. John Bolten is "absolutely sure" that the audience understood the second translation. Some sat, large numbers stood. To Billy it seemed a tremendous demonstration of spiritual hunger. He turned round saying, "I have never experienced anything like this."

More than 16,000 decision cards were taken and returned by post. Peter Schneider of the Berlin YMCA, who had volunteered to organize the follow-up, soon learned that thousands had sent in cards, not because they had made a decision for Christ that afternoon but from curiosity, or confusion of mind caused by the translation. But most of them welcomed counseling, and in a long series of meetings all across Berlin he and his helpers reaped where Billy had sown. One of the converts, whom Peter Schneider thus met, was the girl who became his wife.

When the Team left for Paris the East German Communist press alleged that Billy Graham had visited East Berlin night clubs—it was the night he was lying in bed wracked by pain—and had not paid the bills!

At Paris, where Billy's one sermon in the Palais de Chaillot led to an invitation to hold a Paris crusade in 1955, he had another excruciating kidney stone attack. The Team sailed home from Cherbourg on July 1 and New York harbor gave him a hero's welcome: not only were Ruth and the four children there, but a score of reporters and photographers, TV and newsreel cameras, and at the pier a crowd singing "Blessed Assurance" and "To God be the Glory." Four film companies immediately approached him about a film on his life or on the crusades, including one detailed offer of a multi-million-dollar technicolor, wide-screen production with leading actors: $100,000 outright plus 25 per cent of the profits to Graham. He declined.

At Montreat the small house on Assembly Drive received endless telephone calls, an avalanche of mail, and became a focus for inquisitive tourists. A good rest seemed impossible—until Billy had to go to Asheville Memorial Hospital for removal of the kidney stone, and was ordered to cancel engagements for six weeks, until the start of the Nashville crusade.

While Billy Graham, Cliff Barrows and Bev Shea worked in America, the British Isles were looking forward to the six weeks' All-Scotland Crusade. For the first time Billy Graham would come with the official endorsement of the churches to lead a united effort to reach an entire land—the land of his ancestors.

Out of the ferment of the Second World War the Scottish churches had emerged with a strong emphasis on evangelism. In 1950 and again in 1952 the British Broadcasting Corporation in Scotland, under its vigorous head, Dr. Ronald Falconer, had organized a radio mission. From it emerged the long-term "Tell Scotland Movement," on which almost all the churches were officially represented. "Tell Scotland" was (and is) founded on the principles that evangelism is not a sporadic encounter with the world but a continuous engagement at every level; that the local congregation is the chief agent of this missionary ministry, and that the activity of laymen is crucial. When Harringay created its enormous interest, "Tell Scotland" was approaching phase two of its work, "the recruiting and training of lay forces of the Church for the task of mission." And the Movement, especially its young field organizer, the late Tom Allan, who had previously led a remarkable advance while minister in a working-class Glasgow parish, believed that it could provide a most effective framework for a Glasgow crusade. Harringay, as never before in England, was alerting the laity to their evangelistic and pastoral opportunities; "Tell Scotland" could thus expect to call up its forces and launch its mission in one.

At the General Assembly of the Church of Scotland in May 1954 the presbytery of Aberdeen proposed that the Church itself invite Graham. The assembly decided rather to endorse the invitation of "Tell Scotland," and did so with enthusiasm, despite a strong speech by George MacLeod, founder of the Iona Community, opposing Graham's methods and theology. A few days later Billy Graham addressed a large and intimidating audience of ministers in Glasgow. "They sat there," recalls a young Congregational minister, "mostly in black, arms folded, brows drawn, as if to say, 'You're not going to convince me.' Afterward as we came down the steps I overheard one minister say, 'You would have to be pretty sour not to agree with that!' "

Except for George MacLeod, to whom Christianity was primarily to be expressed in judgment upon and action within the social and political order, and the very small group of ultra-Calvinist Free Presbyterians mainly in the Western Isles, plus some of the leaders of the Free Church, the Scottish churches came together in a remarkable outward expression of unity to prepare for a crusade to be held in Glasgow but aimed to reach all Scotland. The unity, however, was not as deep as it looked. It included those who strongly supported Graham but had no interest in "Tell Scotland," those in favor of both, and those who would not have supported Graham except for their commitment to "Tell Scotland." Deeper still lay a fundamental cleavage on the meaning of the Cross and the nature of the Gospel.

The long-term effect of the crusade would depend upon these hidden tensions being resolved.

Meanwhile Glasgow prepared with the tremendous enthusiasm for which it is famous. The city engineer effected the conversion of Kelvin Hall from an exhibition center to an auditorium; the Parks Commission lent shrubs, tubs of flowers and chairs. A contractor transported extra chairs, free, from other cities of Scotland. All poster sites were donated by business houses, and the bill-posters receipted their own bills. At a central site where no advertising had ever been permitted, the city instantly agreed to a display for the crusade, which a steel firm erected, another firm decorated and a third flood-lighted—all free. Hugh Fraser (now Lord Fraser of Allander) provided offices worth $7,000 a year for £1, fully equipped. The city gave all police services.

The Scots and the Team both organized with such care that sparks flew sometimes as each hammered away at the other's preconceptions, "but Jerry Beavan and I always ended the greatest of friends" recalls the secretary, D. S. K. McLeay. Traditional Scots' thrift was a trifle scandalized when Jerry spent thirty minutes on a long-distance call to London the day he arrived, aiming pads of note paper at a vagrant mouse as he talked. But, says a young Baptist minister who served in the office, "He impressed us tremendously the closer we worked with him. The backroom team as a whole taught us that spirituality and business efficiency could be combined. . . . A deeply spiritual, deeply dedicated, and yet utterly competent crew."

Glasgow had a vital influence on the Graham Team's development by bringing the counseling program a long step forward. In previous crusades interested clergymen had been merely invited by letter to send likely counselors to the classes, and perhaps seven or ten would respond from each church. At Glasgow the clergy were nervous about what might be taught. Beavan and Charlie Riggs therefore visited Glasgow in the autumn of 1954 and explained the training program to six groups, each consisting of about a hundred ministers from the city and surrounding counties. Many of these ministers sent in fifty or more names each: 4,300 people enrolled and nearly 4,000 took the classes. The highest hitherto had been Harringay with 2,500; in America it had been much smaller. Thenceforth, the Team decided, they would always explain follow-up to the clergy first.

A solid cross section of church people began to learn how to be counselors. To a great many this use of the Bible was, in the words of one Church of Scotland minister, David Orrock, "something totally new and impressive. It has often struck me since as being exceedingly odd that I should come through theological college and enter the Christian ministry without ever having been taught how to make a man a Christian by leading him to Christ. Pre-evangelism is dealt with in considerable scope and detail, but when it comes to the point where the man says, 'What must I do to be saved?' this had never seriously been dealt with." Furthermore (in Tom Allan's words ten years later), "there were many people converted in the counseling classes and this is one of the most important aspects of the crusade."

Billy Graham came to Glasgow on the morning of Saturday March 9, 1955, waved to by singing groups as the train from the south rushed through wayside stations, and welcomed at St. Enoch Station by an enthusiastic but more orderly crowd than Waterloo's the previous year.

"Glasgow Belongs to Billy," ran the headline in a paper that evening. During the two days before the crusade opened three incidents seemed to symbolize the width and depth of the preparation.

At the civic reception in the City Chambers, after the speeches, old Lord Provost Kerr, Socialist leader on the city council and not particularly known as a Christian man, suddenly moved across to the grand piano in his civic robes and began to play and sing the 23rd Psalm to the tune *Crimond*. All the guests, moved by this spontaneous and unlikely gesture, joined in.

On the Sunday afternoon, during a blinding snowstorm, a representative and interdenominational congregation gathered in Glasgow Cathedral for a broadcast dedication service of great dignity. Billy Graham pledged himself "to serve the Church, whether it be a humble Brethren assembly or the congregation of this ancient cathedral."

The third incident, entirely private, occurred on the Saturday night at the North British Hotel in the privacy of Billy Graham's sitting room, which to Howard Butt's joy had a large coal fire. (Howard suffered acutely from Glasgow's dank cold, despite frequently paddling his feet in hot water. Communists apart, the merchant city of Scotland rather relished an associate evangelist who was also millionaire vice-president of a grocery chain.) Graham, Butt, Grady Wilson and Paul Rees, after meeting 7,000 crusade workers at the Kelvin Hall, dined alone. "Then," says Paul Rees, "we went to our knees and had a time of waiting on the Lord, and such a spirit of prayer came over all of us! I recall how much liberty the Spirit seemed to give Howard Butt as he prayed, till that room was simply an upper room, a real Pentecost for us, and we were all profoundly aware of the presence of God."

Each began to confess failures, mistakes and sins, till tears ran. In Rees' words, "We were just bowed low before the Lord, 'broken'— that would describe the mood that the Spirit created in our hearts that day." They arose with a sense of being cleansed and empowered, "confident that God was about to do something in Scotland."

Billy had no fear of empty seats the first night of Kelvin Hall. The crusade being intended not for Glasgow only but for towns and villages far beyond, the greater part of the space had to be reserved for organized parties; reserved tickets for the whole six weeks were taken before the start, and an annex with closed-circuit TV, holding 3,000, was hurriedly arranged. For unreserved seats people were queuing outside Kelvin Hall throughout the raw afternoon.

Many ministers had questioned whether Billy should invite public decisions. For inquirers to come forward, rather than to wait behind or file into another room, had never been known and was most un-

Scottish. In reply to Tom Allan's doubts Billy said, "Let's see what happens." Allan could detect in him—and before every subsequent meeting—"an inner and very finely controlled tension. . . . A man under immense strain but somehow living on top of the strain." Once Billy had prayed with his friends and the meeting began he seemed to Allan transformed: "All the strain is gone, and from then on the man has forgotten himself."

The first night, attended by the Moderator and a galaxy of notables, was most unemotional and somewhat chaotic, with coughs, photographers, and constant movement on creaking boards in different parts of the hall. The choir was superb. Bev Shea, recovering from laryngitis, sang one verse only. During the early part of the service Billy had a moment of lost confidence, perhaps because everybody anticipated a great victory, whereas at Harringay they had half-expected failure. But when he rose there was a great hush, a quiet. "I have never felt an audience so close to me before," Graham wrote to Ruth. "It seemed that the hearts were open and the Lord pouring it in. I tried to talk quietly and deliberately. I could feel the power of the Holy Spirit moving in the audience.

"Then came the moment of decision. Would they come? Would they respond?

"I asked them to bow their heads, and then quietly gave the invitation. At first not a person moved. My heart began to sink a little. My faith wavered only for a second, and then it all came flooding back to me that millions of people were praying and that God was going to answer their prayers. Then great faith came surging into my heart, and I knew they would come even before I saw the first one move. I bowed my head and began to pray. Then I glanced up and people were streaming from everywhere. I saw some of the ministers with their clerical collars, on the platform, begin to weep."

---

20 · *Fire on the Heather?*

The All Scotland Crusade did not have to make its way as at Harringay, but was borne along in a floodtide of goodwill and spiritual hunger.

In every audience at Kelvin Hall more than half were not Glasgow residents but came from all areas of Scotland except the remotest.[1] Every audience was a true cross section of social levels. Harringay had reached directly only a small proportion of artisans and manual workers, although by the conversion of the militant Communist, Charles Potter, who thereafter undertook missions to industrial workers until his early death in 1959, it did so indirectly. In Glasgow there was no question, for apart from subsidiary meetings in mills and factories (Billy himself spoke at John Brown's shipyard where Cunard's Queen ships were built), almost all parishes were cooperating, including those mainly composed of dockers and steel workers.

And more at least than any previous local attempt, All Scotland reached the unchurched—because of "Operation Andrew."

Operation Andrew took its name from the words in St. John's Gospel: "Andrew, Simon Peter's brother . . . first findeth his own brother Simon and saith unto him, we have found . . . the Christ. And he brought him to Jesus." The device behind the name had been evolved by Stephen Olford at Richmond and brought to the notice of the Team during Harringay by Bob Pettifer, a young member of the Brethren: a church would charter coaches to a crusade on which members could travel only if they brought along a nonchurchgoer. This concept was further developed by Sanny and Riggs at Glasgow into a scheme whereby churches were invited to book reservations at Kelvin Hall provided they would fill their allotted seats according to the spirit of Operation Andrew. "The idea," says Riggs, "was to go out after the uncommitted, the unchurched, and bring them in a group." In the perspective of another decade of crusade activity the Glasgow scheme was experimental and unpolished, but it did ensure that a large number of the unchurched were present every night.

Thousands of these unchurched found that (in a phrase of Graham's), "the only true joy is living in the center of God's will." Their stories are vividly alive to themselves and those around them. They would overweight a book, and two little incidents must represent the rest.

Billy received a semi-literate letter from a lad, reproduced here verbatim: "I wonder if you could possible put my friends and my

[1] This fact lessens the value, as proof of the crusade's success, of the statistics independently prepared by the Glasgow sociologist, John Highet, which showed a sharp rise in Glasgow churchgoing on the Sunday following the crusade, dropping in the next five years to a level of about half as much again as that of the year previous to the crusade.

own mind at ease But giving us your answer to our Problem. Well Sir as you may know my friend and I made a decision for Christ at one of your Campaigns in the Kelvin Hall, Glasgow. Well, our Problem is that we being young lads we like to keep in style like most other lads for we get our trousers made tighter than they normally are and sometimes our jackets are longer and shoes are rather stylish. Well Sir just recently a friend of ours told us that the Bible says we should not dress as such for it is considered a sin." The letter asked whether they should continue wearing "Teddy Boy" clothes. (Billy replied, "It's the man inside the suit that really counts. . . . When our hearts are right, we will desire that everything we do and say will 'express' Christ.") The lad's letter ended: "P.S. we are praying earnestly for you and your team and we hope God will Bless you in your great work for the People of Glasgow."

When the letter reached Billy Graham it bore a note from the follow-up department: "They are two really tough types, previously belonging to one of the toughest types of gangs in Glasgow. They have been wonderfully converted—are making a terrific witness in their work, despite ridicule, and despite lack of education are studying their Bibles and learning verses every day. Apart from this, they have in the past stolen a considerable amount of goods, without being found out, and are now so convicted about it that they intend making restitution, although they expect a heavy penalty for it.[1]

The second story comes from another rough area of Glasgow. A manual laborer's character had been transformed as a result of his decision. He had begun to attend church regularly. Talking to a tough pal whose face was hideously scarred, he said he too ought to go to church.

"I couldn't go," replied his friend. "There's no place in church for a man with scars like mine."

"Why, Charlie, we follow a Man who had worse scars than you."

On April 1 Hugh Fraser gave a luncheon for Billy Graham to address 400 social, political and business leaders—a unique and representative event.[2]

Yet the crusade influenced clergy more than secular leaders, and influenced them profoundly. Graham was right when he told Dr.

---

[1] I tried to trace these young men but the slum area where they had lived is pulled down and there was no way to discover their whereabouts.

[2] Afterwards a guest happened to return. "I found Billy taking time to go round and speak to the waitresses who had attended at table."

George Docherty of New York Presbyterian Church, Washington, at the close of the crusade, after looking through scores of letters: "Probably the most lasting result will be in the lives of hundreds of ministers." Paul Rees again made a deep impression. Graham gave two notable addresses to ministers; before the first his heart sank when Scottish-born Dr. John Sutherland Bonnell of New York, who was to speak too, whispered, "There is probably a greater concentration of theological brains under this roof than you could get any other place in the world." When Billy rose he acted on Docherty's advice of years before: "When you preach to the preachers, don't try to teach them. Preach to their hearts and they will respond."

They responded to Graham's personality: "There was something clean and elevating and radiant about him." They responded to his sincerity and conviction. They warmed under the glow of fresh life in their churches. They were confronted starkly by the issues of personal evangelism. One incident illuminates this confrontation: a Team member, who took a theater service at which twenty-four inquirers responded, walked across to a group of five ministers to request their aid as counselors, and not one moved. They could preach, but they were embarrassed and incapable when asked to help individuals to faith.

They were also confronted with the Gospel of God's grace, which had tended to be forgotten in Scotland. Many ministers, bred in strong Calvinism, were critical of Graham's emphasis on decision, on the importance of the will, although they recognized that he did not deny or belittle the sovereignty of God, or suggest that the Christian way is soft or easy. Above all, the Scots minister had to face the question of authority in preaching. Scotland no longer could claim the title, "Land of the Book," but the title was dormant rather than extinct; and the crusade proved once again, by its effects on the lives of men, that the authority of the Bible had not been invalidated by Biblical criticism. There was something symbolic in the fact that Glasgow's motto, popularly compressed to "Let Glasgow flourish," was displayed in full over the entrance to Kelvin Hall: "Let Glasgow flourish by the Preaching of the Word and the Praising of His Name."

If Graham left his mark on Glasgow, Glasgow influenced Graham, and in no way more than in his thinking about the social implications of the Gospel.

Tom Allan, a Socialist in politics, stated categorically,[1] "Billy

[1] In an interview in 1965, a few months before his death at age forty-nine.

Graham has one of the most acute and social consciences of any man I ever met. All his sympathies, all his affections, all his personal passion is on the side of the dispossessed, the disinherited, the lost, the hungry, the lonely, the homeless, the downtrodden." Graham had seen poverty in the West Virginian coalfields, and he had not forgotten his stay in South Wales in 1946. Always interested in John Wesley, he had particularly noted Wesley's social concern. In earlier days as a public figure in America Graham had tended to be brash about social problems. In Atlanta in 1950 he had said that the Bible had the complete answer to the local street car strike: the leaders on both sides must be converted and then pray together. But even then, as always in his mature years, he stressed that the Christian life is not only a vertical relationship between man and God, but a horizontal one too, and that a man new-made in Christ will show his love of God by loving his neighbor also.

At Glasgow Graham found himself among men like Tom Allan who had thought deeply about the church's role in society, the outworking of God's Kingdom within the contemporary scene. Just as Tom Allan's ministry was strongly influenced by Graham, so also Graham learned from Allan. "It wasn't that he changed when he came to Scotland," Allan recalled. "It was simply that these ideas and challenges became more strictly focused."

The sharper focus was reflected in his preaching as the crusade continued.

The peak of the All Scotland Crusade was the Good Friday TV and radio broadcast from Kelvin Hall.

The religious department of the BBC, Scottish Region, had arranged its entire schedule for March and April to ensure that the message and atmosphere of the crusade reached Scotland's farthest corners. On Good Friday Billy Graham spoke to the whole United Kingdom, having already the previous week given a nationwide series of five-minute breakfast-time broadcasts. For the staff of the BBC in Glasgow the unforgettable memory is of Billy's interest in each of them personally: in Ronald Falconer's words, his "constant witness of Christian love to all whom he met." Falconer was much impressed by Graham's knowledge of broadcasting, especially Billy's pointing out the near-impossibility of what he was being asked to do on Good Friday: to reach simultaneously, with one message, three audiences, each requiring a different approach: the TV viewers, the radio listeners, and the Kelvin Hall congregation.

All that second week Graham was troubled by a touch of flu and laryngitis. One evening he was depressed. "I just felt I didn't want to preach tonight," he reported, "and I paced back and forth, praying to God, but it seemed that my prayers got nowhere." Then he fell across his bed, slept soundly for two hours and, refreshed physically and spiritually, "had great liberty" in preaching. For Palm Sunday he went to North Berwick on the east coast to throw off his cold. His mind ranging ahead to Good Friday, he invited the foremost theologian in Scotland, Dr. James B. Stewart, Professor of New Testament Language, Literature and Theology in the University of Edinburgh, and a future Moderator, to spend much of Sunday with him. "Most of our talk and discussion was of a theological nature," writes Dr. Stewart, "especially relating to the doctrine of the Atonement." Dr. Stewart did not realize at the time that Graham was working over with him the theme of his upcoming TV sermon, determined that nothing should be theologically unsound or ill-digested. His aim was to "glorify Christ and make the Gospel so simple that the smallest child might understand."

On Good Friday itself, in his hotel room, Billy read and reread the story of the crucifixion. "When I read of His suffering and death by crucifixion it overwhelms me," he wrote that afternoon. "I have knelt down more than once during the day, feeling my unworthiness and sinfulness."

His sermon that night on the Cross was probably one of the greatest and most influential Graham has ever preached. With a television audience second only to the Coronation, it was unquestionably the vastest audience addressed by a preacher in Britain. In public houses rough men sat with eyes glued to the screen in utter quiet; at football matches next day it was the chief topic at half time. The service was watched and heard in Buckingham Palace and in tenement rooms. Not only was it (in the professional opinion of *TV Mirror*) "unmistakably superb television," but the content was crystal clear, proclaiming Christ's death in man's stead so plainly that the issues, even if rejected, could not be misunderstood.

Few of those who were touched by that telecast became known to Graham personally. A Yorkshire vicar, however, wrote to Graham on Easter Day: "I have been ordained 20 years—and I have only just found Christ for whom I have searched ever since I was little more than a kid of 12. I want to tell *you* this because I think you have been the mediator of my findings." He described some recent steps in his search, including watching a Billy Graham film, and studying the parables. "But now I *know* I have found Christ—that He has for-given the sins—the really awful sins—of the past. I seem to have new life. I *know* He is Risen. I watched you last Friday night in a friend's house—and then I went back to Church—just to *know*. . . . Maybe I shall come down the mountain, but I know this time I shall not come down alone.

"My heart is so full of joy and peace—but it isn't easy to find folk who understand. I know you can and will."

In Easter week the crusade became truly All Scottish by means of the broadcast relay mission.

Dr. D. P. Thomson, an Evangelist of the Church of Scotland, con-ceived a brilliant development of the relays by telephone lines since Harringay's had been unpremeditated and therefore haphazard. From Kelvin Hall the relays were concentrated on the six nights of Easter week and into thirty-seven strategic centers. Each local relay center had its appointed "missioner," and the week began and ended with united rallies on the Sundays. "For ten days," wrote Tom Allan, "the whole country from Scotland to the borders and from Stornoway to the east coast was bound together in one great national mission, and under the sound of the eternal Gospel." At Edinburgh, where the relay mission was followed up by a great meeting in Tynecastle Sta-dium addressed by Graham, Thomson himself trained the 600 coun-selors, thoroughly and in depth, with each one interviewed separately before final acceptance. Later 1,000 persons attended central follow-up courses.

At the end of the All Scotland Crusade Billy Graham made a spe-cial point of visiting D. P. Thomson's home at Crieff to sit at his feet. "I never met a man," Thomson said many years later, "who was so open to constructive criticism, fresh suggestions and ideas."

For the final two weeks the crusade was extended by telephonic re-lays to England, Ireland and Wales, attended by over one and a half million people—each relay center prepared by committees drawn from the different denominations, their counselors trained with the aid of tapes recorded by Lorne Sanny. In Glasgow the crusade ended in a blaze of glory in two immense stadium rallies on April 29 and 30.

The Grahams (Billy had been joined by Ruth) had a short holiday and then went south. After a short second London crusade at Wem-bley, Billy and Ruth returned to be guests of the Duke of Hamilton as Lord High Commissioner to the Church of Scotland when he went into residence at the palace of Holyrood House for the General Assembly. Billy delighted in the ceremonial and the historic significance of the court, and in meeting distinguished fellow guests, though there was nearly a calamity when he discovered his evening dress trousers left behind and all the shops shut. Hugh Fraser came to the rescue: the manager of his Edinburgh branch, recalled from the golf course, had a pair fitted and made in a few hours. In the dimly lit banquet hall everyone Billy met "seemed to be Lord Somebody." "I shook hands with one man and said, 'How do you do, my lord.' The man stuttered, blushed and said, 'I'm sorry, sir, I'm your waiter.' " Ruth sat next to the Earl of Home, the Grahams' first meeting with the future Prime Minister.

The General Assembly of the Church of Scotland gave Billy Graham a thunderous welcome when he replied, in a speech of one minute, to their strong motion of gratitude for the crusade. As the son of staunch Scottish Presbyterians Billy considers their welcome "one of the most historic moments of my entire ministry."

The All Scotland crusade had seen a great reaping where others had sown. It had created immense expectancy throughout Scotland. The heather seemed dry, Graham had lit a fire and departed, his part done. And the heather did not blaze.

Once again the churches were not truly ready for their opportunities, and many converts did not grow to maturity. More Scottish clergy entered into the work of crusade than had their brethren in London, and thus more churches benefited. Where counselors and converts came together in regular Bible studies they grew together, but the crusade did not lead to a continuing revival, gathering momentum each month. The hope of Graham, Allan and many others that it would set in motion a progressing evangelism through local congregations was not fulfilled.

That the crusade had been part of the "Tell Scotland Movement" produced unforeseen complications and tangles; had it come at another time, had there been longer to prepare, the effect would have been greater. And unity did not outlast the crusade. Though many thousands of lay people had indeed been revitalized, by conversion or rededication or by their experience as counselors, "Tell Scotland" found itself unsure of its course. Some tried to work on as if no crusade had occurred; others assumed that mass evangelism was the only object, the only way, and attempted to recreate locally the conditions of the crusade with local "Billy Grahams."

Nor was the basic theological tension in Scotland resolved.

Had Graham stayed as long as Moody and Sankey, whose six months' campaign of 1874–5 in Edinburgh and Glasgow had an incontrovertibly deep and lasting influence on Scottish churches, the dissension over the meaning and content of evangelism might have been ended by the sheer weight of the cumulative evidence of changed lives. For it could not be denied that these lives had changed.

Yet though the hopes of those who planned and carried out the crusade, both Scots and Americans, were not totally realized, much was accomplished. In 1954 and 1955 Graham said it took two years for the results of a crusade to be evident; experience has now led him to say not two years but at least five. By 1960 there was evidence enough, for those who knew where to look. There were projects which derived directly from the crusade, such as D. P. Thomson's Lay Training Centre at Crieff; Tom Allan's transformation of St. George's Tron, a nearly empty church in the center of Glasgow, which he built into a powerful bridgehead of evangelism and witness with intensive activities to reach the surrounding unchurched; and the summer Bible school started by Brethren Assemblies. There had also been the lasting encouragement and rededication which the crusade brought to scores of ministers. But undoubtedly the greatest result was to be found in the lives and careers of the young.

By 1959 the Bible Training Institute in Glasgow had more students than it could house; and when, in 1961, nineteen students then in Church of Scotland theological colleges signed a letter to Graham saying they had been converted in the crusade, their letter symbolized the scores of young men and women whose conversion or activity at Kelvin Hall put them on the road to full-time Christian service. When Alan Redpath took the pastorate of Charlotte Baptist Chapel, Edinburgh, as late as 1962 on his return from America, he found a steady trickle of new members joining whose spiritual pilgrimage had begun in the crusade.

The heather is still dry, and Billy Graham, whose name is far from forgotten by the ordinary Scot, may yet be the man who sets it unquenchably alight.

An influential younger minister of the Church of Scotland summed up well, nine years later: "I'm convinced that the All Scotland crusade had a very profound and a very lasting effect on the church life of Scotland. I don't think it's quite the sort of effect that we would have wished for, but I think it will have lasting results over the next generation at least, and possibly beyond."

21 · *"And Fear to Launch Away"*

In England during the winter of 1954–55 the direct influence of Billy Graham had continued through the widespread showing of two films: *London Crusade,* a documentary, and *Souls in Conflict,* the color feature based on three conversion stories, including that of Joan Winmill who played virtually her own experience.

The mood in England was expressed by Hugh Gough, Bishop of Barking, at the 121st annual Islington Conference of Anglican clergy in January 1955: "Quite clearly we are witnessing the beginning of another Evangelical Revival in this country." Not only could the Bishop affirm, "Hardly a week goes by without my getting fresh evidence of the deep and lasting effect of the Greater London Crusade and of similar evangelism," but, as the former president of the Baptist World Alliance, Townley Lord said: "the atmosphere and attitude of England toward religion have perceptibly changed from prevailing coldness and indifference to increasing warmth and growth." Even the Socialist weekly *New Statesman,* no friend to Christianity, admitted, "People talk about religion without embarrassment more freely than used to be thought seemly."

There were private indications that Church leaders, especially in the Church of England, were about to place themselves squarely beside the fresh evangelical emphasis as a proved means of combating irreligion; as a practical implementation of the famous 1945 report, *Towards the Conversion of England;* and as part of the fulfillment of the Archbishop of Canterbury's hope expressed at the Queen's accession, that England would see again a Reformation as profound and Scriptural as in the reign of the first Elizabeth.

And then they hesitated.

In the spring of 1955 the aged G. K. A. Bell, Bishop of Chichester and ecumenical leader, told the American journalist Stanley High of *Reader's Digest,* "Of Billy Graham's great and enduring service to our country there can be no doubt. Spiritually, England was waiting for such a challenge. There are evidences all about, many in my own diocese, that clergy and laymen have been aroused by that challenge and that the message of the Church to the nation is being given new force and authority." But when Billy Graham came to Wembley Stadium for seven nights of May 1955, no great dignitary of the Church attended.

The Wembley crusade was such a daring innovation that Billy Graham had doubts: he had never before returned to a city for a second crusade; no stadium of comparable size had been taken for seven nights. "I only pray to God we are doing right in coming back," he had written to Roy Cattell at the beginning of the year. On the day Wembley began, in a note dictated for a brief-lived diary, he admitted "great fear. There has been a great silence on the part of the forces of opposition and the Devil, yet I know he is getting his big guns loaded, and I know that he is going to blast away with all his might. But I also have a feeling that God is going to do something unusual."

Every factor weighed against the Wembley crusade. The new Prime Minister, Anthony Eden, had decided on a general election; Billy drew greater crowds—50,000 or 60,000 every night—than any politician, but the election campaign inevitably absorbed energies and interest. The London newspapers were recovering from a prolonged strike and gave the crusade little coverage; Graham refused to create news by sensational comments or actions. The sole sensation during the actual week was the abortive attempt of John French, former fiancé of Joan Winmill, who had broken off a relationship she knew could not bring happiness, to assault Graham in a hotel lobby.[1] Graham, surprised but friendly, seized French's hand in a warm handshake before it could strike; French, a successful actor, stayed to be counseled and became an evangelist in America and the Orient.

Graham was guest of honor at a private luncheon given by George Goyder, head of a newsprint corporation, at which the editors of nearly all the great national papers were present. "What impressed this very critical and unusual audience," writes George Goyder, "was Billy Graham's complete sincerity, which enabled him to receive critical questions and answer them quite impersonally. His love of our Lord shone through everything he said, and I do not think there was a single editor present who was not moved as well as impressed." Graham handled a severe attack by the editor of one of Britain's most popular dailies in such a way that to some of the others it seemed the editor was "almost converted on the spot."

Wembley's greatest difficulty was the English weather. Every night except two it poured, and those two were bleak. Many who had taken free reservations stayed away to leave empty seats; the rain at least weeded out the idly curious, the crowd-followers and sensation-seekers. Yet though attendance far outpaced Harringay, even the final

[1] Joan Winmill had married Bill Brown of Philadelphia, an associate crusade director on the Billy Graham Team, in April 1955.

congregation of 80,000 seemed a contrast to the unforgettable close of 1954. The rain did not stop inquirers swarming across—in numbers that also dwarfed Harringay—at the close of each service, about 3,000 a night. In terms of statistics Wembley was no failure. As Archbishop Gough could remark nine years later, "There are thousands of men and women in the Kingdom today because of it. Therefore can we say it was a mistake?" Moreover, it gave a fine opportunity to converts of Harringay, some 400 of whom were counselors at Wembley. To many of the organizers, looking back, it was, however, a disappointment. Billy Graham himself found Wembley one of his hardest crusades, quite apart from the rain, for it was the first he had conducted before an audience so far away as to be almost impersonal.

All adverse factors would have been outweighed had the foremost leaders of the churches identified themselves with this new attempt to reach the unchurched.

While religious leaders hesitated, other hands stretched out in friendship. The British royal family do not extend invitations lightly. To be received by royalty constitutes an accolade of national acceptance.

On the morning of May 17 Billy and Ruth Graham spent forty-five minutes with the Queen Mother and Princess Margaret at Clarence House, and were touched to discover not only a detailed knowledge of the meetings in London and Scotland but of their family life. Much of the conversation revolved round spiritual matters. On May 19 the Duchess of Kent (Princess Marina) paid a private visit to the Wembley service. On the following Sunday Billy Graham preached before the Queen.

The invitation had reached him in Scotland, to be kept strictly confidential. Billy prepared a sermon on the text from Acts 27:25, "Sirs, be of good cheer, for I believe God, that it shall be even as it was told me," and had put his notes on extra large paper. When he filed into the Royal Chapel, Windsor Great Park, with the Dean of Windsor (the chaplaincy happened to be vacant) he saw that there was no pulpit—he must preach from memory to the Queen and the Duke of Edinburgh, the Queen Mother and Princess Margaret, and a small congregation of royal household and estate workers. "I preached in utter simplicity. . . . I had prayed so much that I knew that however simple and full of mistakes my sermon was, God would overrule it and use it."

At luncheon in Windsor Castle with the Queen and Duke, the only other guests were the Dean and Mrs. Hamilton, and two members of the household. When the Grahams returned to London, the Palace had released news of the visit, and they were besieged by pressmen. One reporter broke down the door of Billy's hotel room in an unsuccessful effort to make him disclose his conversation with the Queen. Some of the papers thereupon made up their own versions— for example, that Billy had patted the head of Prince Charles (whom he had not even seen).

During the summer of 1955 the Team was again in continental Europe: five days in Paris, the first crusade (as distinct from rallies), in which Billy Graham preached by interpretation, followed by another whirlwind tour of twelve cities in Switzerland, West Germany, Scandinavia and Holland. Again there were great crowds, with press coverage varying from sympathetic to ludicrous. Graham spoke also at three American military bases. The senior chaplain of the European command wrote, "Your trip . . . opened many doors which had been formerly closed for many years: policy doors, doors to offices of commanders and doors to the hearts of many thousands of our service personnel and their families."

Later that year came the three weeks' Toronto crusade, notable for the Team's first use of that magnificent hymn of God in creation and grace: "How Great Thou Art," a translation by an Englishman, Stuart Hine, of the Russian version of a Swedish poem, set to a Swedish folk melody. Cliff Barrows had been given a mimeographed copy in London in 1954. "Strange to say we did not choose to use it," he recalls. It had been sung in America since 1951, but was not well known when Cliff conducted it with Bev Shea and the Toronto crusade choir in 1955. Helped by Shea's RCA Victor recording and by regular use in crusades, "How Great Thou Art" became in time the most popular hymn in North America, and is now sung around the world. "I love that song," wrote Billy Graham during the New York crusade of 1957, at which Bev Shea sang it more than a hundred times in sixteen weeks. "It gives the glory to God and directs our thinking to Him."

While Graham was in Toronto a controversy was brewing in England about his scheduled return for a short, limited mission to Cambridge University in November 1955.

The previous December he had hesitated before accepting the Cambridge invitation because, instead of coming at the behest of a representative group of clerical and lay leaders, he would be missioner of the Cambridge Inter-Collegiate Christian Union (known by its initials, CICCU, pronounced *Kick-U*), an undergraduate body of long and honorable but controversial history, which had been growing vigorously in recent years. CICCU had traditionally rejected unity with other student religious bodies in order not to blunt its own evangelistic thrust, a policy which had been strikingly vindicated but meant that Graham would not have the wide support normal to his crusades. The majority of chaplains and members of the theological faculty would be at best neutral, at worst highly critical.

In the summer of 1955 the projected Cambridge mission became a matter of national controversy through a correspondence in *The Times* initiated by headmaster of Durham School, Canon H. K. Luce, which began: "The recent increase of fundamentalism among university students cannot but cause concern to those whose work lies in religious education," and concluded: "Is it not time that our religious leaders made it plain that while they respect, or even admire, Dr. Graham's sincerity and personal power, they cannot regard fundamentalism as likely to issue in anything but disillusionment and disaster for educated men and women in this twentieth century world?"

The Times Literary Supplement, reviewing a book by Canon Luce, once commented that if his view of Christ and the New Testament was correct, "what was the point of the crucifixion?" Luce's letter, however, brought weighty names into correspondence. It was plain that many who attacked Graham's "fundamentalism" used the term in a sense which he repudiated, for he did not believe that the Word of God came by the suppression of the Scriptural writers' personalities; Graham's belief on inspiration was better expressed by a sentence in the Second Epistle of Peter: "Holy men of God spake as they were moved by the Holy Ghost."

The fundamentalist correspondence, and the discussions and debates which it evoked wherever clergy gathered, crystallized round a fear that Graham and those like him stifled thought; that "decision for Christ" was a matter of emotion and will divorced from intellect; that the convert would slam the door of his mind and henceforth live a narrow life of faith and zeal which precluded intellectual growth.

Those who fostered this fear were tragically prisoners of history.

In the nineteen-twenties, reacting to the extremes of modernism, many evangelicals, especially at universities, had indeed refused to think. The period was long over, but the taste of it remained. The kind of anti-intellectual, hidebound "fundamentalist," from whom the educated youth of England must be protected, had virtually disappeared; it was his ghost that haunted episcopal palaces and masters' lodges.

As the Cambridge dates drew closer, Billy Graham nearly cabled cancellation. He could look back to many student occasions: memorable meetings at the invitation of the president of Princeton Seminary in 1953; the Royal Albert Hall filled by attentive London University men and women; Edinburgh students, a notoriously difficult audience, hearing him in complete absorption. Before students "I usually have far more liberty and power of presentation than at most other audiences." Cambridge, however, loomed as a den of intellectual and theological lions. He was far better read, far more intelligent than many writers to *The Times* assumed, but not theologically trained. And he knew what was at stake. "I have never undertaken a mission in my life for which I felt more inadequate and unqualified and in need of prayer," he wrote on September 30. "I think it will possibly be one of the most crucial weeks of my entire ministry. The eyes of all British religious life are now focused there, and what happens there may well decide which way the tide will turn in Britain."

When he reached New York to sail to England he was tired and nervous. Then he learned that his old friend Stephen Olford was around, shortly returning to England. Billy telephoned at midnight and persuaded Olford to sail next day as his guest in a suite which had been given him by the steamship company: "I want you to be chaplain to my soul for the whole of this trip because I'm scared stiff of this Cambridge mission. I want to spend time in prayer with you."

Olford recalls those days on board ship as "next to Pontypridd the holiest time we ever had together."

The Cambridge mission had been thoroughly prepared. To support Graham CICCU had enrolled a team of clerical and lay assistant missioners headed by John Stott, London rector and later an honorary chaplain to the Queen. Stott had won a double first at Cambridge (in modern languages and theology) and was an experienced university missioner. No one ever doubted that Stott appealed to the mind. Graham knew him well, admired him and at Cambridge sought to emulate him.

In September the Bishop of Barking had written: "I can well understand your feelings of apprehension about Cambridge, but Billy do *not* worry. God has opened up the way so wonderfully and has called you to it, and so all will be well. If I may be bold enough to give one suggestion, I would say, 'Keep to the simplicity of your message.' Do not regard these men as 'intellectuals.' Appeal to their *conscience.* They are sinners, needing a Savior. *Conviction of sin,* not intellectual persuasion, is the need. So many preachers fail at this point when they speak to university men. So, Billy, keep to the wonderful, clear, simple message God has qualified you to preach and which He honored wonderfully in London and Glasgow."

But Billy, as he prepared, tried to turn himself into a John Stott, and when the two men were together the process continued. "I was really feeling boxed in and inadequate," comments Billy. "I felt that John ought to be the preacher, and I should have been his assistant. John is one of my dearest friends, but he can also be a critic. And I felt in the first two or three nights I was preaching to please John rather than the Holy Spirit."

To Stott himself it did not seem that Billy Graham at Cambridge pandered to the intellect of his hearers. Dons who, on those first three nights in the ancient University Church, detected Billy's unease presumed it arose from his being confined to a pulpit and a Geneva gown, without Barrows or Shea or a thousand-voice choir. When they mentally appraised his sermons as theological exercises the marks awarded were low. Though undergraduates listened hungrily, Billy knew that he was not getting through to their hearts.

Billy Graham is the most uncontrived of men. He must be himself and no other. He had been a little contrived at Glasgow when he began, but the warmth of welcome from the Moderator and the Scottish theological leaders and from humble folk had swiftly and painlessly melted his self-consciousness. In Cambridge he had to win a battle with himself. Following the third sermon, the day after his thirty-seventh birthday, he wrestled once more with this desire to make an appeal to the intellect. This time he threw aside the prepared sermons and on the Wednesday night preached once again as if before the most ordinary audience in the world. At last he broke through.

In its impact on the University and in numbers who sought counseling and affirmed decision to trust in the Living Christ, Graham's week in Cambridge was undoubtedly the greatest since D. L. Moody's historic mission of 1882. Unlike Moody's it did not affect noticeably the tone or direction of Cambridge life. But Graham on his side has never forgotten the lesson learned at Cambridge. Since 1955 he has preached at Harvard, Yale and many other American universities. And has never repeated his mistake.

Despite the effect on many students, Cambridge in fact strengthened the opposition. It did indeed decide which way the tide in England would turn—outward. "If I had gone to Cambridge and just been myself in those early days. . . ." This is one of the "ifs" of history.

An element of classic tragedy is weaved into the Billy Graham story. God had sent a man and shown how He could use him with and for the Church. The Church drew back.

The crusades had influenced England enormously. Any observer who supposes that this influence speedily evaporated forgets that Graham has deliberately refused to found a network of disciples, such as that forced by circumstances upon John Wesley, which constituted tangible evidence of the Methodist Revival. Nor was London or Glasgow dramatically changed. Graham once claimed that crusades transformed cities—London's amazing shift of mood in 1954 must have seemed proof—but he later withdrew the claim. "I think," he wrote in 1959, "the great result of these crusades is not in the changing of a city's life but in the individuals whose lives are permanently changed, the many churches which are revived, and the ministers who receive a new vision."

All three results were abundantly demonstrated in England of the later fifties. The sharp rise in the number of ministerial candidates and of recruits to missionary societies owed much to the crusades. Evangelism became an important part of many parishes and church programs. Christian Unions sprang up in business houses and elsewhere, such as the House of Commons Christian Fellowship which began in 1957 on the initiative of a Harringay convert.

The list of incidental results could be lengthened. More important was the new spirit. As one London clergyman put it in the sixties, "The whole Church moved up. Before 1954 the Church was holding onto its seat. After the Harringay crusade the Church realized it had a mission. We had the will to win."

In the prevailing religious indifference of the early fifties, which the crusades had done much to shatter, any advance seemed notable; and it did not become evident until the end of the decade how much England lost through the hesitation of those in high places who failed to maintain the momentum generated by the events of 1954–55, but drew back, belittling or doubting the validity of what had happened.

In doing so they provided an excuse for clergy to whom the crusades had presented a dilemma: if Billy Graham was right, much of their preaching and activity needed redirecting. They must turn round in their tracks, however painful the process. And many did so. Others resisted and delayed, but might have taken the humbling step in time, if their leaders had encouraged them. But when these leaders began to belittle or ignore the effect and value of the evangelism demonstrated in the crusades, such lower clergy could justify themselves.

"Britain was greatly blessed through the Graham Crusades in 1954 and 1955," Bishop Hugh Gough summed up in 1959. "But, to be honest, I think we missed what God intended for us. Many in the Church doubted and even opposed, and as a result I fear the words must be spoken of this country, 'Thou knewest not the time of thy visitation.' "

IV

The Wide World
1956-1959

---

22 · Eastward to India

In Billy Graham's room at the Statler Hotel in New York on Sunday January 15, 1956, the bags were already being carried out for the plane to Bombay. John Bolten, who was to travel with Billy, arrived from Boston. He brought a message of encouragement from Harold Ockenga, centered on Joshua 1:5: "As I was with Moses, so will I be with thee."

"Billy was quiet for a moment," recalls John Bolten. "I could see his eyes were moist, and he looked out of the window over Manhattan. And then suddenly he got up from his chair, and said, 'As He was with me in Scotland and in England and in Germany and in France and in America, so will He be with us in India.' We shook hands. Nobody said a word. There was a feeling as if the Presence of the Lord had come over us and given Billy this promise, as He had truly given it to Joshua at that crucial time."

An invitation from the Evangelical Fellowship of India had been endorsed by almost every church and mission except Roman Catholic, the first time in India's history that such multiplicity of Christian endeavor had united behind one man. Having accepted India in preference to elsewhere (invitations were coming from all over the world at an astounding rate) Billy Graham characteristically read all he could lay hands on about the country, its peoples and religions. The intinerary had been arranged by two Englishmen. The Team was small: Bev Shea did not go, and Cliff Barrows joined only for the later meetings.

Graham's arrival at Bombay coincided with the language riots. (He promptly rushed off to the danger areas.) At police insistence the great stadium rally was canceled, though Billy spoke to a packed indoor meeting of ministers. The outstanding memory was of the press conference. Graham had been warned that because of the riots a handful of reporters would come, but forty attended, almost as many as for Bulganin and Khrushchev a few weeks earlier. He expected questions on communism, the American race problem, or on Goa, especially as he was known to have been called to Secretary of State Dulles shortly before departure. After Graham had spoken of his purpose in India the first question was, "How does a man commit his life to Christ?" A British missionary commented: "I could hardly believe it. Questions on such themes continued for nearly an hour, until the chairman had reluctantly to bring the conference to a close." As the reporters shook hands they thanked Graham for his frankness. "So many of you Christians hedge. You don't give us exactly what you believe."

Spiritual hunger in Bombay was a foretaste of events all around India. Preparations had been made on a scale never before known. ("He made us live in peace for three days!" was the cryptic comment of the Church of South India Bishop of Madras.) Meetings were of a size unprecedented for a Christian preacher, and public interest was almost as great among Hindus as within the Christian minority. "We watched Billy Graham when he was preaching and when he was just talking to people," said one of them. "He was always smiling. He was so happy. The thing he has fills him with such joy that we want whatever it is he has, and he says Christ can give it to us." Another said: "Our religion is a religion of myths and traditions. This man is telling us of a historic Christ. He deals with absolute certainties, and we are convinced that what he tells us is true, and we want to have our lives anchored to something that is sure."

Graham had prepared a simple sermon on John 3:16: "God so loved the world, that he gave his only begotten Son, that whosoever believeth in him should not perish, but have everlasting life." At each place he preached basically the same address, couched in short sentences for easy interpretation. (At Madras every sentence was translated twice, into Telegu and Tamil.) "When I gave the invitation," he wrote to Ruth from Madras, "all you could hear was just the tramp, tramp, tramp of bare feet and sandled feet as they were coming forward quietly and reverently. . . . I have never seen such sincerity and devoutness on the faces of people. This was God. Yes, the same God that was with us at Wembley and Harringay and Kelvin Hall has been with us here in India." To Billy Graham it brought renewed conviction "that human nature is the same the world over, and that when the gospel of Christ is preached in simplicity and power, there is a response in the human soul." [1]

The spell of India captivated Billy from his moment of landing. He warmed to the indefinable sense of exhilaration in the India of the cold weather season. He loved the sights and sounds of the East, the jostling of ancient and modern, the gracefulness of the people, the teaming life of the cities and the placid timelessness of the villages. Its poverty tore at him and he had to be rescued from scattering rupees, refusing to remember warnings about professional beggars or that giving a rupee is like handing an American tramp a twenty dollar bill.

In the last days of January he reached the state of Kerala, the heart of South India's ancient indigenous Christianity. There in the city of Kottayam, jammed with visitors for the meetings, he spoke in the cathedral to a congregation of clergy that included the Jacobite Catholicos of the East in his red robes, bearded Mar Thoma bishops in purple or white, and the famous Bishop Jacob, leader in the formation of the Church of South India and a vice-president of the World Council of Churches.

Billy had been awakened early by the blaring of amplifiers in the specially enlarged college athletic field below the bishop's house. He peeped out and saw a great prayer meeting in progress under arc lights. He preached that night to a concourse which could not be counted, but was believed locally to be far in excess of 75,000. The white of their clothes reflected the powerful lights. The quiet reverence and intentness, even the silence of food vendors and bookstall keepers during the service, brought home to Billy the strength of

[1] One of the many Hindus converted at the Madras crusade was a young man called Jacob Paul. Under severe pressure from his father and village he twice renounced Christ, and twice repented immediately of this forced apostasy. He had to leave home. He is now an evangelist among Hindus. He told his story to Robert Ferm in 1959 (see *World Wide Witness*, published by B.G.E.A., pp. 52–58).

Graham's Tamil interpreter, Victor Monogoram, says that as the sermon progressed he became so involved in evangelizing, as distinct from merely translating, that his own ministry received new power, and thereafter the audience at his evangelistic meetings greatly increased.

Christianity in South India. He saw for a certainty that the key to the evangelization of India lay among Indians themselves. Bishop Jacob had already told him that South Indians were going as missionaries to North India. Billy Graham resolved to do his utmost to aid Asians to preach Christ to Asians—a resolve deepened during a short service of Holy Communion conducted by the bishop in his private chapel on the Sunday morning.

When Graham at length reached New Delhi he found that the interpreter into Hindustani was an outstanding intellectual, the head of the Henry Martyn School of Islamics, Dr. Akbar Abdul-Haqq, whose father had been a convert from Islam. Akbar Haqq, a Methodist who had received part of his education in America, had nearly refused to interpret, partly because he had never done such work, but mostly because "I was not interested in this sort of outreach at all, even though I was curious to find out how God was using Billy Graham, and how this method of evangelism was being blessed of God." During the first of the Delhi meetings Billy sensed that his interpreter was "God's chosen vessel for this type of evangelism in the Orient."

When Haqq came to the hotel room next night to become familiar with the points of the sermon, Billy startled him by saying, "Oh, let's forget about it. Let's talk about your coming to America to be with me." Billy told Haqq: "I'm not the man to be used for spiritual awakening here. It has to be an Asian. I think you are the man."

Haqq visited the Louisville crusade later in 1956 as Graham's guest, "and God spoke to me in regard to my deeper commitment to His cause." At the end of the year he held a mission in Graham style at Kanpur in North India, the first of many. The present Metropolitan, Lakdasa de Mel (then Bishop of Kurunagala) called Haqq's mission in Ceylon in 1959 "a splendid job, especially among intellectuals and university students. He got a lot of half-baked Christians warmed up! Because he is one of us he can do what Billy Graham never could have done. He can do such a great job in Asia."

Not in Asia only can he do this job. Akbar Haqq believes that missionary work has been too much a one-way traffic. "The whole world is a missionary field, and we Christians have to band together to confront the East and the West with God."

Billy Graham and his Team spent less than four weeks in India, yet their visit stirred and heartened the churches as few other incidents in living memory.

His constant underlining that Christ had been born in Asia and did not belong to Europe or America but to all men encouraged national Christians to discard the defeatism engendered by taunts that they were mere relics of the British imperial rule. The respect and interest of government and press helped reassure missionaries who were recovering from a recent scare of expulsion. Graham's focus on a Christlike life challenged the mass of nominal Christians whose failure to live according to their beliefs is a particular handicap often referred to by the Indian churches. Some fifteen thousand people, including many non-Christians, had registered decisions. Graham on leaving emphasized, "The 5 per cent effort to win men to a personal committal to Christ is over; the 95 per cent effort to bring them to maturity in the fellowship of the churches is about to begin."

His legacy to India was a trifle marred late in 1956, months after Graham's departure, by a violent attack in the Indian press on the book written by the American newsman George Burnham. Burnham had been sent by his newspaper, *The Chattanooga Free Press,* to cover the tour, and his articles were carried by 600 American papers. He traveled with the Team on condition that he have complete editorial freedom. The late George Burnham was an able, colorful reporter and a Christian who had once been "a drunken newspaper bum." Without previous experience of India, he wrote for an American public for whom he measured all things Indian by a strictly transatlantic gauge, rather as Gulliver looked on the people of Lilliput. Some of his remarks on customs and religion caused offense in India. Moreover Graham allowed him to quote from diary-letters sent home to Montreat, without realizing that one or two spontaneous comments written for Ruth without thought of publication could be misinterpreted. Worse, Billy had contributed an introduction to Burnham's book without reading it, an error that caused him to be attacked in India as having insincerely lauded the land in his speeches while smearing it in his heart. His disclaimer, in a letter to the Madras *Sunday Standard,* was a model of firmness, regret, and charity in face of that paper's unfair and bitterly worded comments. To the Englishman who had organized the tour he wrote, "I have learned a lesson and it will never happen again."

The Prime Minister, Nehru, who had given Graham an interview, did not join in the criticism, for he knew Billy Graham to be a warm friend of India who, immediately on his return, had made strong representations on India's behalf to President Eisenhower.

Indeed, Graham has always been a friend of India. The influence of the tour continued after he and his Team had left. "The message," wrote the chairman of the Evangelical Fellowship of India, "has spread in ever widening circles through the tape-recordings, and also through the heart recordings voiced in towns, villages, hospitals and homes. It is heartening to hear of those who have returned to their homes and, by personal testimony, won souls." Before long, teams of nationals began traveling across the land to evangelize non-Christians and to bring renewal among Christians. "One of the most remarkable impacts of his visit," Akbar Haqq had said, "was this consciousness of the need for revival and evangelism in India which came to the Indian church as a whole."

Billy Graham capped his tour of India by one-day meetings in Manila, Hong Kong, Formosa, Japan, Korea and Hawaii during February 1956. When it was over President Eisenhower said at a press conference that he saw Billy Graham as "a man who clearly understands that any advance in the world has got to be accompanied by a clear realization that man is, after all, a spiritual being. He carries his religion to the far corners of the earth, trying to promote mediation instead of conflict, tolerance instead of prejudice."

For Billy Graham himself the tour had further broadened his horizon. The wide world seemed open to the message, and in his heart was peace.

---

23 · A New Home and a New Magazine

Billy Graham returned from India to a new home up the mountain.

The house on Assembly Drive had long been too small and too public. Tourists not only peered through the hedge—the Haymakers counted thirty one August Sunday—they forced themselves into the yard, even into the house, and gave the children money to pose for photographs. In 1955 friends at Montreat and elsewhere surprised the Grahams by raising a fund for the building of a house on the land which Billy had bought at $12 an acre years before. Ruth's romantic sense of history came into full play: she scoured the mountains buying old timber from disused cabins and brick from an ancient schoolhouse to build a place which fitted exactly into its background. Soon it looked a hundred years old, even to the split rail fences. Inside she evoked an informal country house atmosphere which spans the centuries. "I want it to be a home that everyone can feel at home in, whether mountain folk or the wealthy."

Meeting with Negro clergymen, Montgomery, Alabama, 1965.

Closing meeting at Hawaii Crusade in Honolulu Stadium, February 1965.

Ruth Graham is met by her husband at Los Angeles International Airport as she arrives for the closing meetings of the Southern California Crusade in September 1963.

Los Angeles Memorial Coliseum, November 23, 1963. Climax of the Southern California Crusade. Attendance 134,254.

Press conference, Copenhagen, May 1965.

Intent listeners at the Copenhagen Crusade, Denmark, May 1965.

The Billy Graham Pavilion at the New York World's Fair, 1964–1965. RIGHT: *Filming* Man in the Fifth Dimension *on location in San Francisco, 1963, with producer Dick Ross.*

LEFT TO RIGHT: *actor Randolph Scott, former Vice President Richard M. Nixon, Billy Graham, and Freeman Gosden of Amos 'n Andy fame.*

Latest picture of the Team, taken in Atlanta, December 1964.

KNEELING FROM LEFT: *Forrest Layman, Tedd Smith, Howard Jones, Ray Gustafson, Dan Piatt, Lane Adams, Joe Blinco, Norman Pell.*

SEATED: *Fernando Vangioni, T. W. Wilson, Walter Smyth, Grady Wilson, Billy Graham, V. Raymond Edman, A. W. Goodwin Hudson, Cliff Barrows, George M. Wilson.*

STANDING, FRONT ROW: *George Clark, Sherwood Wirt, Charles Ward, Jacob Stam, Bill Brown, Harry Williams, Ralph Bell, Don Hustad, Lee Fisher, Robert Ferm, John Wesley White, Victor Nelson, Robert Root.*

REAR ROW: *Maurice Rowlandson, Jerry Schochenmaier, John Corts, David Barr, Stanley Mooneyham, Wesley Boyd, Irv Chambers, Charles Riggs, John Lenning, Paul Cedar, George Bev Shea, John Dillon, Hank Beukema.*

Forty-seven years old. "He has unbounded opportunities. He has many temptations. Billy Graham is resolved to continue crusades for as long as he has the strength—a servant of God, the Church and his fellow men."

Here when a crusade ends (and Billy always leaves a city the night after the last meeting) he can return to "recharge his batteries," reveling in the woodland sights and sounds, the superb view and the North Carolina mountain air. Rest and quiet for Billy are the prime factors of the house, Ruth says. The study, designed by a friend in Greensboro, prefabricated by his firm and shipped to Montreat, is so placed that no one need shush the children and their friends when Daddy is working. And all the time he can squeeze from the relentless pressure of preparation and correspondence, of telephone calls for discussion, reports and decisions, and interviews with those who seek his advice or aid, Billy spends with the children, except for the golf which keeps him fit. The two Grahams (with the aid of Beatrice Long, their patient, unruffled daily maid, and John Rickman, the caretaker, who works with his heart as well as his hands), had set themselves to bring up a family which should be normal and happy, a family capable of nourishing each child's spiritual perceptions and loyalties. Ruth once described their home as a "Noah's Ark of happy confusion"—children, dogs, a cat called Moldy, and at one stage three Hampshire sheep. "They can keep down the grass," said Billy, "and we've got to have sheep and goats and things like that so the kids will learn the facts of life." "Bill," replied Ruth with a smile, "why don't I just tell them and save us all that trouble?"

It was when Billy was feeding this small flock with apples that an ungrateful ram butted him down the steep rocky hillside; he sustained a painful hairline fracture in his left tibia, torn ligaments of the left knee, cuts, bruises, and much hilarious kidding from all over the world.[1]

"Although we don't have a normal family life," Ruth can remark, "we have a very happy one." For her the work of bringing up the children and making a true home for Billy between crusades is a mission by divine appointment. Her knowledge of Scripture, her love of literature (with a gift for writing poetry), and her fund of common sense is reflected in Billy's preaching: "Some of my best thoughts come from her."

Her neighbors say, "She's been with the Queen, she's been with the President, but she's the most unaffected woman. Ruth is just Ruth."

---

[1] Billy's love of animals is a part of his character. Ruth has often seen him deep in spiritual conversation with a visitor while kittens play around his legs. When he was ill she sometimes found one of their big dogs lying on the bed beside him. The St. Bernard, Heidi, which they have had since 1960, watches TV with him, her head moving as she follows the action on the screen.

A small boy in St. Louis won a newspaper competition on "Whom I want to be like," with an entry choosing Billy Graham. Billy wrote to the boy, Dan Fotsch, "I am greatly honored and humbled. . . . I, too, chose a Man a few years ago to be like. I have failed miserably on many occasions, but with all my heart I am praying that I will continue to grow and be like Jesus."

Jesus the Man that Billy Graham knows was well described in a letter he wrote to a Dallas crusade convert, a former television actor and night club owner, who was planning to produce a film on the life of Christ: "Please get a man with great strength in his face. I have seen so many pictures of Jesus as a weakling that I am sick of it. He was no sissie and He was no weakling." Graham was sure Christ must have been the most perfectly developed man physically in the history of the world. "No sin and mar had come near His body. He must have been straight, strong, big, handsome, tender, gracious, courteous," and His eyes could pierce the hypocrisy of a Pharisee yet had such tenderness that He could break a sinful woman's heart.

If those closely acquainted with Billy Graham by 1956 were asked in what ways he approached his ideal of the Christ-life, they might have used the words of Dr. James S. Stewart: "Dr. Graham exemplifies wonderfully in his person the basic New Testament paradox, namely, the union of the most profound humility and the most blazing conviction." Like his Master, Graham spoke boldly, with authority. And as Christ sought His Father's glory, so Graham genuinely wanted Christ to have the praise. "You have no idea how sick I get of the name 'Billy Graham,' " he wrote to Wendell Phillips, "and how wonderful and thrilling the name 'Christ' sounds to my ears." Louis Zamperini remembers an informal gathering at the Grahams which included prominent ministers attending local conferences. The friend who opened the proceedings built up Billy so high that all eyes were glued on this second Elijah. Then Billy began "and completely turned everybody's eyes off himself without being too obvious about it, and when he got through everybody was Christ-conscious"—so much that during the discussion nobody noticed when Billy Graham left the room.

Graham has soaked himself in the spirit of I Corinthians 13, St. Paul's chapter on Christian love. "There's no doubt Billy believes that love is the great mark of the Christian," John Stott has said. This shows itself not only in his friendliness, his total absorption in whomever he is with, however brief the encounter or unimportant the person, but in his seeking the best in every man. A strong sense of loyalty can blind him to faults in those working with him. "He has a tendency to just ignore that which doesn't fit into the pattern of the best," one of his associates has said. "When he loves you it's almost as though you can do no wrong." A strong pastoral care for his staff had led now and again to the retention of services which others urged should be dismissed. "I cannot help remembering," he said of one case, "that Jesus kept Judas in the apostolic band although He knew he was a traitor."

Billy Graham took a long time to learn to say No, because every request that reached him pulled at his heartstrings or seemed deserving. His tendency to superlatives also springs at least in part from love. "I have heard him in many places say, 'This is a wonderful city; I would like to live here,'" comments George Wilson. "He really means this. He falls in love with people and so enjoys people that he would be at home in almost any city." Superlatives also arise because, as Lorne Sanny remarks, "Billy is totally absorbed in whatever he is doing. He has great vision for tomorrow but he doesn't live for tomorrow. He lives for today. I was with him in twenty-four crusades, and at every crusade there was some reason why this one was the greatest crusade, the most strategic, the one that could start the world-wide revival. He believed it. And he'd work towards that crusade and preach in it and give himself to it as if he was never going to have another, was going to die afterwards." This total involvement with the moment makes any setback a disaster, any gain a triumph— though his sense of balance in due time corrects the bias.

By 1956 Billy Graham no longer was merely an American preacher. What he said, or did, or was, could make for good or ill across the world. He had been nearly seven years in the forefront and was not yet forty. His continuing influence would depend on whether his personality, his mind and spirit, grew or desiccated under the unremitting heat of public life. "With all my heart I want to grow, learn and expand so that I can be of the greatest possible use to the whole Kingdom of God."

The Billy Graham Evangelistic Association was certainly growing and expanding.

By 1957 it had an office staff at Minneapolis of over one hundred and twenty-five and had reached the limit of rented space. Opportunity came to buy the Standard Oil Company's building on the same street at such favorable terms that the Association obtained twice their previous space at less annual cost. Office staff and Team alike gave generously to finance the building, which George Wilson fitted with the latest mechanical office equipment. As he says, "The Lord's business deserves the benefit of the finest methods men can devise."

There were critics who murmured "commercialism," or like Judas thought the money should have been given to the poor. The commercialism charge was made even by those who strongly approved of proper equipment for overseas missionary hospitals or schools, but failed to see that the B.G.E.A. applied the same principle—using the best technical aids to bring men within sound and sight of the Gospel. The issue resolved itself into whether the thousands upon thousands of letters addressed to Billy Graham by converts and radio listeners should be answered speedily, the senders' spiritual problems counseled, their gifts acknowledged. Without the efficiency of the Minneapolis staff chaos would have throttled the Graham ministry, which was expanding so rapidly in the mid-nineteen-fifties that income only just kept ahead of expenditure, both rising steadily.

Graham was master in his own house though he seldom went to Minneapolis. Adept at delegation (when George Wilson told him they needed the new building Billy replied, "Well, man, if you need a building, go ahead and buy it; don't bother me with details"), Graham kept his finger on the pulse through daily reports from Wilson. "I have worked with a number of ministers and a number of businessmen," Wilson comments, "and I think Mr. Graham has more business sense than the average businessman and certainly far more than any preacher I have ever met. He can calculate a budget very carefully. He remembers figures very well." And Graham insisted on the highest business standards, on "truthfulness, honesty and a complete above-board handling of finances."

Graham's mind was forever ranging for fresh ways of proclaiming or consolidating the Gospel. In one sense he is a man of impulses, moving to the moment. Grady Wilson jokes that "Billy's mind must be very clean; he's always changing it," and Paul Maddox used to say his job was to keep up with the changes. For Billy Graham's small personal staff, flexibility is vital. Ruth admits that his quickness of decision "sometimes drives people crazy who are not adjusted to it. Some might call it vacillating. That's not it, he's flexible. I think that is why God uses him. If a man is stiff and set in his ways it would be more difficult for God to use him. But he's not changeable, he's flexible."

In another sense Billy does not move until he is sure of his ground.

He has an idea, a vision, and is prepared for the wait and the work which sifts the idea and transmutes the vision into reality.

In no way was this more evident than in the founding of *Christianity Today*.

As early as 1953 Graham saw the need for a "strong, hard-hitting, intellectual magazine" which should propound the evangelical view as strongly and intelligently as, for two generations, *The Christian Century* has put the liberal. During his West Coast tour in January 1954 he had discussed it with Wilbur M. Smith, the encyclopedic Bible teacher and writer of Pasadena, who, he found, had long wanted such a magazine, one to be read widely by ministers. In October 1954 James de Forest Murch, then editor of *United Evangelical Action*, spontaneously urged Graham in the same direction: "You are in a position to bring such a journal into being."

These seeds of thought germinated at Christmas 1954 when Billy and his father-in-law, Dr. Nelson Bell, discovered an identity of vision of such force that Billy immediately wrote to a few of his friends who could provide the intellectual or material wherewithal to create *Christianity Today*, as Billy already had christened it. He gave a larger list of names to Nelson Bell, who wrote all over the world for support and was soon eating and sleeping the magazine, finally surrendering his surgical practice in order to be executive editor. In September 1955 a board of trustees was formed in New York. Many of Graham's friends urged him to make the new magazine a house organ of the Billy Graham Evangelistic Association. He nearly did so, but finally decided against it.

Christianity Today, therefore, has been independent, editorially and in every way, from the start, but it owed much to Graham's judgment in its early days. Its aim, as he expressed it before publication began, would be to articulate evangelical doctrine and conviction "with scholarly competence, clarity and vigor," and to "apply the Biblical revelation vigorously to the contemporary social crisis, by presenting the implications of the Gospel message in every area of life." A worldwide panel of contributing editors and correspondents would make it a universal rather than an American magazine, an ambition that was slow to be realized. In policy it should be "pro-church and church-integrated, tied to no one denomination or interchurch council, and would aim to present the truth forcefully but in love."

Professor Carl F. H. Henry of Fuller Theological Seminary, a former secular editor and the author of numerous theological books, was appointed editor. Publication began fortnightly from Washington, D.C., in October 1956.

Gifts great and small from more than a thousand donors, including the B.G.E.A., enabled the first issues of the magazine to go free to every Protestant minister in North America and Great Britain for a year, and to a large number thereafter. Jerry Beavan had pointed out from the first that British clergy would not be attracted except by a British-based edition, which was not feasible; there is little doubt that in 1956–57 the free issues of a magazine with a slant that was then predominantly American tended to swell British clerical wastepaper baskets.

Christianity Today is disliked by extreme fundamentalists, despised by extreme liberals and mistrusted by many moderate liberals. But tangible evidence of its growing impact on Christian thinking is the rapid rise of its paid circulation, at first a minute proportion of the 160,000 copies distributed; by 1962 it had passed *The Christian Century's* 37,500. In the next three years the magazine leaped ahead; paid circulation is now about 145,000 out of a total distribution of 260,000. It has stimulated new writers and thinkers, provided a forum for the sifting of ideas, helped lift evangelicals out of their anti-intellectual mire, and has directed or clarified the theological views of many ministers and laymen who were trudging aimlessly in a welter of secondhand liberalism.

In its desire to be thoroughly theological *Christianity Today* became at one time almost obtuse, and Donald Grey Barnhouse suggested it had read the verse, "Feed my sheep" as, "Feed my giraffes." But it settled down to become a strong, intelligent medium of news and opinion which in the words of *Time* magazine "tries to make traditional Protestant theology clear and interesting—and nearly always succeeds."

24 · New York, 1957

On leaving London in 1954 Billy Graham had said, "I have never had the faith to tackle New York, Chicago or Philadelphia, but if God can accomplish this in London, He can accomplish it in other cities." From the summer of 1955, when a firm, broad-based invitation reached him in Paris, Billy's thoughts were increasingly dominated by New York. The crusade would begin on May 15, 1957, in Madison Square Garden.

New York with its polyglot population, its fierce competitive spirit, its hustle and sophistication and absorption in things material—to come to the city of Wall Street, of Broadway, Madison Avenue and Harlem and all that those names connoted might be to court disaster. Protestants were in a minority to Roman Catholics and Jews, church-going in Manhattan was low, and it was the opinion of Jesse Bader, from his experience of twenty-three years as executive secretary of the Department of Evangelism of the National Council of Churches, that "to do evangelistic work in New York is like digging in flint."

The invitation came from the Protestant Council of the City of New York, representing 1,700 churches of 31 denominations, and from a number of independent bodies. As in Glasgow, all the important churches would cooperate, at least in name.

This invitation brought upon Graham's head some of the most violent opposition he had ever experienced. He was not disturbed by the attacks of extreme liberals. *The Christian Century,* which at that time was still in full tilt against Graham, derided the forthcoming crusade as a "trumped-up revival," which would "spin along to its own kind of triumph because canny, experienced engineers of decision have laid the tracks, contracted for the passengers, and will now direct the traffic which arrives on schedule. . . . The Graham procedure . . . does its mechanical best to 'succeed' whether or not the Holy Spirit is in attendance. As this strange new junction of Madison Avenue and Bible Belt, the Holy Spirit is not overworked; He is overlooked."

Far more painful were the strident calumnies hurled at Graham by the extreme fundamentalists led by Carl McIntire, John R. Rice and old Dr. Bob Jones. They attacked him for being sponsored by "modernists," although the crusade was not being organized by the Protestant Council (which included many of liberal leanings) but by an executive committee of fifteen men who shared Graham's basic outlook and aims. And no one controlled the preaching except Graham, who intended "to pull no punches in presenting Christ and Him crucified." The extreme fundamentalists were not content to oppose Graham by setting forth their own viewpoint. They put out false rumors, such as that the Navigators had been voted out of the counseling room to please the liberals.

Dr. Bob Jones, Sr., was reported to have said that Graham was too inexperienced and immature for a New York campaign, and that his preaching was merely a matter of glamour and not under the power of the Holy Spirit because he pursued an unscriptural policy in co-operating with men who did not hold fundamentalist views. Yet, though Jones reportedly denied it, Graham was following the policy of D. L. Moody and Billy Sunday. And the truth is that Dr. Bob Jones, Sr., in his own campaigning days demanded in each city the cooperation of every Protestant minister—as Willis Haymaker, who had been on his staff, well remembers. In a Texas city where the ministerial association sponsored Dr. Jones, he had made no protest though its president was well known as a liberal; and in a New Jersey city Dr. Jones had been boycotted by the fundamentalists because he wanted such widely based support.

The extreme fundamentalists did not conduct their controversies against Graham in the spirit of charity. "Dr. —— continues his merciless attacks," Billy Graham wrote to his father-in-law in December 1956. "Some of the things he is saying and doing are almost unbelievable. Every inclination within the 'old man of me' wants to answer him, but the still, small voice says, 'Let the Lord take care of it.' " Luverne Gustavson, after mailing this letter, told her parents that it was the closest her boss had ever come to being ruffled "by all the criticism that gets hurled at him."

Graham believed God had used Bob Jones greatly in the past, and as in the Bible David would not harm King Saul because he was the Lord's anointed, so Billy Graham refused to attack or refute Bob Jones.

When the New York crusade began, Dr. Jones informed Nelson Bell (and distributed copies of the letter) that no Bob Jones students would be permitted to hold a prayer meeting to ask blessing on Billy Graham in New York, for that would be a repudiation of the purpose for which the university was founded. A young Billy Graham convert was expelled, ostensibly for minor infraction of rules but in reality, as he believed, for standing up for Graham.

While enduring attacks from the far left and the far right Billy Graham met a succession of problems that each seemed at the time gigantic, "far too big for me, that could destroy the crusade." In the summer of 1956 Dawson Trotman was drowned in a boating accident at Schroon Lake, New York. Graham was in Tulsa for a one-night meeting during the Oklahoma City crusade when Lorne Sanny brought the news about five in the afternoon. Billy was resting in bed. His immediate reaction was, "Lord, I want to rededicate my life."

Sanny would have been in charge of counseling preparation, but
henceforth must give most of his time as president of Navigators in
Trotman's place, so Charlie Riggs took over in New York, where
4,300 counselors registered for training. Then early in 1957 Jerry
Beavan, on whom the general organization depended, resigned for
personal reasons, though he would return later to do special assignments.[1]

Charlie Riggs became crusade director. "I did not think Charlie
could do it," Graham recalls, "except I had this peace—that Charlie
so depended on God and the Holy Spirit that I knew the Lord could
do it through Charlie."

Meanwhile in New York churches were becoming increasingly
wholehearted, largely through the work of Leighton Ford.

Leighton Ford, a Canadian ordained in the Presbyterian ministry,
was only twenty-five at the time of the New York crusade. He had
majored in philosophy at Wheaton and been president of the senior
class at Columbia Presbyterian Seminary. He was fast developing into
a powerful preacher whose intellectual grasp was balanced by ability
to convey his meaning to the simplest listener. He had known Billy
Graham since Youth for Christ days in Ontario, and at Wheaton fell
in love with Jean, Billy's younger sister. On their third date they had
gone to hear Billy at Cincinnati, and Billy took Jean aside: "You
hold on tight to him; don't let him go. I could walk around the world
a hundred times and I'd never find a fellow I'd rather have for my
brother-in-law!" Fortunately Jean was already in love with Leighton
and they were married at Charlotte in December 1953 by Billy, who
has never been allowed to forget a superb verbal stumble during the
ceremony, when he uttered the words: "Now that Leighton and Jean
have exchanged wings—oh, I mean rings."

Leighton Ford went to England for the Wembley crusade and
spent the summer of 1955 on follow-up work in Scotland, returning
to join the Billy Graham Team at Toronto as associate evangelist.
In New York he held the new post of director of ministerial relations.
He not only won the clergy's confidence to a marked degree but pio-
neered the policy that a crusade must initiate its work among the
local ministers months rather than weeks before the opening night.

It was Leighton Ford who, during the Team's devotional retreat at
Wainwright House at Rye, New York on Long Island Sound, as the
crusade drew near, gave a "searching, challenging, convicting mes-

[1] Among these assignments were the overall direction of the Australian and
New Zealand crusades, and the African tour. He left the Team finally in 1962

sage," through which, wrote Graham, "we were all broken by the Holy Spirit." They ended on their knees in penitence and tears. Next day the Scotsman Ralph Mitchell spoke. "It happened all over again. We felt as though the Lord had cleansed our hearts, filled us with the Holy Spirit and anointed us for the special task in New York City."

When Billy Graham reached New York (after another visit to President Eisenhower at the White House) for the start of the crusade on May 15, 1957, he felt physically fitter and spiritually better prepared than before any previous crusade, yet "more inadequate and helpless." Once again he was conscious of waves of prayer in New York and across the world, from great meetings and from humble individuals like the young farmer in Buckinghamshire, England, who wrote: "In case I am too tired to pray at night, I have made it a rule to pray for Dr. Graham whilst I am milking each day, and I always think of him the moment I sit on the milking stool." There had been ample predictions that Graham would fail in New York. "From human viewpoint and by human evaluation it may be a flop," Graham commented. "However, I am convinced in answer to the prayers of millions that in the sight of God and by heaven's evaluation it will be no failure. God will have His way, and in some unknown and remarkable way Christ will receive the glory and honor."

"We have not come to put on a show or an entertainment. We believe that there are many people here tonight that have hungry hearts —all your life you've been searching for peace and joy, happiness, forgiveness.

"I want to tell you, before you leave Madison Square Garden this night of May 15, you can find everything that you have been searching for, in Christ. He can bring that inward deepest peace to your soul. He can forgive every sin you've ever committed. And He can give you the assurance that you're ready to meet your God, if you will surrender your will and your heart to Him.

"I want you to listen tonight not only with your ears, but the Bible teaches that your heart also has ears. Listen with your soul tonight. Forget that there's anyone else here. Forget me as the speaker, listen only to the message that God would have you to retain from what is to be said tonight.

"Shall we pray: *Our Father and our God, in Christ's name we commit the next few moments to Thee, and we pray that the speaker*

---

and is now vice-president of the Rexall Drug Company. He remains close friends with Billy Graham, who often seeks his advice.

shall hide behind the Cross until the people shall see none, save Jesus.

"And we pray that many tonight will re-evaluate their relationship to God, others will consider, for the first time perhaps, their need of God, and that many shall respond and surrender themselves to Him as they did 2,000 years ago on the shores of Galilee: for we ask it in His name. Amen."

Billy Graham's prayer on that opening night was answered.

From the start the New York crusade, despite a quiet undercurrent of opposition, broke all records for attendance, for decisions, for impact on the city, and had such outward success that its critics, determined to assert a failure, were forced to argue that it was a flop in the sight of God and by heaven's evaluation. *The Christian Century* called its message a "violation of the wholeness of the Christian faith." They said that most of the crowd (about 18,000 nightly) were Christians anyway; and that the decisions were invalid because not "preceded or succeeded by action by the church,"—two charges which in effect canceled each other out. The great theologian, Reinhold Niebuhr, stated in *Life* magazine for July 1 that "this new evangelism promises a new life, not through painful religious experience but merely by signing a decision card," a charge that must have sounded odd to the increasing thousands who signed cards in token of costly decision, and completed the Bible courses or came to the regular studies for converts, and were finding their way through the adjustments inevitable in a life which had turned from self to Christ.

Dr. Niebuhr's further charge (without supporting evidence) that the bulk of those attending were not from New York City at all, was decisively disproved by a show of hands taken on subsequent nights which demonstrated that 80–85 per cent lived or worked in the city or the surrounding metropolitan area.

His third main criticism was that Graham's evangelism "neglected to explore the social dimensions of the Gospel." Though Niebuhr admitted that Graham "had sound personal views on racial segregation and other social issues of our time," he alleged that "he almost ignores them in his actual preaching." Niebuhr based this opinion of Graham on the newspaper accounts of the crusade and on occasional attendance. But the Associated Press religious writer, George W. Cornell, sitting at the press desk night after night, disagreed with this view. He wrote a private letter to Graham: "I have read various criticisms of you from those who say you do not stress the full social implications of Christ's demands (the horizontal aspects, as you put it), but I have concluded that the critics simply have not paused to listen to you, but have been so dazzled by your external successes that they don't see its roots."

Nevertheless, Niebuhr's criticism was taken to heart by Graham, who increasingly touched on a whole range of social issues, from the race question and juvenile delinquency to alcoholism and the housing problem. "Billy Graham's preaching," said Dan Potter, the director of the Protestant Council, "has more social content than that of the average New York minister. He says things that no minister in Manhattan dares say." "Men have been made aware of the sins of the heart and of society," wrote the president of Princeton Theological Seminary, Dr. John A. Mackay. "It is unfair, however, to demand that Billy Graham should have offered a blueprint for the solution of complicated social issues in our highly industrialized mass society."

But this was just what his critics did demand, for they rejected his belief that the root ill of human society is the unregenerate human heart.

The crusade was aided by the extensive coverage given throughout by the New York press. *The New York Times* printed the entire text of Graham's sermon on several occasions. The *Journal-American,* before the crusade, ran a very friendly series about Graham by the noted columnist, the late Dorothy Kilgallen, and made the first nights at the Garden front-page news. *The Herald Tribune* allowed Graham space on the front page to write on any subject whenever he wished during the four months of the crusade.

The press naturally featured Billy Graham, but as always the crusade was the operation of a Team, which included several associates brought in specially for New York. The principal Team members now had years of experience behind them. Cliff Barrows was far more than a song leader. He produced the weekly *Hour of Decision* broadcast; he produced the daily *Prayer Time* program on a local station; he arranged the tape-recording of all Graham's sermons. Rehearsing and conducting the choir each evening, guiding the service and bringing the whole audience into partnership made him well known. Yet it was probably behind the scenes, as unofficial link between all the different components of a crusade—Graham, Graham's personal assistants, Team associates, the office administration, the committee—that Cliff did his finest work.

Cliff frequently appeared on *Impact,* a brief epilogue conducted from a studio by one or other associate evangelist and televised over a local station, followed by telephone counseling—an imaginative and effective strategy.

Impact was only one of several new ventures for which the crusade was notable.

New York's high schools and universities were a focus of evangelism based on the crusade, with specialized preparation and follow-up; Akbar Haqq came over from India primarily for this. Another special approach was to men and women in show business, led by Lane Adams, a former fighter pilot and night-club singer, who had postponed ordination in the Presbyterian ministry for this work.

Eight years later, at a conference for ministers in Bellingham, Washington, preparatory to Leighton Ford's Vancouver crusade of 1965, Adams saw smiling at him a man he had not met since 1957— Bob Dayton, a Shakespearean actor now a minister. Adams went across and said to him: "There are a lot here who say, 'Do the converts last?' Instead of arguing we'll call on you for a testimony." Bob Dayton first gave a rendering of Hamlet's *To be or not to be,* and repeated it in a Texas accent, "and they were in convulsions of laughter. Then he gave a stirring testimony of how Christ had invaded his life in the New York crusade."

Bob Dayton had been a member of the Christian Actors' Fellowship founded during the crusade, with Jerome Hines of the Metropolitan Opera Company as president and about two hundred members.

Ethel Waters, the Negro blues singer and actress, had made a spontaneous retort on a television program to the question whether the crusade would fail: "God don't sponsor no flops!" Lane Adams offered her a seat in the reserved section. During her long stage and screen career Ethel Waters had never lost the consciousness of God that had come when she was converted at the age of twelve, and as she walked into Madison Square Garden that first night she "felt that my Lord was calling me back home." After the first week she joined the choir of fifteen hundred voices in order to secure a reserved seat every night, and sang at each service for eight weeks. "So many things I had pondered about for a lifetime, the Lord cleared up during these weeks." Cliff Barrows learned of her presence when she signed a choir petition for the extension of the crusade, and asked her if she would sing a solo. She sang the song that she had made famous on Broadway: "His Eye is on the Sparrow." "This time, however, it was to be very different. The glitter and heartache of the stage had disappeared. . . . There was just myself, standing before 18,000 people, saying, 'I love Jesus, too,' the only way I could say it—by singing 'His Eye is on the Sparrow.' "

On five nights in the final eight weeks Ethel Waters sang that song. When the crusade ended she had readjusted much in her life, for "I found that I could no longer act every role I was offered and continue to glorify my Lord." She played in the feature film based on the New York crusade, *The Heart is a Rebel,* and has visited crusades year by year, at her own expense, to sing in her inimitable style.

The most significant breakthrough of New York was entirely unpremeditated.

A few days after the crusade began Fred Dienert said to Billy Graham: "Wouldn't it be wonderful if we could take this crowd to the nation, if the people at home could see what's going on, and the people coming to Christ." Graham, recalling the great influence on Britain of the Kelvin Hall telecast on Good Friday 1955, agreed. Bennett and Dienert sounded the networks about televising the crusade coast-to-coast, but encountered skepticism, even politely veiled ridicule. Then the American Broadcasting Company offered time. To pay for the initial contract of four weekly telecasts Billy Graham received from a foundation the largest single gift ever made to the Association—$100,000.

The hour-long telecasts from Madison Square Garden on Saturday June 1 and each following Saturday (seventeen in all) were a revelation to America. The very fact that the pictures emanated from the country's best known arena made them doubly impressive. As a television ministry it was a thousand times more effective than the Graham Team's studio program of earlier years, for the crowd in the Garden created a strong sense of participation for the viewer, who was not eavesdropping an event, not watching a contrived half hour of song and talk.

A friend of Lane Adams, Tedd Seelye, well expressed the value of these telecasts to a country where churchgoing and religion were becoming increasingly popular: "When the average, moral, reputable American sees Dr. Graham in a studio telling him he needs to be 'born again' his first impulse will be to discredit him as a religious fanatic. But if the viewer sees thousands of respectable, normal people listening and consenting to all this he hears, and then sees hundreds voluntarily get up and walk to the front in response to a low-pressure request, he'll begin to consider the message and situation with some sincere, honest interest. It's much easier to say a single speaker is wrong than to discredit the conviction and decision of thousands."

After the first telecast over 25,000 letters were written to Billy Graham, to encourage or thank him or tell of decisions made for Christ while viewing. Each succeeding Saturday widened and deepened the influence of the television crusade. In Chicago, at Polk Brothers' display of TV sets at the Chicagoland Fair, so many people watched those sets that happened to be tuned into the crusade, and ignored the others, that the sales representatives went down the long line and turned all sets to the crusade. In Buffalo the Council of Churches reported the criticism of the New York crusade had been swept away and that church attendance had reached an unprecedented figure for the time of year.

The first television crusade proved a turning point in the Graham Team's ministry. More than one and a half million letters were sent to Billy Graham in three months. He had been a household name for some years, but only those who lived near a city which had held a crusade had become fully aware of his message, despite millions who listened to the *Hour of Decision*. Now his ministry came right into homes across the nation. By the end of this first television crusade no less than 30,000 Americans had voluntarily written in to state definite decisions made for Christ during or after the telecasts; and by the network's assessment of the normal proportion of letter-writers to viewers after any telecast, the total number of decisions were probably considerably more.

---

25 · *Yankee Stadium to Times Square*

Numbers in New York were greater than in any previous crusade. The final total of attendance was 2,357,400, the highest for any event in the history of Madison Square Garden.[1] The number of decisions, apart from those of telecast viewers, was 61,148.

A New York minister wrote afterward: "The real results of the crusade are not in statistical form or in ways that can be measured. You cannot tell what the crusade did for the morale of us ministers, the new confidence it gave us, the motivation it supplies for the preaching of the Bible and Christ crucified." While the crusade con-

[1] The directors of the Garden presented Billy Graham with a plaque to this effect.

tinued, however, the mounting statistical figure meant a mounting nightly heap of individual cards. Each decision card involved informing a minister promptly of a convert, and contacting him later to see whether pastoral responsibilities had been accepted. Each card meant follow-up literature for the convert and the grading and returning of his first Bible lessons—and further aid as required until he was integrated in the life of a church.

With the number of cards rising in their tens of thousands, and the follow-up department slipping into chaos, Charlie Riggs secured the services of Colonel Robert C. Root, a former B-29 pilot and squadron commander in the U.S.A.A.F., who resigned as senior design engineer with North American Aviation at Los Angeles in order to overhaul the administration of the mailing and filing operations.

He was soon known among the Team as "Flow Chart Root" because he drew up work-flow charts in the manner of a big administrative organization, until every member of the follow-up department knew exactly what to do and when. "Since our procedures," Root writes, "were based on original concepts, we had a great deal of trouble operating smoothly and efficiently, and a lot of the work was done the hard way."

The following year, before the San Francisco crusade, Bob Root established the "Co-Labor Corps," drawing his inspiration from Haggai 1:14, which tells how the leaders and the lesser men of a community were stirred up by the Spirit of the Lord: "and they came and did work in the house of the Lord of Hosts, their God." Root approached businessmen and laymen accustomed to heavy administrative responsibility, and each would recruit his own corps and train it with the aid of a manual drawn up by Root. Thus at San Francisco the widespread duties that had accumulated in the follow-up and other departments were all efficiently and swiftly carried out.

Bob Root's reorganization, together with Charlie Riggs' work to train counselors, ensured that from New York onward the counseling and follow-up department could expand to handle inquirers no matter how many came forward.

Despite its record figures of attendance, despite the flow of decisions, New York was difficult from beginning to end. "The tremendous satanic power in this city has sometimes pressured me beyond endurance," Billy Graham wrote about halfway through. "The crusade seems to have moved in tides. One week would be tremendous blessing, and the next it seemed Satan had moved in somewhere. Then all of a sudden, in answer to deep intercessory prayer, it seems that Satan would flee and the power of God would come in great power." People would be moving forward to make a commitment even before the invitation.

It had been intended to end after six weeks. An option, however, had been taken on Madison Square Garden by the New York executive committee for five months. The Team and the executive committee became certain they should extend beyond the last week of June. For the closing rally on July 20 they booked Yankee Stadium, the home of the New York Yankees baseball team. The temperature inside the stadium that day was 105 degrees. More than 100,000 attended, with another 20,000 outside the gates, listening by loudspeaker. This remains the largest crowd in the stadium's history, for at Pope Paul's visit in October 1965 the crowd was not packed in so tightly.[1]

Vice-President Nixon brought a message from President Eisenhower, addressed the crowd before Billy Graham's sermon, and was much moved by the immensity of the turnout and the reverence of the service.

Billy Graham and the executive committee, after much prayer and an all-morning discussion on the previous day, had already decided to extend again until August 10. Some of the committee had been afraid of an anticlimax after Yankee Stadium. Billy had replied that he could find no Scriptural basis for troubling about that. Christ's entry into Jerusalem was a great climax; His death the following Friday was from a human viewpoint "a great anticlimax, yet it proved to be the turning point of history."

"Mr. Graham anticipated," wrote Luverne Gustavson on July 26, "a terrible drop in attendance this week, with no large delegations booked, but it's been amazingly full! And hundreds still come forward. There is a 'deeper' tone to the whole services, it seems. And Mr. Graham's messages are largely to Christians, so a lot of the early converts are getting established in the Christian life. His subjects on Prayer and the Holy Spirit have been exceptionally good."

Billy was exhausted. He had been preaching ten weeks nightly without a break. He now cut out other engagements, spent most of the day in bed, sometimes would almost cling to the pulpit. "I had nothing to give, I had exhausted my material, I had exhausted my body; I had exhausted my mind. Yet I'm sure that everyone would agree that the preaching had far more power. It was God taking sheer

[1] *Applications* to attend Pope Paul's Mass, however, were reported to be considerably in excess of 120,000.

weakness—it's when I get out of the way and say, 'God, You have to do it.' I sat on the platform many nights with nothing to say, nothing. Just sat there. And I knew that in a few minutes I'd have to get up and preach, and I'd just say, 'Oh, God, I can't do it. I cannot do it.' And yet, I would stand up and all of a sudden it would begin to come —just God giving it, that's all."

On August 10 they extended for the third and last time. "Not even the most vocal critics," Billy wrote on August 26, "can now say that it was publicity, organization or showmanship. There is an element of the Spirit of God that is beyond analysis and rationalization." The crusade ended after sixteen weeks with a rally in Times Square on the evening of Sunday September 1.

This rally, being held in a complex of intersecting avenues and streets, was one of the occasions when exact and accurate figures were not obtainable. "The police arrived well before the start of the meeting," recalls Jerry Beavan, "and said that our total crowd would be 75,000. I argued with the inspector that they couldn't possibly know that far in advance, but they set that figure and released it to the press. They did their 'estimating' in a squad car, two blocks from the platform and more than one hour prior to the start." A United Press International reporter estimated the crowd at 200,000, and this figure, announced on television before the police inspector's, was brought to Billy Graham on the platform. Beavan's own figure, "based on quite a few years of estimating crowds," was 160,000, which he maintained in face of press insistence that it was higher.

The Times Square rally is almost certainly the largest gathering Graham has ever addressed, and one of the most remarkable. The "crossroads of the world," under the flashing lights of Broadway, was turned, in *The New York Times*' words, "into a great cathedral." The crowds stretched shoulder to shoulder down Broadway as far as the eye could see, and spilled into the cross streets, their singing echoing beneath the commercial buildings, hotels and movie theaters.

"Let us tonight make this a time of rededication," said Graham. He began, once again, to preach Christ, "who died for our sins and paid the supreme sacrifice that we might have life."

The crusade had cost, including television, two and a half million dollars, yet there was a surplus at the New York committee's disposal. It had cost Billy Graham physically even more than London's twelve weeks in 1954. "Something went out of me during New York that I seemingly cannot recover." He has always been slow to heal, either from an illness or from prolonged and exceptional exhaustion.

The Protestant Council of New York was in no doubt that the crusade had fulfilled its purpose. On March 21, 1958, some six months after the close, its executive secretary, Dan Potter, wrote to Graham that the four objectives had been "met in a miraculous way: to win men to Christ; to make the city God-conscious; to strengthen the churches; to make the city conscious of moral, spiritual and social responsibilities."

Plenty of detractors were claiming already that the crusade had been a passing wonder, a prodigious effort of infinitesimal consequence, an excessive publicity for a partial Christianity. In regard to these detractors the late Samuel Shoemaker, nationally known Episcopal minister of Pittsburgh, wrote (September 20, 1957) to the late Jesse Bader: "I simply cannot understand the people [critics] who expect Billy to do in four months what they have not done in forty years, and to cover everything from the multiplication table to binomial theorems, when it is all so obvious he is talking to the spiritually unlettered of the world. There is a kind of apostasy in some of these critics, a kind of fighting against the Holy Spirit Himself as He chooses to use Billy Graham. It really frightens me. It is so proud and pharisaical, instead of being grateful for something done that may not be their way of doing it, with parts of which they would probably disagree, as would you and I, but not to be thankful for that great Protestant witness to New York, knowing it as you and I know it, is to me almost to be something less than Christian."

Billy Graham frankly admitted he had only scratched the surface of New York. He knew too that it would be years before a valid assessment could be made. Five months after the close, on January 28, 1958, *The New York Times* published a survey under the headline "Graham Impact Held Fleeting as Ministers Appraise Crusade." The survey was based on a mere 159 replies received to a questionnaire sent to 504 ministers picked at random. Some who replied had not cooperated with the crusade except in name, one had revealed his attitude by the remark that the crusade had "set back the Christian cause by several years." Four were Unitarian or Universalist, who not surprisingly called the campaign's results "completely negative." The ministers were only asked three questions: How many cards had you received? How many of these were new names? How many are attending service regularly? No convert had been contacted directly.

On May 15, 1958, one year to the day after the opening of the crusade, the Protestant Council held a united rally at Madison Square

Garden. Billy Graham sent greetings on tape from the San Francisco crusade. When his associate evangelist, Joe Blinco, whom he had brought onto the Team from England in 1955, asked converts of the previous year's crusade to stand, it seemed almost half of the 17,500 present were on their feet.

Dr. Robert O. Ferm, dean of students at Houghton College in New York State, was not surprised. He had just completed a survey of results, conducted as fully and fairly as he could.

He had interviewed 231 ministers. Nearly a quarter had begun meetings of members for prayer or Bible study. Others assured him their existing meetings had been strengthened. Ferm also met clergy who regretted the crusade, for they had lost members. (Ferm's conclusion, after his talks with many converts, was that some had left the churches of extreme liberals because they were no longer satisfied with a truncated or nebulous Christianity; others had left the churches of extreme fundamentalists because of regret at persistent opposition to a cooperative crusade.)

As in London, so in New York: the more a church had entered into the work the more harvest it was reaping. Norman Vincent Peale, the well-known minister of the Marble Collegiate Church on Fifth Avenue, gladly and frequently affirmed publicly what he wrote to Billy Graham on October 22, 1957: "My spiritual life is stronger and deeper as a result of your marvelous preaching. You have done me more good than I can possibly express. Our church has profited in a wonderful way from the crusade."

Robert Ferm went to the follow-up office, and from the files of the 61,000 decision cards selected at random a group from each letter of the alphabet. He contacted 500 by telephone. "Without exception they were pleased to have been contacted. More than ninety per cent clearly reiterated their original decisions. Only seven per cent appeared to be uncertain or confused." To another 500 he mailed questionnaires. Ten per cent had moved without leaving an address. Of the rest, runs Ferm's report, "the overwhelming majority still adhere to their decision, whether they have been nurtured or neglected by the church."

Ferm "found converts among the socially prominent and the outcast, the rich and the poor, the illiterate who could not sign their own decision cards and the university professor; racial lines were freely crossed and Negroes and Puerto Ricans were among the large groups. . . . The utter fascination of listening to the reports of converts would convince the skeptic that a work of grace had been done.

The person who actually made the decision retains a warm and vibrant faith that has been able to survive and persist through many discouragements and above many obstacles. His enthusiastic affirmation of faith is heart-warming. It is a twentieth-century wonder that the Church has failed to reach out and draw him into her fellowship."

"For here," Ferm continued, "the great tragedy becomes apparent." More than half the converts he contacted had been entirely neglected by any church, despite the cards sent to ministers and their assurances to the follow-up department. Less than a quarter had been visited; another quarter a pastor had contacted by telephone or letter, but they had not been treated as babes in Christ, to be cared for (in St. Paul's phrase) "as a nurse cherisheth her children." Some had found their way to churches notwithstanding; others knew that they should, but not having yet done so were retarded in spiritual growth.

Billy Graham commented on this failure of vision and concern in the churches: "This has become the great bottleneck in our evangelistic crusades."

He was, however, soon to see what a crusade could do for a nation whose churches removed that bottleneck.

---

26 · *Under the Southern Cross*

When Billy Graham agreed to conduct nationwide crusades in Australia and New Zealand during those countries' late summer and autumn, February until May, of 1959, it was the first time since Scotland that he had been invited officially by all the major churches of a land.[1]

Graham and Jerry Beavan knew little about Australia. Their original plan was for five weeks in Sydney, a week in Brisbane and another in Melbourne. But Jerry was soon made aware that Melbourne deserved a full-length crusade. His final strategy imaginatively took advantage of the full talents of the Graham Team, now much more

---

[1] The invitations came separately, and in different forms, from each of the six Australian states and from New Zealand, but the effect was that Graham and his Team went to both nations as official guests of the churches. In Scotland, 1955, the invitation had come from a movement ("Tell Scotland") on which the churches were officially represented, and was endorsed by their formal resolutions.

than one preacher and one associate, together with a song leader and a soloist. Beavan planned two full-length crusades in Melbourne and Sydney led by Billy Graham, and shorter crusades in the other Australian state capitals and in three New Zealand cities. The supplemental crusades would be conducted by an associate evangelist—Grady Wilson or Joe Blinco or Leighton Ford—with Graham coming for the last two or three days.

Whether at Melbourne, Sydney or elsewhere, the crusades were expected by the Graham Team to be small.

With a population approximately that of Illinois, and less than that of New York City, scattered over a land mass the size of the United States without Alaska, Australia did not seem to Graham the likely scene of a crusade that would move a nation as had Harringay or Kelvin Hall or, in a different way, Madison Square Garden. The fact that a vast preponderance of the population lived on the Southeastern seaboard, especially around Sydney and Melbourne, did not at the time seem specially significant. Moreover the Australians, still predominantly British or Irish in background, with an expanding economy, an exceptional emphasis on sport and the outdoor life, and a worldwide reputation for independence and self-sufficiency and bluntness of speech, had not previously proved receptive to evangelists, especially those from abroad. An American Pentecostal, for example, had been forced to close his mission prematurely and leave Melbourne in 1956. Moreover, during the San Francisco crusade Billy Graham received a gloomy report from Edwin Orr, lately returned from an evangelistic tour of Australia, and this was only partly offset by the more optimistic report of another American evangelist, Larry Love, who said he had found some great men of God.

In May 1958 Jerry Beavan and his family moved to Sydney. "It was Jerry's vision to touch the whole country," Graham says. "He put tremendous energies into it. I think probably Jerry's finest work with us was Australia."

It was Beavan who foresaw that by landline relays, tape recordings, and the extensive buying of time on radio and television, together with a full use of Operation Andrew and special transport near the crusade centers, most of the people of Australia might be touched. As he traveled around the continent he began to sense a high degree of expectancy. "Bill," he wrote on August 8, 1958, "I really believe that we are right on the verge of a national spiritual awakening here in Australia.... There are so many evidences that God is doing an unusual thing that we are constantly overwhelmed by His blessing. . . . There is more prayer right now in Sydney than there was in New York City at the height of that crusade."

All over Australia people were praying. Office workers from suburban bungalows would remember Billy Graham as they knelt at their bedsides before catching commuters' trains. In the pastoral lands of the north and the west, when the day grew too hot for stock to move and the musterers rested in the shade, here and there a stockman would withdraw a few yards and in the peace of the vast distances pray for the coming crusade.

Similar intimations of a national stirring were provided by the pattern of gifts. Walter Argall, a Sydney banker and treasurer for the crusade, drew up a Share Partner scheme whereby numbers of donors who could not offer large amounts convenanted to give $2.80 a month ("No more than two packets of mints a day"). Sydney alone raised $62,000 this way. Australian public opinion, however, had memories of foreign evangelists who lived lavishly and took big sums out of the country. The Billy Graham Team chose modest accommodations; they waived their normal custom whereby the local committee met the cost of hospitality and travel, and instead bore all their own expenses—a substantial contribution on the Team's part to the crusade budget, and an effective answer to criticism.

The first crusade was to be held at Melbourne—cultured, wealthy, conservative; a quietly self-confident city that might graciously allow Billy Graham a hearing, and little more, although the chairman of the crusade executive was the Dean of the Anglican Cathedral, Dr. Stuart Barton Babbage, and the vice chairman was President-General of the Methodist Conference, Dr. Harold Wood.

For crusade director Billy Graham sent Walter Herbert Smyth, a minister from Philadelphia who had worked with him in Youth for Christ and subsequently in Graham's film distribution office. Smyth, whom a crusade chairman in New Zealand described as combining "the efficiency of Jerry Beavan and the sweetness of Billy Graham," impressed the Melbourne committee because, in the words of Harold Wood, "he was tactful in his approach and very careful not to obtrude his own point of view, but he was always there in a very brotherly and cooperative spirit." The Australians appreciated the refusal by Smyth, Charlie Riggs and Dan Piatt to impose a pattern.

Despite Australian zeal, the Americans continued to expect a small crusade. Melbourne's autumn weather being chancy, they chose the largest indoor arena, the Stadium (now the Festival Hall) out in West Melbourne, which seated 7,500 for boxing. By building a temporary aluminum annex for closed circuit television, accommodations were increased to 10,000.

The year of 1958 had been busy for Billy Graham. Soon after the birth of the Graham's fifth child and second son, Nelson Edman (Ned) in January, Billy went to the Caribbean and Central America. This three-week crusade had a lasting significance far beyond the countries visited because it led to the late Kenneth Strachan's scheme known as "Evangelism in Depth," which adapts the principles of counseling and follow-up to long-term missionary evangelism. Strachan and Graham traveled together and spent many hours talking about the problems of evangelism, particularly as they related to Latin America. "Evangelism in Depth" emerged from their discussions.

After the crusade Strachan worked out the principles of "Evangelism in Depth" in the Latin American mission fields, and from there the scheme has spread to other continents.

In the summer of 1958 came the seven-week San Francisco crusade, followed by the week at Sacramento in July, with one- or two-day stands in four other California cities, followed in the fall by the crusade in Graham's native Charlotte. Besides all this he had his weekly radio sermon, gave dozens of long-promised individual addresses, and broke into his free periods by accepting still further speaking engagements. Along with so full a schedule came constant new problems brought by the growth of the Association, and he was already giving serious thought to the founding of a Christian university.

Early in 1959, with Australia only a few weeks away, Graham was in Dallas for the Texas State Baptist Evangelistic Conference. While he was playing golf, his left eye suddenly began to hurt badly and he could see only straight ahead. He was found to be suffering from blockage in a blood vessel (angio-spastic edema of the macula), a condition brought on entirely by overstrain; he might have had a thrombosis instead. All engagements before leaving for Australia were canceled. Cortisone and another powerful drug, nica, were prescribed. To give Billy a complete rest in the sun, the Grahams went to Hawaii. The opening at Melbourne was postponed by a week to February 15, the Sydney crusade shortened by a week. Billy was ordered to reduce his daily schedule in Australia to little more than the evening preaching, and to swim or play a short round of golf on most days.

On the opening Sunday afternoon, February 15, 1959, the 10,000-seat Stadium could not contain the crowds that flocked to West Melbourne to hear Billy Graham, who during the service went outside and addressed, in a sudden rainstorm, an overflow crowd estimated by the police at 5,000.

After five days the committee abandoned the Stadium (and had to pay the hiring charge of $420 a night for the remaining three weeks) and moved the crusade to a new open-air auditorium inaugurated the previous week, the Sidney Myer Music Bowl in King's Domain, across the Yarra River in the center of the city. Its unusually shaped aluminum roof covered only the platform and some 2,000 seats, but the Bowl was so designed that a great audience could sit on the new-sown grass slopes and look down to the platform, and more thousands could stand behind in a wide arc. The acoustics and amplifying were perfect: the fringes of the crowd, though unable to see, could hear every word of song and sermon, and Melbourne spilled out to King's Domain in such numbers that Team and Committee marveled at the littleness of the faith that had been content to book the Stadium.

"We are seeing God do a mighty thing," wrote Grady Wilson to Dr. John R. Wimbish of Tampa, the morning after the first meeting at the new site, at which 25,000 had gathered around the Bowl. "When Billy gave the invitation, immediately they began streaming down the aisles from all directions. There were more than 3,000 that came forward, and finally Billy threw up his hands and said: "Stop, ladies and gentlemen, there is no more room. If you want to give your life to Christ, go home and drop me a letter in the mail and we will send you follow-up literature that will help you in your Christian life. It has been simply fantastic what God the Holy Ghost has done here."

As hundreds of that 3,000 crowded on the platform a police inspector urged John Robinson, the crusade committee's secretary, to get them off it: "The platform won't stand the weight, there'll be a collapse." After Robinson had passed on the necessary instructions he asked the inspector what he thought about it all, for the man had previously indicated that the whole crusade was both nonsense and a nuisance. The inspector answered, in awed tones: "There is something here I don't understand. There is something here with depth that is beyond me. It can only be God at work."

Numbers at the Myer Bowl on the Sunday topped 70,000, and

whereas the crusade and Billy's sermons were reported fully in newspapers read throughout the state of Victoria, all Australia read the headlines' news of the smashing turnout.

The crusade services were being televised in Victoria. At the end of each service a telephone number was flashed on the screen, which viewers could call if they wished to speak to a counselor. It has been claimed that after the first telecast, "up to ten thousand calls were banked up in the hopelessly jammed system." This figure was not precisely true: counseling took time, the ten lines available could all be busy up to twenty minutes while every disappointed caller might try twenty times to get through, each attempt being automatically registered. To handle the load the committee then set up several panels of counselors sitting in stores or places of business. When an inquirer rang the number shown on the TV screen he would be immediately answered, "You will be called back by a counselor in a few minutes," and his number passed to one of the panels.

The Music Bowl was a perfect place for the nonchurchgoer. A solicitor to one of the banks told a lawyer on the crusade committee, Harold McCracken, "I would be uncomfortable in a church, but people like me find it very easy to go along and listen to Billy in these surroundings. Everything is so natural. This is how I think Christ must have preached when He was talking to the people of His day." Bill Dempsey, another committee member, recalls watching a young man of a rough sort (in Australian slang, "the bodgie and widgie type") on the fringes of the crowd trying to drag his girl away. Later Dempsey saw the man being counseled after coming forward. Billy Graham had won the heart of Melbourne. Even drinkers outside a hotel called to him as he passed, "Good on you, Billy, we're for you!"

E. W. Tipping, Melbourne's leading newspaper columnist, a Roman Catholic (the Roman Catholics were markedly friendly in Melbourne), recalled vividly five years after the crusade how Graham would "take his text straight from the Scriptures and then in very, very simple language he would get that message across. That was what appealed to me most. He's a rhetorical speaker with a big audience, but I don't think that the essence of his appeal is his rhetoric so much as the simplicity of his message and the way he rammed it home."

Graham's message reached the irreligious, such as the Jacksons. Their marriage was breaking down—night clubs, racing and alcohol being unable to disguise their incompatibility. The husband, George Jackson, an ex-prisoner of war and a foreman in a clothing factory, was alternately violent and moody, refusing for days to speak to his wife or daughters. Jackson was a confidence trickster as well as gambler and blasphemer, but inwardly knew such misery that he actually wished he could be back in the Japanese camps on the Death Railway, "that I might hide myself away and die in a wallow of self-pity." When the crusade began George was so incensed by the publicity, so convinced that Graham was "out to make fast money with a good gimmick," that he wrote and told him to "get out of the country."

The Jacksons denied God's existence, but the wife, Dawn, went to the first night at the Music Bowl—"a completely new experience for someone of my background. Yet I dared there to believe that Jesus was a real person and could change my then very miserable life." George was amazed when she told him she was converted, but he could not deny the change in her life: "She had what I had always wanted, peace of mind." He continued to sneer and refused to go to the Bowl "until I thought I had saved enough face." He then went wearing dark glasses.

In 1965 the Jacksons sailed to Borneo as missionaries.

The Crusade also reached men of position and morality. The president of the Church of England Men's Society of Victoria, John Bishop, the head accountant of a chain store, had attended the opening meeting in duty bound, and went again the third or fourth night. Billy preached on John 3:16. "The thing that hit me," Bishop recalls, "was the fact of my complete unworthiness and my complete incompetence and the incapability to do anything myself before God; that only by the saving grace of Jesus Who died for our sins and Who asks us to believe in Him, could I ever hope to be reconciled with my Creator. That's the way it hit me. It was a shattering experience, because I had all the pride and arrogance and conceit of a person who, in the eyes of the Church, had achieved one of the most important posts that a layman can achieve. I'd come from a humble home, but worked hard and studied hard, and became a qualified accountant and got a good job in the company. I'd really arrived. And then this hit me, that I was just a miserable sinner bereft of everything."

This prominent layman never went forward ("I didn't have the courage") and has always wished he had. Instead, in the privacy of his room, he faced his dilemma ("Can this man be right and I wrong?") and committed his life to Christ; then he doubted, then again prayed. Certainty of forgiveness and new birth did not come sensationally. "The conviction just grew and grew. I couldn't stay away from the crusade meetings and that built me up."

Billy Graham, Cliff Barrows and Bev Shea had always been happy in their work, but Melbourne brought them a new happiness, all the stronger for being unexpected. The crusade was taking wings, and Jerry Beavan was assuring them that Sydney would rise even higher. It was now nearly a decade since Los Angeles '49, and Christ seemed to be saying to each of the Team what He said to Nathanael: "Thou shalt see greater things than these."

The whole Team warmed to the friendliness of the Australians, as the Australians to theirs. Billy Graham's left eye troubled him a little, but Paul Maddox managed to get him often to a specialist for check-ups, and subsequently the eye made a complete recovery. Except for the eye Billy felt fine. Whereas the New York crusade was a battle, Melbourne—and all Australia—is remembered through a haze of happiness. Cliff and Bev, too, won a large place in the affections of a nation that loves to sing. "They created a wonderful atmosphere in the early stages of each meeting," runs the memory of a businessman convert, "and that atmosphere helped us to realize fully the joy and love of Christianity."

The Melbourne crusade executives were struggling to keep pace with events. John Robinson, who could remember no such feeling of strain since the first days of the Japanese war, when he was a staff officer at Australian general headquarters, would work all day until the crusade service—sorting the innumerable problems created by the change of site, or the wholly unexpected flow of inquirers, or the stream of up-country parties coming in by train and coach. After the service he would return to his office in Carlton, than dash home for a few hours sleep and be back before the family was out of bed. For Robinson it meant not only severe fatigue but the temporary rupture of a regular devotional life. One morning at his desk he buried his face in his arms. "I can vividly remember saying to the Lord in prayer, 'Lord I've got my hands full. I've just got to trust you, and here we go. You'll have to look after me.' And of course He did, of course He did."

In the third week the Myer Music Bowl had to be vacated because of Melbourne's annual Spring Festival, named Moomba, which in it-self was expected to be a strong counter-attraction over the final ten days. The crusade moved to the Agricultural Showgrounds, far from the city center and the residential suburbs—too near freight yards, power stations and a slaughter house. A third move, especially to such uncongenial surroundings with bad acoustics, might have proved a handicap; but the crowds ranged from ten to twenty-eight thousand, and the crusade continued to be the main topic in Melbourne.

Then came the torrential rain of March 2. On March 3, a youth night, the rain was if possible worse, yet about 25,000 attended. The platform was not under cover. Billy's tie-microphone went out of action and he preached crouching over a low microphone on the dais. Most of the people were in the stands, but those who came forward had to plough through the mud in the open. "I found myself wondering whether anybody at all would venture out when the appeal was made," recalls Leon Morris, vice-principal (now principal) of Ridley College and head of the follow-up department. "But I don't think I shall ever forget the sight as they tramped out in the rain to make their decision," 1,200 of them, almost all young people.

Meanwhile at Myer Music Bowl the rain had washed away the loose earth on the slopes, where Billy's audience had trodden bare the new sown grass, and poured down to flood what had been the counseling area. Had the crusade stayed there one more night it would have been drowned!

At the end of the week the Showground management refused the crusade committee's offer to buy out the Saturday night trotting races. The Team therefore arranged, instead of a service, a special television program over the commercial channel.

The final meeting of the crusade, on Sunday March 15, was scheduled for the Melbourne Cricket Ground, scene of cricket Test Matches and, in winter, of the big games of Victorian football, which to the uninitiated looks like a mixture of rugby and soccer, with a touch of American football too. Much of the Olympic Games of 1956 took place there, one of the largest and best designed stadiums in the world.

The most people the Cricket Ground had ever contained was 115,802 at a football league final in 1956. The few scoffers still vocal in Melbourne said the crusade could never fill it because the nightly crowds of 20,000 or 30,000 had been "the same people coming over and over again." John Robinson's fears were the reverse. The Team had been following their normal custom of distributing more tickets than there were seats, on a theory proved in America that when tickets are free, 20 per cent will be unused. Robinson knew that if an Australian holds a ticket he uses it.

No one was quite prepared for the sight that sunny afternoon.

Long before the arrival of the governor of Victoria, Sir Dallas

Brooks, the stands were full and people were still crowding into the gates. The secretary of Melbourne Cricket Club, Ian Johnson, made history by allowing women and children to enter the Members' Stand. He made history again by permitting thousands to sit on the turf. He was quoted by one newspaper as saying the total admission was 143,750, by another that it could not be exactly estimated but was over 130,000.[1]

The governor read the Twenty-third Psalm and Billy, before his address, gave out a special message from President Eisenhower. Billy was overwhelmed by the size of the crowd, greater even than that of Wembley in 1954. Luverne Gustavson, far back in one of the stands, echoed the thoughts of the Team when she wrote that evening: "It was a stirring sight to see so many people gathered so reverently for a gospel service. Then at the end of the service when the congregation joined to sing 'God be with you till we meet again,' my throat got all lumpy. For certainly most of these people would never meet again until in the Presence of Christ."

More than four thousand inquirers came forward at the invitation: with the counselors beside them, it was an amazing sight in itself. Counseling was held up briefly when with typically British touch "God Save the Queen" was played at the departure of the Queen's representative.

Even more than the governor's presence, another action seemed to spotlight the city of Melbourne's reaction to the crusade. Close behind the Cricket Ground lies one of the main suburban railway lines of Melbourne. Normally, red trains and green trains clatter noisily by at frequent intervals. That afternoon they were strangely muted. The committee learned afterward that the Chairman of Commissioners, Victoria Railways, had personally ordered trains to proceed slowly in the vicinity during the service.

Seven weeks after the Graham Team had left Melbourne, the Chief Justice of Victoria, Lieutenant-General Sir Edmund Herring, echoed in a private letter to Billy the public comments of churchmen: "Your crusade here," he wrote, "has had tremendous repercussions. All the churches have new recruits to look after, and all I have been in touch

---

[1] The police had opened the gates again just as the service began, to relieve the pressure in the streets, and the thousands who thereupon swelled the crowd already in the standing room at the back of the stands never passed through the turnstiles, and thus were not counted.

with are doing everything they can to make them welcome and keep them in the fold. But, quite apart from the number of people who have either been brought into the churches or brought back to them, we all owe you a debt for sweetening our own lives and making the great bulk of the people who are, sad to say, outside the Christian World, pause and think for a minute of where they stand." In 1964 Sir Edmund Herring could strongly endorse his 1959 letter. "I would say that in all sorts of ways and all sorts of places the influence of Billy Graham is still felt here."

To go to Melbourne after five years is to be left in no doubt that the crusade of 1959 has had a continuing impact. Even people who had little contact with the crusade remember it for the extraordinary atmosphere of goodwill that covered the city, while leading church-men, such as the Methodist Dr. Harold Wood emphasize the mas-sive contribution to a Christian unity which transcended differences of denomination and of theological interpretation. "We were all con-scious," he wrote, "that we were one in Christ; all animated by the desire to communicate Christ; and also conscious of the great need in the community. . . . In the years since that remarkable time I think there is still a continuing feeling of unity."

In Melbourne 28,105 decisions were recorded, of which some 19,000 were "acceptance of Christ." Dr. Leon Morris, head of the follow-up section, gave as his personal impression after five years that "the majority would have stood firm. I am continually meeting people now who were converted in the crusade and who are going on in the faith, and I'm not aware of any considerable number that have slipped back." He points out that for an accurate assessment on 28,000 men, women and children a very wide survey would be needed, and that an objector could certainly dig up some who lapsed. As in any movement, or even in the ordinary life of a church, there were those who were "caught up in the excitement of the moment and registered a commitment of some kind that didn't go deep, and they fell away." But the widespread impression in Melbourne is that most of the converts stood.

Any writer or sociologist or theologian in the mid-nineteen-sixties who wants to challenge the value of a Graham crusade ought first to make a detailed study of Australia in and after 1959.

27 · Through New Zealand Eyes

From Melbourne Billy Graham went to Tasmania for two one-night meetings, then took a week's rest on Queensland beaches. In the meantime preparations in Sydney suggested that even the Melbourne crusade would be dwarfed. But first he was due in New Zealand.

In going there the Graham Team was responding to a unanimous invitation from New Zealand's National Council of Churches. Ironically they might never have accepted had not a South Island layman, in Sydney on business when Beavan had arrived on his exploratory trip, disabused him of an impression that New Zealand was a couple of islands off the coast of Australia.

Grady Wilson, well suited for the go-ahead bustle of Auckland, New Zealand's largest city, led off on Easter Sunday, March 29. Leighton Ford's scholarly approach was most appropriate for Wellington, the capital. In South Island Joe Blinco, the English Methodist, had a close affinity with the most English place in New Zealand, Christchurch, on the Canterbury Plains, the famous sheep country with its backdrop of the Southern Alps. The strategy of associate crusades, first attempted in New Zealand, was thoroughly vindicated; but local organizers noted how each associate evangelist brightened when Billy Graham reached them. The crusade had been arranged so that Billy could speak at each center at the climax—Auckland on Friday and Saturday, Wellington on Sunday, Christchurch on Tuesday. The response was on a scale totally unexpected, for New Zealand has never been much moved by religious efforts. Professor E. M. Blaiklock of Auckland University believes that, had Billy Graham stayed there longer, "It is not at all unlikely that there might have been at least a city-wide revival. . . . The converts of that few days' effort are visible all over the place."

Twenty per cent of New Zealand's population attended the meeting in the three cities, and Billy Graham preached face-to-face to more people in six days than in any other week in his ministry. Jerry Beavan has said that New Zealand's response was "the nearest to a national awakening I have ever seen." The influence of the crusade, directly or by landline relays, was felt right through the dominion.

The Dean of Nelson, across the straits from Wellington, at evensong on the following Sunday, invited any of his congregation "who weren't sure in their own minds whether they really belonged to Jesus Christ or not," to come forward and join him as he knelt at the altar rail. "There was no pressure and no begging—just a simple invitation to join me—and the response was tremendous. At least 200 people came forward. A great number were married couples. . . . The effect of the Graham crusade in our Cathedral Church has been continuing and good." The same verdict after five years is given by clerical and lay leaders of other denominations.

Although much was lost because many individual churches failed to learn in time that a crusade should not be a single burst of activity but part of a continuing program of evangelism, Graham's visit is seen in retrospect as a peak of church unity and the beginning of new vigor. The memory remains so vivid that churchmen almost forget that the actual crusade was only eleven days long. No informed New Zealander disputes that a large number of children, young people, and adults, of all social levels, became active, enduring Christians.

In 1964 a man and a married couple analyzed what happened to them before, during and after the 1959 crusade. They are only three out of more than 17,000 who came forward, and all were of professional background in Auckland. But their memories and perceptions throw a flood of light on a Graham crusade from the angle of the man and woman in the stadium seat.

Terence Nolan was forty-four years of age at the time of the crusade. Son of a substantial sheep farmer and educated at an Anglican boarding school, he had seen action throughout the war in North Africa, Greece and Italy, winning a D.S.O. and a mention in dispatches, and winding up as a lieutenant-colonel on the staff. He married in England and after the war entered a manufacturing business, rising to become chairman and managing director. For two years he was also an honorary A.D.C. to Lord Freyberg when governor-general. The Nolans live in the Auckland suburb of Rumuera.

Terence Nolan's parents were not churchgoers, but he had been a regular communicant in his regiment, and his English wife, who had been a Baptist but was confirmed as an Anglican when they returned to New Zealand, was a committed Christian. Noland became a churchwarden at their Anglican parish church, "but I hadn't opened a Bible since I left school, and said my prayers only very spasmodically."

The Nolans' vicar, Canon Austin Charles, was vice-chairman of the Auckland crusade committee. His parishioners, however, showed less enthusiasm than their vicar at the prospect of Billy Graham, while in Nolan's weekday world of business and society "there was little interest other than mild curiosity" about a man who had drawn such crowds. Mrs. Nolan, through friendship with nonconformists, enrolled in counseling classes. The two often discussed what she learned there; her husband "scoffed at them but I think I was taking it in." Except that he decided to take one look at Graham, "I said I didn't really think I would bother to go along to the crusade because it wasn't for me, it was for other people. I thought it a lot of nonsense. I considered that I was an adequate Christian. My wife was extremely annoyed."

Nolan went to Grady Wilson's opening service to please his wife. He was immediately impressed, as a former staff officer, by the smooth arrangements and by the crowd of 15,000; by the singing of the choir and the soloist, Martha Nixon; and by Grady Wilson's words. "When at the end Grady Wilson invited all those who wanted to commit themselves to come forward, I felt a most extraordinary urge to get up and go. It was almost as if something was lifting me up in my seat to come forward. But I wouldn't go. I thought, 'I'm an Anglican, and Anglicans don't do this sort of thing—it is quite ridiculous—I am a Christian already.' And so I stayed where I was. But I was very unhappy about it, and when I got home that night I was in absolute mental turmoil because I felt I should have gone forward. I then went back—I had a business meeting I had to go to and I missed one night—but I went back every night, and I still couldn't make up my mind whether to go forward or not."

The crusade, Nolan recalls, had immediately become "the main topic of conversation: business people were suddenly aware that people were definitely interested. The actual campaign itself made a tremendous impact on the city and on the business community." And every night Mrs. Nolan was talking about her experiences as a counselor. Terence Nolan still hesitated to go forward when Billy Graham preached for the first time on the sixth night, Friday. "I knew that I had been called to go and I knew that I had to make up my mind whether I finally would go or I wouldn't. And so I went along each night to try and get it clear in my mind. I had never been quite so worried about anything before. I couldn't eat and I couldn't sleep."

On the Saturday, before the final service, Nolan went alone to his beach cottage at Orere Point, on the Thames coast—at that time of year deserted except for birds. He wandered away into his acre of bush, "quietly trying to think it out, because I realized that if I did go forward I would have to change my attitude to a lot of things, and I would have to actively commit myself as a Christian very much more than I had in the past. It came back to: Did I really believe in Christ and in God, or didn't I? That's what the essential battle was. I really think I faced up to it for the first time in my life. By the time I came home on that Saturday night, I knew that when Billy Graham invited those to go I would go forward with them."

The after-effects of the crusade were everywhere evident to Terence Nolan. He attended a special service for converts who were linked to his parish church. "Some of them fell by the wayside, but a number of our parishioners who were only scarce or tardy churchgoers before that time are still committed. Our parish church was definitely strengthened. The vestry was quite a different atmosphere after the crusade because at least a third of the vestry had gone forward. One of them in particular, a young chap who was always very anti-everything, became a tower of strength after the campaign."

In Nolan's factory over half of the staff of 500 attended the crusade. A number, including several senior men, went forward. "There was a bond between us. We all knew who had gone forward, and talked about it, and I feel that those men, two or three of whom I know well, would still have not have been churchgoers had it not been for the Graham campaign. Because of it they are all in official positions in their churches. They have an impact on those who work under them, and therefore the campaign must have done good, because those men are better than what they would have been had Billy Graham not come."

As for Terence Nolan, looking back after five years, "The whole outlook of my life has altered ... a tremendous sense of security, more assured of the future, a greater sense of peace. ... My attitude to people in less fortunate circumstances has altered and my sense of stewardship, helping others. They talk about racial equality in New Zealand, but I was always rather scathing of any native race here, but my attitude to that has altered. And I was, I suppose, arrogant and dictatorial before, and I am sure I am much more tolerant to other people's views. In fact, I think I am a completely different person."

The memories of Dr. and Mrs. Dennis Spackman form a contrast to those of Terence Nolan.

In 1959 Dr. Spackman was twenty-nine and his wife Rowan a year younger. They were happily married, with children, living a life normal to a young doctor already rising fast in his profession. They were nominal Anglicans but not churchgoers. When Dennis had gone to medical school, "any faith that I had smartly went down the drain," and since their marriage Rowan had discarded the religiosity which had been briefly intense as an older schoolgirl attending a ritualistic church. They were not anti-Christians: "We just didn't give it a thought."

They went to the crusade because an Auckland doctor had circulated all six hundred doctors in the city, offering tickets. The Spackmans were merely curious: "Here was Billy Graham, a world figure; this man must have something!" On Saturday morning they read in the paper that over 2,000 had gone forward. The doctor exclaimed, "Goodness me, just like a pack of sheep." Deep in Mrs. Spackman's mind, however, was "a feeling that possibly I might find the God that I knew was controlling everything." Her basic reason for dropping religion had been, "I thought a Christian should live up to a standard, and I had kept falling short all the time."

Because of the universal interest in the crusade that Saturday, the Spackmans were by now excited and went to the stadium in mid-afternoon to get good seats. By the time the stadium had filled and the singing had begun, the Spackmans, independently, were both reacting the same way. "We thought the singing wonderful, the songs alive and vibrant; but there was a sort of electric air in the stadium which was new to us. It was more than just a sense of reverence—an all-pervading sense of expectancy, and yet at the same time of calmness. Before a ball game or a football match it's entirely different; there's expectancy but you don't get the peace."

They were impressed too by the way "the people taking part weren't exalting themselves. They were pushing themselves into the background." Billy Graham came onto the platform unnoticed, and although they were in front of the stand, "Billy Graham was just a small figure over there. He wasn't prominent at all. It was what he was saying that was so prominent."

The sermon reached Mrs. Spackman immediately. "I just knew that this was the answer to life." For Dr. Spackman the way was less sure: "Here was an intelligent man who believed the Bible. He kept saying 'The Bible says this', 'the Bible says that', and I didn't believe the Bible. . . . I realized if the Bible was what he said it was, then there was no element of doubt in it at all. But I was an ardent evolutionist. I couldn't believe in Adam and Eve or the Garden of Eden, or even the Resurrection or the Virgin Birth.

"I wasn't convicted of sin, because if you had told me that I was a miserable sinner I would probably have had a standing fight with you.

Billy mentioned sin of course, vice and corruption and crime and so on—he hammered that quite a lot—but that didn't worry me because I was a better man than my neighbor. That wasn't the thing. It was more, so far as I was concerned, getting to know this Someone that he preached about. I had never heard of Somebody Who died on a Cross for me. I never knew that anybody had died on the Cross for Dennis Spackman. I wanted to know this Person. Billy didn't scare me into the Kingdom of Heaven, he appealed to my common logic to taste and see. I hungered for it, but I had a few problems about the Bible to be disposed of first."

At the invitation, Mrs. Spackman had no hesitation. The doctor knew he wanted to go forward, but would have hesitated had he not heard Billy speak of taking one step at a time: "If God is only whispering to you, and if you can't even understand it, you had better come forward. Do it now."

The Spackmans left their seats. While waiting for a counselor the doctor thought the singing of "Just as I Am without One Plea," which he had never heard before, entirely appropriate and moving. Both were fortunate in their counselors. The doctor's was a schoolteacher and a member of the Open Brethren assembly on the North Shore. "He didn't start laying down the law, he didn't bail me up in a corner." Next week the counselor wrote a personal letter. This was much appreciated, for the Spackmans had run straight into difficulty.

They had entered on their decision cards the local Anglican church they never attended. The assistant clergyman of the church acknowledged receipt of the cards to the follow-up office, who naturally thereupon recorded the Spackmans as being "followed up by their minister." But all the clergyman did during a twenty-minute call "was to talk about his bunions, because I am a doctor. Billy Graham's name was not mentioned, and he never gave us one thing about Christianity." When they brought up the subject, "he sort of looked at us and turned back to his bunions. We were terribly upset."

The Spackmans decided to begin reading their Bibles. The follow-up literature was helpful, especially the notes and corrections when their first lesson was returned. "We were beginning to understand the Gospel. Within a week we realized we were sinners, and that it is by faith only that we are saved."

They went to the parish church "determined to do everything in our power to cooperate in going on in the Christian life."

Each Sunday they listened carefully to the sermon but found nothing to bite upon. "We would walk home disappointed, genuinely upset and disillusioned." The vicar came to tea or after-dinner coffee several times. "He deliberately undermined any belief in the Bible. We asked him key questions and all the way through he was very negative, and when Billy Graham would be mentioned, he would sort of shrug his shoulders. Often it wasn't what he said so much as what he didn't say." Because the Spackmans were eager to learn they organized a small Bible class in their home; the vicar sent them a Church Army captain to conduct it. "He was sincere, but it was a case of the blind leading the blind."

Of the crusade inquirers who were referred to their church, the Spackmans believe that they remain the only two active Christians. (Long research would be necessary to corroborate this conclusion.) On the basis of evidence from crusades all over the world many of those lost to sight because of an unsympathetic attitude of a church found a spiritual home elsewhere, sometimes after a temporary lapse.

The Spackmans themselves nearly fell away. Dennis Spackman had not yet reconciled intellectual problems with the growing daily evidence of a Christian experience. "We were getting ourselves hopelessly befuddled. Billy Graham had told us these things, and we believed them implicitly, yet here was a professional clergyman undermining it all. The time was coming when something had to crack."

At that point Dr. Spackman was invited to attend a Bible study meeting in the home of one of his patients. He found some thirty adults being taught with the aid of a blackboard by George Curle, a member of the Brethren. Week after week thereafter the Spackmans learned about the great Bible doctrines. Not surprisingly after the welcome they had received, the Spackmans left the Anglican church. They became Baptists, though the church work they have since undertaken in the midst of a thriving practice, and at considerable monetary sacrifice, has been interdenominational.

George Curle lent Dennis Spackman books "to satisfy the scientific mind, to bridge the gap from the extreme materialism which I had before. I didn't have to turn a blind eye or bury my head in the sand." He found that "if a man who has an intellectual problem with anything in the Bible is prepared to investigate it a little bit further, with somebody who can help him, the answers will be there. Christianity doesn't stifle the intellect, it encourages it to grow."

28 · *Sydney: The Pattern Crusade*

The Sydney crusade of four weeks in April and May 1959 was firmly consolidated as part of the continuing mission of the Church.

The crusade had been awaited since 1954, when the late Archbishop of Sydney and Primate of Australia, Howard Mowll, first approached Billy Graham. Mowll, a strong evangelical and a leader in the ecumenical movement, was so trusted by other denominations that virtually the entire Protestant Church community was officially committed to support. Archbishop Mowll died during 1958. His successor was Hugh Gough, Bishop of Barking, who had not yet arrived from England but who naturally endorsed the coming of Billy Graham. No less than 9,400 persons enrolled for counseling classes, a figure more than double that in New York, with its far greater population, though dwarfed by Los Angeles in 1963, which enrolled 23,000. Of the 6,000 people selected as counselors or advisers, over half were Anglicans, from 160 parishes.

However well led, the classes cannot entirely eliminate unwise, hasty or inappropriate counseling of inquirers. (A high-court judge in Sydney found himself counseled by his local tailor, who was too overawed to be of much use!) But the Australian crusades introduced a major and overdue development, the provision of specially trained counselors for children.

That numerous children under fifteen should come forward, often in groups, or because to a child any great service is inevitably emotionally charged, has been a source of criticism—criticism justified only if children's counseling and follow-up are left in inexperienced hands. Where there is a background of Christian teaching in home or school, the crusade will often be the focal point at which the child moves from unthinking acceptance to personal trust and allegiance. Even without this background, a crusade may be the start of a child's lasting and growing commitment, as the records of missionary and ministerial candidates show. On the other hand, scores of children at any crusade are bound to be confused, their coming forward representing no more than a desire to do what seems right, a groping response to the claims of Christ. Others simply follow their friends. Still others merely want a closer look at the evangelist.

All this represents a pastoral opportunity if properly followed up by sensitive and sympathetic counselors. The Scripture Union leaders in Melbourne had some initial difficulty in convincing the Americans that children need special care; Sydney improved upon Melbourne, and Brisbane upon Sydney. Charlie Riggs freely acknowledges, "A lot of the procedures of working with children came to us in Australia," and the children's department he set up has been improving its ideas and materials year by year since 1959.

Sydney taught the Graham Team a further new concept: the pre-crusade city-wide visitation—the intention being that every home in the entire city be visited by a church member bringing an invitation to attend the crusade. This, together with the enthusiasm generated by Sydney's "Men at Work" scheme (similar to the Co-Labor Corps), and the thousands of small prayer meetings in homes, and the press coverage from the Melbourne crusade, all raised expectancy to a high pitch. The Sydney press had been Billy's ally ever since his first press conference on his way to Melbourne, and it covered the crusade as no other event since the Queen's visit.[1]

Before Billy Graham arrived, Gordon Powell, minister of St. Stephen's, Sydney, the principal Presbyterian church of Australia, and vice-chairman of the crusade committee, made a prophecy: at the end of the crusade it would be said, "Never before in human history had one man preached the Gospel to so many in one place in so short a time, face to face." He was right: attendances reached just short of 1,000,000 (980,000) in four weeks. (In Los Angeles in 1963 Billy preached to 910,000 in a crusade lasting three days less.)

Yet on the first day of the Sydney Crusade, when 50,000 people came to the Royal Agricultural Society's Showground, few of the committee quite expected their "city of happy pagans" to show much response. Nearly 1,000 came forward, and so it continued day after day. From the platform it was "always deeply moving," writes Bishop Marcus Loane, "to watch the solemn audience suddenly break up when the invitation was given, like a giant human anthill stirred to life, as thousands rose from their seats in the arena or in the farthest

---

[1] Walter Argall, the crusade treasurer, particularly recalls Billy's answer to the last question at the airport press conference, "Are you looking for converts?" Billy answered, "Yes, certainly," and the pressmen came back, "Australians don't like the suggestion that they should be converted—it's old-fashioned." Billy claimed that *converted* was quite a contemporary word; in fact, he said he had been converted during his trip to Australia during the last two or three days: he had traveled by Qantas, he liked its comfort, its competence and the friendly service; if he was coming this way again, he would use Qantas—he had been converted to Qantas. "Conversion is simply a question of finding the right line and going with it." Even the police broke into grins.

stands to go forward." From the follow-up office at the top of the Members' Stand, with the whole arena in view, it looks "like the blowing of the wind across a field of wheat; this sudden movement in the vast crowd, and then the streams of seekers converging on the platform—like a movement of the breath of God." This movement was essentially an individual action: one here, another there, pushing past the row of friends or strangers to the aisle; then, at the platform (though a host of inquirers and counselors were all around) the convert conscious, as was often testified afterward, of no other people around. The prayer of committal would be repeated as if alone with God.

More than once heavy rain turned the Showground into a quagmire. Roy Gustafson, Billy's old friend of Florida days, had gone to Australia as his guest, "with some big question marks. Just because numbers are large is no proof that God is in it. Goliath was big. . . ." On the first Friday at Sydney rain fell intermittently during the service. At the invitation, "the rain came down like a tropical storm. You couldn't even see the people in the stands. They couldn't see the platform. We were under the marquee, fortunately, and I said to myself, 'Why don't you say *Amen* and let these people go, and trust the Holy Spirit to do the work?' And Billy started the appeal. I said to myself, 'He must be crazy. No one will come tonight.' But 1,700 people came, and stood in water and mud up to their ankles. I remember an official in one of the banks, a counselor, drenched to the skin, with half a dozen people under an umbrella, and he in the middle standing with a Bible. Water was coming through in a fine mist and ruining the Bible, but he was pointing the half dozen to the Savior. That night I was absolutely convinced that God had laid His hand on Billy."

Billy Graham wrote that week: "I feel that I am a spectator watching the Spirit of God at work. It is beyond our control. 'This is the day the Lord hath made; let us rejoice and be glad in it.' " Alex Gilchrist, the crusade committee's secretary, sensed as they drove back each evening to the Wentworth Hotel that Billy was "tired physically but rejoicing in what he'd seen God doing; and he seemed like a man that wanted to spend much time with the Lord." Billy's times of prayer, alone in his room from mid-afternoon until the service, were inviolate. In Sydney, however, with his health almost normal and the eye causing no trouble, Graham could put much into personal interviews. He spent many hours with Gordon Powell, who despite being vice-chairman of the crusade, and despite his prediction, had been little more than a benevolent neutral at the beginning. Powell's attitude had quickly become more positive. Although one of Australia's most famous preachers, he was not ashamed to acknowledge, during the crusade and after, Billy Graham's influence on his preaching. They talked together about the authority of Scripture and the importance of decisive evangelism. "I realized," says Powell, "that evangelism was his 'magnificent obsession.' He turned every subject back to evangelism sooner or later." As often with Graham, the gain of that talk was mutual. "I got a great deal from him," Graham comments, "and we became very close personal friends."

Graham met press and television men, public figures from the governor downward, and an old Dutch immigrant dying of cancer, in poverty, split apart from his family because they could not find a home. A reporter said the man had expressed a wish to hear Billy Graham before he died. Billy called on him and, relates Gilchrist, "had the joy of leading him to Christ. As the result of a special plea made in one of the meetings, Christian friends found a home for this man and his family, and so he ended his days a few weeks later in happiness and peace."

The crusade treasurer, Walter Argall, was badly injured in a car smash returning from the Showground. When the night sister of the danger-list ward hurried in and said, "Dr. Graham wants to see you," the distraught Argall thought it was yet another medical inspection. "And then I heard a long striding step coming down the corridor into the room. Billy said, 'Well now, Walter, you know all these things happen for a purpose, and behind this God will have something for you,' and so on, in quite a loud voice, until I was a little disturbed as to the condition of the other patients. Then he prayed, and it was a prayer for me, and for everybody in the locality."

As Billy strode out of the room a patient said in a voice of disgust, "Ah! get to sleep!" In the morning Argall apologized. Another man answered, "You're wrong. I haven't been able to sit up since I've been here, but I got my ears clear of the pillows and I listened, and it was for me, and I liked it—I wanted it. I feel all of us are of the same mind." There was a chorus of approval. Argall renewed his apology to the patient who had said, "Get to sleep." The patient replied, "You're wrong. I wanted to stop him as he went past my bed. If any disgust was in my voice, it was that I didn't do it. Because what he had to say was for me."

The Sydney crusade shook the city even more than the earlier crusade had shaken Melbourne. It reached many society leaders, men and women, who previously would have been embarrassed, amused, or indignant at any suggestion that they would walk forward among the inquirers.[1]

Billy Graham reached the working man, too, but only where the local clergy were prepared to work on the assumption that he would.

Ken Childs, a young Anglican minister, had lately gone to a weak parish of railwaymen and car factory workers. "The clergy of the district had grave doubts as to whether Billy Graham was really going to touch the working men, but I looked upon this opportunity as one given to us by God, and started to 'talk' the crusade as much as possible." Despite perfunctory interest or open criticism wherever he visited, Childs arranged bus loads every night, and soon learned that his parishioners' mistrust of organized Christianity, their belief that the Christian faith is tepid and weak-kneed, dissolved on hearing Billy Graham. "The overall impression that Billy gave was of a man utterly sincere, who is really speaking with the voice of God. Authority is the word. This is what the working man is looking for because he is used to it. The Crusade meetings gave them an opportunity to look over the fence at the Christian faith, an opportunity we can rarely give in the local parish setting."

Ken Childs shaped his whole parish work around the crusade. For every working man who went forward, dozens stayed uncommitted though convinced that here was real Christianity. . . . Where the Church failed to follow on from that point, these people didn't become Christians. His own congregation's numbers grew from 60 to 200 in the next five years.

Billy Graham has been criticized for failing to make an impact on the dockers, the core of lower class secularism in Sydney. Ken Childs, though he wished Graham could have gone among them more, and to more factories, would say that the criticism was misdirected: "Where the Church was awake, the crusade showed that people weren't really against the churches as we thought."

Graham has been criticized also for failing to indicate more precisely the relevance of Christianity to the Australian economic and social situation. Yet he touched on social concerns in every sermon, whether on the right use of sex, on the Christian view of marriage (outstanding was his sermon on marriage and the home) and on economic ethics. Mr. Justice Richardson recalls a man who had secured

[1] Joe Blinco, conducting follow-up Bible classes in a shed at the Showground before a crusade service, was told by one wealthy woman that she was learning about Jesus Christ in the exact place where her cattle had been stalled during the Agricultural Show!

an unfair advantage in a contract: "On being converted at the crusades he went immediately to the other party and handed over a check to restore equity and good conscience."

Whether Graham, however, is to attack specific blemishes of a country where he is a guest raises a delicate question, which was underscored by two trivial incidents in 1959. Grady Wilson, preaching in Perth, Western Australia, said that on Anzac Day he had never seen so many drunks in his life. The comment was splashed across the eastern papers, and Billy was at once on the line: "You cannot say that! We're guests here." Six weeks later Graham in London (where he had a long private talk with the Queen) made his famous and apt comment to the press, "It looks as though your parks have been turned into bedrooms." In the ensuing uproar Grady felt the score was even.

At the final service of the Sydney crusade, on May 10, 1959, no less than 150,000 people were present: 80,000 in the Showground and 70,000 in the adjoining Cricket Ground, linked by amplifiers. It was estimated that a further one million Australians listened either by landline or by the live radio broadcast. There was an exciting added touch to the service when the two choirs, one of 1,500, the other of 2,000, with Bev Shea sang "How great Thou art" in alternate verses, one from the Showground, the next from the Cricket Ground. Billy preached on "The Broad and the Narrow Way," and the inquirers streamed forward. Gilchrist saw Billy on the platform "absolutely overwhelmed." "What a sight! what a sight!" Billy repeated, "to see these hundreds coming through the rain. You who are in the Cricket Ground, you come forward too. Come and stand around the fences, and you who are listening to the landline relays, come and stand at the front of the auditorium where you are"; 5,683 people made decisions. "The thanksgiving prayer in the follow-up room," writes the follow-up committee chairman, "when all the cards had come in and were being processed, was unforgettable."

The Sydney crusade and its climax had stirred all Australia. The associate crusade followed, with Billy traveling across the continent to conclude them—Perth (Grady Wilson), Adelaide (Blinco), and Brisbane (Ford), where a weary but happy Graham preached his final sermon in Australia.

The effectiveness of these brief associate crusades varied according to the unity and thoroughness of local preparation and follow-up.

But, as Gordon Powell puts it succinctly and, by the evidence, accurately, "The whole country was rocked by the Graham phenomenon." Owing to Australia's unique distribution of population, a majority living in and around five big cities, it is probable that 50 per cent of the country heard Billy Graham in person or through landlines, and almost all the rest at least once on radio or by television. Indeed, Graham's own opinion is that it "was through television that we most touched the major cities of Australia."

Australia had never previously known a nationwide religious revival. The total figure of those who signified a committal to Christ in the crusade exceeded 130,000—no less than 1.24 per cent of the population. John Robinson of Melbourne wrote to Billy: "This must represent such a flood of new life and power into our whole religious force, which will surely go on to challenge the ungodliness and immorality about us." Five years later Robinson was sure (and Sydney men agreed) that the crusade had proved no flash in the pan: "I believe that in a very real sense, and to quite a degree, this nation came to a place of repentance." Robinson believes, too, that Australia, a great bastion of Christianity in the Far East, a nation with the Gospel in its hands, accepted a new responsibility "for the people to our North. The impetus given to the work on the mission field is being felt more today than immediately following the crusade, for wherever you go you meet converts now in missionary service."

Britain's failure, in the years following 1955, to maintain momentum or to reap the full harvest was not repeated in Australia. In Sydney, with its 56,780 decisions, the work of the crusade was integrated into the continuing mission of the Church, with a new emphasis on evangelism and a new conviction of the power of the Christian gospel. "It has been a thrilling experience here," wrote Archbishop Gough to Graham on July 22, 1959, "to come across so many people who have entered into spiritual life through your crusade. Literally thousands of men and women are now being built up in the fellowship of our Anglican churches, and I had the great joy the other Sunday of confirming as many as 350 in the Cathedral."

In the year following the crusade the Archbishop confirmed 1,000. In 1964 he stated: "As I go round I'm constantly finding men in positions of leadership in the parishes who are crusade converts." The Anglican theological college had a steady influx. On December 20, 1962, the principal, Dr. D. B. Knox, wrote to Graham that out of 100 then in residence, eight "attributed their conversion and spiritual awakening directly to the campaign, six others regarded the campaign, whether by way of attendance or counseling, as directly contributing to their call to the ministry."

Gordon Powell's church, St. Stephen's Presbyterian, had 646 people referred to them and took 404 new members on to the communion roll—believed to be a world record for instant growth in a single church. Six of the new members were prominent Sydney doctors. Two years later Powell found that more than half the new members of 1959 were regular and enthusiastic churchmen. Nearly a quarter had dropped away but, as in the Parable of the Sower, the good seed sown in the good ground was bringing forth a harvest that more than made up for that which was lost. In 1964 Powell could state categorically, "The lasting impact on the churches which cooperated, such as St. Stephen's, is unquestioned."

The continuing influence of the crusade was shown by the response to the follow-up mission of Leighton Ford and Joe Blinco in 1961, and to the sacred concert tour by Cliff Barrows, Bev Shea and Ted Smith in 1965. Another evidence is the high listener rating of the *Hour of Decision,* and the flood of correspondence which descends on the *Hour of Decision* Australian office when a television crusade is shown. Furthermore, the ordinary membership work of the churches has continuously brought in men, women, and young people who attest that the crusade was a first step in their pilgrimage.

The crusade of 1959 has a further and wider significance for those who will face it. This has been well expressed by the chairman of the Sydney follow-up committee, Harry Orr: "It settled, as far as this generation is concerned, the effect of mass evangelism. I do not think that anybody can deny the very evident results, and the place of mass evangelism in the program of the church."

V

The New Age
1960-

---

29 · Election Year, 1960

An unfriendly American book about Graham asserted in 1960: "On the whole it now looks as if Billy Graham's revivals have lost their luster." The Australian crusades are dismissed in one line and a footnote.[1]

Graham had long before reflected upon—even with relief—the prospect of being returned to comparative obscurity. He therefore commented to the critic: "I am not sure what the Lord has in the future. I am willing to be His man in whatever department of His kingdom He wants to thrust me. I have no personal aims." But the book's dire assessment of Graham's future was as quickly proved wrong as similar pronouncements in the past. In the new age of sputniks and astronauts, of increasing racial and international strife, of ferment in thought and morality, Billy Graham's influence and stature increased, however much his views and achievement might be debated.

The nineteen-sixties began, for the Graham Team, with the Africa tour from January to March. The timing was fortunate: when Gra-

---

[1] P. 223 of *Billy Graham: Revivalist in a Secular Age*, by William G. McLoughlin, Jr., New York, 1960. Apart from factual errors and quotes taken out of context, the book is weakened by denigration of motives and the imputation to Graham of a craftiness which even the strongest opponents who have personal knowledge would not recognize in him. A student of the book should check back on its source materials to which the author supplies references.

ham two years earlier had accepted the African invitation in preference to others, it was not obvious that early 1960 would be the last opportunity for such meetings, before gathering political storms would make it impossible to organize them in many of the lands he planned to visit.

Graham went at the request of nationals and Christian councils, not merely of missionaries. Every meeting was integrated. "Because of the race problem," Graham wrote to the managing editor of *Life,* "we have turned down an urgent invitation from the churches of South Africa. We feel it will be a greater sermon to them leaving out South Africa from our itinerary." Nor would he fly via Johannesburg, the fastest route from Nigeria to Southern Rhodesia, because in that city the Negro member of the Team, Howard Jones, would have met difficulties.

Beyond the direct impact of the integrated meetings, the African tour had important incidental results. One was the prize-winning documentary in color produced by Dick Ross, *Africa on the Bridge.*[1] It was designed less to feature the achievements of the Team than to bring to the home countries an understanding of Africa and to evoke a missionary response. Another useful result was the opening of Ethiopia to large scale evangelistic meetings, previously prevented by the Coptic Church, although Protestant missionary work had long been permitted. Beavan and Riggs on their advance tour found a discouraged committee which had been refused permission for a meeting in the capital city, Addis Ababa. A cable from Graham to the Emperor had not been shown to him. After a prayer meeting, the Americans were about to leave for another country when fortunately they met a Norwegian businessman named Mosvold who knew Billy and who had an invitation to dine with the Emperor that evening. Mosvold volunteered to talk with Haile Selassie about Billy. As a result of Mosvold's intervention the Emperor put his own Royal Stadium at Graham's disposal and ordered the schools to be closed all day so that every child over twelve could attend the morning meeting. Graham later spent ninety minutes with the Emperor, who invited him to hold a crusade throughout Ethiopia. Howard Jones and the singer Bob Harrison, another Negro member of the Graham Team, have since held two crusades in Ethiopia.

Wherever Graham went in Africa, as in other parts of the world, national and political leaders received him warmly. And always he presented Christ's claim upon their personal allegiance.

[1] Winner of the Golden Reel Award for Documentary Films, 1960.

Graham recognizes that sovereigns and prime ministers, the world over, seldom are faced directly with spiritual matters. In Africa or Asia, especially, a national clergyman who is received in audience is cautious. A missionary is inhibited by his status as a guest in the land, and a foreign church leader must use his brief audience to discuss the specific local problems or needs of the Christian community. Graham, as soon as preliminary courtesies are finished, takes the first opening to explain why he has come. Then, following the example of Paul the Apostle before King Agrippa, he begins by telling how he met the risen Christ Who transformed his life: "I'm not perfect, but I believe I have a resource of power and joy and peace that will take me even into the face of death. I have seen people everywhere having this same experience, and it is available to anyone."

It was when he used such words that Pundit Nehru, who had sat glum through the early part of their meeting in New Delhi in 1956, began to ask questions and became alert. "When," Graham says, "you make it personal about yourself and apply it to the other man, and then take a few incidents from the life of Christ, I've found that very few are not interested." Of all the leaders Graham has visited, throughout the world, only one, the Moslem ruler of a then self-governing state within Nigeria, has been resentful; he stated in no uncertain terms that he did not need Christ.

More often Graham is told that he is the first clergyman who has talked to them about spiritual matters on an intimate level. On one tour the ruler of a great power, who spent a long time discussing the Bible with Graham, remarked that clergymen never seemed to raise these subjects in personal conversation, and told him how refreshing it had been. Even then Graham had wondered whether in this instance he had gone too far, but has been proved wrong by subsequent conversations.

As Graham comments: "Whether the story of Christ is told in a huge stadium, across the desk of some powerful leader, or shared with a golfing companion, it satisfies a common hunger. All over the world, whenever I meet people face to face, I am made aware of this personal need among the famous and successful as well as the lonely and obscure."

During the summer and autumn of 1960 Graham was almost fully engaged in Europe. The only crusades in the United States that year were short: a week in June at Washington, D.C., and three days at

Madison Square Garden in October for Spanish-speaking New Yorkers.

While preaching in Switzerland (a week each in Berne, Basel and Lausanne, and two days in Zurich) Billy and his family lived near Lausanne in a house lent by the Swiss-Armenian financier, Ara Tchividjian. In 1955 Tchividjian had picked up a copy of *Peace With God* and "found the answer for a lifetime of searching. . . . After I made my decision, God kept His word, Jesus Christ became my Savior and my Lord, and I saw the evidence of this new life in my thoughts, my desires, my actions. My family must have seen it too, for one by one they followed me in this decision. All seven of them." His eldest son, Stephan, met Virginia (Gigi) Graham during this visit. In 1963 they were married, and in 1964 they made Billy Graham a grandfather at forty-five.

After Switzerland the Graham Team passed to Germany. Of the three 1960 German crusades the week at Berlin proved historical, for the great tent was pitched at the Brandenburg Gate, less than a year before the building of the Berlin Wall. Without the Wall, East Berliners were able to stream across, despite tank movements, police interrogation and the campaign of hate against Billy in the East Berlin press. The Communist newspapers repeated their old charge that he frequented night clubs, and added an embellishment: he was accompanied, they said, by a "blonde called Beverly Shea!" They accused him of attacking communism. But in Berlin he refused to speak against it, although his conviction that communism is an evil force, bent on destroying the political and spiritual foundations of the West, was already known. Instead Graham was able to read publicly a telegram of greeting from the leaders of the Baptist Church in Moscow which he had visited as a tourist in 1959.

Special precautions were taken to prevent police reprisals on inquirers from East Berlin. These were told not to give their addresses, but only the name of their pastor. Lists of inquirers were carried across the line each night by several pastors as they returned, so that if one pastor were stopped by the police, searched, and the list confiscated, others would get through. The lists were then sorted, and parish clergy would shortly receive a plain postcard suggesting a visit to this or that parishioner; each clergyman knew why. Correspondence follow-up was not feasible.

The final meeting, on a warm early October day, was held in the open in the immediate shadow of the Reichstag. On the façade of the

Reichstag are engraved the words, "To the German People." On the crusade banner, hung behind the platform, was woven a text. By a coincidence of perspective, most of the audience saw the stone inscription and the text of the banner one above the other, and many people commented on the aptness of the message: *"To the German People* Jesus said, I am the Way, the Truth, and the Life."

In the course of his address, which Peter Schneider translated sentence by sentence, Graham said: "We stand at the center of history, in front of this historic Reichstag. If Germany has a mighty spiritual awakening and the people turn to God, we may have another mighty Reformation that can sweep throughout the world. And my plea to you today is that you come to a strong belief in the Bible as the Word of God. Martin Luther was reading this Book when God spoke to him, and it changed the course of history. You come back to this Book, begin to read it, study it, and God will speak to you and, through you, perhaps history can be changed. . . . I believe the young people of this generation who cannot remember much about the war are searching for something to believe in. They are looking for a slogan that they can say. They are searching for a flag to follow. They want a leader to follow. Let that leader be Christ. Let that flag be the Christian flag. Let the slogan of the German people be Christ; and if that happens, Germany can lead the world spiritually."

Graham remained abroad for much of 1960 because he did not wish to become involved in a partisan way in the Nixon-Kennedy presidential campaign.

Had he returned, his involvement somehow would have become almost inevitable. His position as a Christian statesman has earned him the highest respect of government leaders. These found that on his travels across the United States and abroad Graham assessed the public mind accurately, that he was forthright and honest in stating his conclusions on current affairs. The former Vice-President, Richard M. Nixon, though he respects as right Graham's determination never to leave his spiritual ministry, refers to the qualities that would have made Graham an able President of the United States: Graham is a conciliator; he is a skilled picker of men; he has great administrative ability and he is decisive; he has a wide understanding of foreign affairs and he can absorb documents rapidly. To correct his areas of weakness he will draw freely on the advice of experts. "He is adept at picking up from the other man what he knows, and he has almost a photographic memory." As a background to these qualities Graham has his sense of history. Mr. Nixon writes: [1] "I could tell in my conversations with him that he was a great student of history, and consequently he was able to evaluate current events with rare perspective and insight. This is one of the reasons his predictions of political trends usually prove to be strikingly accurate."

During the Eisenhower years Graham visited the White House many times for serious discussion. The former President writes: [2] "For years I have know the Reverend Billy Graham and have enjoyed every visit I have had with him. As I see him, he is a man who is both a devoted Christian and an evangelist who can relate his basic spiritual beliefs to the tough problems of the day.

"One of the reasons that I have valued my contacts with him is because of his out-giving personality. He is an interesting conversationalist, and one can easily feel his devotion to the higher things of life and his deep faith in the Bible and its teachings. Frankly, I think that both by word and action he has been a splendid influence in the United States—indeed in other areas of the world also—and I most sincerely hope that he will remain active for many years to continue the work to which he has dedicated his life."

Most of Graham's political friends are Democrats. Among them, however, the closest is Richard Nixon, the Republican Presidential candidate in 1960.[3] In the strong conviction that Nixon would make the better President, Graham personally was for Nixon.

Before Billy left for Europe he was urged by Nixon not to come out for him publicly, despite the help it would be, "because your ministry is more important than my getting elected President." On August 10 Billy Graham wrote a letter, marked strictly confidential, to John F. Kennedy from Switzerland in which he denied the rumor circulating in the Democratic party that he intended to raise the religious issue publicly during the presidential campaign. On the con-

[1] In a letter to the author, October 5, 1965. The other points were made in an interview with the author in New York, December 1964.

[2] Letter of General of the Army Dwight D. Eisenhower to the author, dated Palm Desert, California, February 8, 1965.

[3] Once after a golf round with Mr. Nixon at the Burning Tree Country Club near Washington, Billy was having a shower when President Eisenhower, who had been playing in an earlier foursome, sent for him. The President, in full decorations, in preparation for a state dinner to the President of Mexico, chatted in the dressing room for fifteen minutes with a Billy who was wearing a towel.

trary, he commended Kennedy for facing it squarely and courageously. He would probably vote for Vice-President Nixon for several reasons, including a longstanding personal friendship, and was sure Kennedy would understand. If Kennedy should be elected President, Graham promised to do all in his power to help unify the American people behind him. "In the event of your election you will have my wholehearted support."

Graham did not publicly endorse the controversial conference of evangelical clergy which met during the electoral campaign, at Washington, but its sponsors, who knew of his personal feelings for Nixon, had Graham's private encouragement, for he felt that the religious issue must be lifted out of the gutter into which it had fallen. It was Graham who encouraged Dr. Norman Vincent Peale to attend.

Graham returned to America early in October, from Berlin, for the three-day crusade to Spanish-speaking New Yorkers. He declined to comment on the religious issue to the press. When, however, he called on Henry R. Luce and mentioned his wish that he could testify to Nixon's merits without being partisan or revealing which way he himself would vote, Luce suggested that it might be better done in a magazine article rather than on television; if Graham decided to write an article, *Life* would of course be glad to publish it. Graham hesitated; the pull to help Nixon was at odds with his right instinct to stay out for the sake of his ministry to all Americans regardless of party.

Back at Montreat he dictated an article. Luce was delighted and on the telephone said he would feature it in the coming issue, two weeks before the election. Graham then replied: "I'm not happy about that article. My wife is totally against it." On Luce's insistence he agreed to let it stand.

"On Thursday night—the night *Life* magazine goes to press—Ruth and I got on our knees and prayed, 'O God, if it is not Your will for this article to go—stop it!' " On Friday morning Governor Hodges (Democrat) of North Carolina called on the telephone and asked if the rumor about an article were true: "It's getting you into politics and you've stayed out of politics." Half an hour later another Democrat, Graham's close friend Governor Frank Clement of Tennessee called, and said, "I'll love you no matter what you do, but I hope you don't publish it."

Governor Clement had no sooner left the line than Mr. Luce called to say that at midnight he had pulled the article. Senator Kennedy had called him up, protesting the proposed Graham article, and asking Luce to see one of the Kennedy staff, who had suggested that it would be only fair to wait a week and run a parallel article about Kennedy by another prominent Protestant clergyman.

"Mr. Luce," said Billy, "I'm so relieved I feel like shouting. Let me write another article on Why Every Christian Should Vote."

Luce was not interested. Billy insisted he would write it anyway. The article appeared in the *Life* issue dated November 7—"We are Electing a President of the World."

The narrowness of the voting has led many in retrospect to conclude that Billy Graham's original article, in a magazine of such wide circulation, might have swung the election to Nixon.

Graham's support for Nixon took one public form only—when he led in prayer at a Nixon rally in Columbia, South Carolina, at the urgent request of former Governor James Byrnes, one-time Secretary of State, who insisted (quite wrongly) that the gesture would not be interpreted as public endorsement but merely as an act of personal friendship.

Soon after his election John F. Kennedy invited Graham to meet him in Florida to play golf together. The engagement had to be canceled because the Kennedy's son John was born the previous night, but it was renewed five days before Kennedy's inauguration, when the two men had a vigorous exchange of thought, the first of several conversations in a developing friendship, in which religious matters were constantly among the subjects discussed. At President Kennedy's funeral service in the cathedral Graham was invited by Robert Kennedy to the seats reserved for the late President's personal friends.

Lyndon Baines Johnson and Billy Graham are friends of long standing. President Johnson is the great-grandson of the evangelist Baines who led General Sam Houston, the Texas hero, to Christ. Since 1963 Graham has stayed several times with the President, who has written warm appreciation of his counsel and prayers. When Graham, after the Denver crusade of September 1965, was in the Mayo Clinic for the removal of stones from his prostate gland, the President called him by telephone four times. Billy was being attended by a little Filipino nurse when the nurses' supervisor came in to say the White House was on the line. Billy picked up the bedside telephone and after the President and he had talked a while, Billy said, "Mr. President, I have a lovely little Filipino nurse standing by my bedside who has been taking excellent care of me." "Put her on the phone," said the President.

30 · The Race Question

On Inauguration Day 1965, at the invitation of President Johnson, Billy Graham preached at a special and unprecedented interdenominational service in the National City Christian Church, Washington, before the President, the Vice-President-elect, members of the cabinet and their families, the governors of all fifty states and the mayors of the hundred largest cities of America.

In his sermon Billy Graham spoke to the nation as being "abundantly endowed with material blessings, but . . . in danger of losing its moral moorings and its spiritual perspective. Christ, in Whom are hid all the treasures of wisdom, said, 'What shall it profit a man, if he shall gain the whole world, and lose his own soul?' This applies to nations as well as to individuals, for a nation that loses its spiritual courage will grow old before its time. Even if we gain all our material and social objectives, but lose our souls, it would be disastrous. . . . I know the leaders of this administration well enough to know that they believe that our problems are basically spiritual and that they require a spiritual solution."

These words before the President epitomize Graham's concern and perception on social issues—an area in which he has been the object of continual criticism.

He admits that since 1949 "my belief in the social implications of the Gospel has deepened and broadened. . . . I am convinced that faith without works is dead." But he has "never felt that the accusations against me of having no social concern were valid."

The accusations are made by those who have not much *listened* to Graham. On the other hand Joe Blinco, whom no one has ever accused of not having an acute social conscience, has listened much. And he states that Graham's preaching "is deeply socially involved. It strikes at the root of the social situation, which is the unsaved and therefore the unsocial state of the human heart without Christ. Billy hits at the root of the matter here. Secondly, in his own country, he goes right down the line about morality in government, morality in business, morality in race relations, morality inside the family, morality in unions. I have heard Billy spell this out as clearly and as definitively as anybody ever has—at a personal level, at a communal level, at a national level—spelling out the social righteousness of the Gospel and the social righteousness as seen in the prophets."

This is not enough for those who replace the Biblical concept of a prophet—whose preaching of social righteousness is in the context of repentance and faith—by a different conception, that of a religious man primarily concerned to change the social order by social and political action. *The Christian Century* in 1959 lumped Graham together with Pope John, Bishop Fulton Sheen, Norman Vincent Peale and Oral Roberts, and dismissed them as each having "steered clear of advocacy of prophetic Christianity." There is also the charge against Graham by churchmen whose real complaint is that he is not a nuclear disarmer, a pacifist, or soft on communism, or a socialist in political views.

A lack of social content in Graham's preaching is regularly asserted by Unitarians and by others who reject the need and reality of the new birth. Graham, however, is "more convinced than ever before," as he wrote for *The Christian Century,* "that we must change men before we can change society. . . . The task of the evangelist is not merely to reform but to stimulate conversion, for conversion puts man in positions where God can do for him, and through him, what he is incapable of doing for or by himself." [1]

In his early days Graham tended to think that if a man were converted he would soon know how to put the world to rights—that men, money and push could transform entire nations. As he grew older he learned that being born again does not make a man an expert in economics or politics or in the multifarious disciplines needed in a modern state. But as Graham's perceptions grew more precise, his conviction was strengthened that the primary task of the Church is not social but redemptive, to proclaim Christ, Who alone can change men. As he writes in *World Aflame* (1965), "We have been trying to solve every ill of society as though society were made up of regenerate men to whom we had an obligation to speak with Christian advice. . . . If the church went back to its main task of preaching the Gospel and getting people converted to Christ, it would have far more impact on the social structure of the nation."

His own ministry he sees as narrowly specialized: that of an evangelist, in the strictly New Testament use of the word, who so preaches the good news of Jesus Christ that men trust in Him as Savior, one by one or in crowds, but each by individual repentance and committal. Just as the early apostles, refusing to "leave the Word of God, and serve tables," would not be diverted to the economic needs

[1] "What Ten Years Have Taught Me," published in *The Christian Century,* February 17, 1960. I have worked from the original unedited script, dictated late in 1959.

of widows, yet did not fail to arrange for their care, so Billy Graham
has kept steadily to his primary task of bringing others to the point of
new birth, yet has stimulated thousands to serve the bodily and social
needs of humanity.

Billy Graham insists that Christians have two responsibilities:
"One, to proclaim the Gospel of Jesus Christ as the only answer to
man's deepest needs. Two, to apply as best we can the principles of
Christianity to the social conditions around us." He fulfills the second
responsibility continually in his newspaper column (hence *My Answer* [1960] is a mine of Christian ethics), in his radio and other
sermons, and by his comments on current affairs, where he has the
advantage of being one of the best informed American churchmen
because statesmen and leaders of governments at home and abroad
value his opinion and trust his discretion.

In contrast to the views of critics, the feelings of the average American toward Graham were well expressed by Governor John Connally
of Texas in a speech of October 31, 1963, three weeks before he was
shot and wounded beside President Kennedy: "Billy Graham is more
than a preacher, more than an evangelist, more than a Christian
leader. In a greater sense, he has become our conscience."

Graham's attitude and action on social issues may best be exam-
ined in relation to the race question: any genuine inquirer as to Graham's worth to his fellow men should look squarely at his record.

Since the New Orleans and Nashville (1954) crusades Billy Graham has kept to his intention of never again holding a segregated
meeting. While Northern churchmen who would later march in the
South were still silent and inactive, Graham was making a definite
contribution to racial reconciliation. At Richmond, Virginia, in 1956,
a white who had enrolled as an usher heard that Negroes were to sit
where they liked. "To hell with your revival!" he said as he threw in
his badge and resigned. Before the first week was over he had made a
commitment to Christ. He soon asked if he might regain his usher's
job. "You know," remarked a rich young white to Graham at Oklahoma City during the crusade of June–July 1956, "you said one night
that it would make a difference in the way you look at the race problem. I came forward last Monday night, and it's already made a
difference."

Graham at this time was becoming more certain than ever that the
problem was fundamentally moral and spiritual. Attempts to force a
change of view on either side of a racial minority, whether in America, India or elsewhere, merely deepen prejudice. "But if," Graham

urges, "you go and preach the love of Christ and the transforming power of Christ, there is not only a spiritual change but a psychological and moral change that takes place in a man who receives Christ, and he forgets all about race when he's giving his life to Christ."

Graham did not only preach and state his views in magazines.[1] During the spring of 1956, after President Eisenhower had talked with him at the White House in March, he went quietly to work among religious leaders of both races in the South, encouraging them individually to take a stronger stand for desegregation and yet to demonstrate charity and patience. He advocated, a year after the Montgomery bus boycott but three years before the lunch counter sit-ins, the ending of all segregation in public transportation, restaurants and hotels. "During the past few weeks," he reported to President Eisenhower on June 4, 1956, "I have addressed a number of annual Protestant religious conferences. I have also spoken at Negro universities. On each occasion I have laid before them what I consider to be a sensible program for bettering race relations. I believe the Lord is helping us, and if the Supreme Court will go along slowly and the extremists on both sides will quiet down, we can have a peaceful social readjustment over the next ten years."

By these approaches, as well as by his crusades, Billy Graham was doing more than Northerners who pointed out the faults of the South from their ivory towers and, at that time, ignored discrimination in their own cities. Graham had taken up the position regarding race which he has maintained consistently: conciliate, and strike at the roots of the problem, which is basically spiritual. As an evangelist to all America he would not become a partisan for one or other side in the strife, and thus was abused by both. Supremacists held him a traitor to the South; extremists who wished to rush integration and civil rights considered that he dragged his feet. Moderates in the South, especially the numerous local ministers who have not yet received proper acknowledgment for their work of restraint when community tensions rose, were encouraged by Billy Graham's example and by his insistence that integration must advance in love, hand in hand with conciliation. Southern churchmen who tried to avoid the racial issue were goaded into facing it by the inescapable attitude of their fellow-Southerner Billy Graham, who in the middle nineteen-fifties was far ahead of his own denomination's position on race. And it is signifi-

[1] His article in *Life* magazine, October 1, 1956, was the earliest of several he has written on the subject in national magazines.

cant that the leading Negro magazines, such as *Ebony* and *Jet-Age,* always write favorably of his work.

In the summer of 1957 the name of Little Rock was blazoned round the world. Billy Graham, in addition to public statements, worked behind the scenes for peace. "Among the Southern clergymen who moved forward most resolutely," commented *Newsweek* (October 7, 1959), "was, characteristically, the Rev. Billy Graham." He offered a full, integrated crusade. Plans were drawn up, but a year later had to be postponed. The local Little Rock Committee, Graham told Beavan, "felt it would be impossible under present conditions to hold a meeting."

The Team's five-week Charlotte crusade in the fall of 1958 was a clear contribution to race relations. More Negroes attended than at any time since Graham had stopped segregated crusades. When someone expressed surprise to a white woman inquirer who had been counseled by a Negro, she replied: "Why, I didn't even realize that she was a Negro. I had not even noticed the color of her skin." On the evening after the crusade, Graham was to go to South Carolina for an evangelistic rally at Columbia. Because he insisted that it should be integrated, the only possible site was the statehouse grounds. Governor George B. Timmerman immediately announced that permission would not be given to the "well-known integrationist"; the rally, the governor said, would also violate the separation of Church and State. Graham replied, "I am certain no citizen would object to people being won to Christ on the capitol grounds." As for Church and State, his sponsors pointed out that Graham had already, in 1950, addressed the legislature inside the statehouse. The governor answered that this was before Graham's anti-segregationist stand. He would leave it to Graham's "conscience whether he would trespass on state property."

The general in command of the nearby Fort Jackson military base then invited Graham to hold the rally there. Sixty thousand attended, the first nonsegregated mass meeting in South Carolina's history. Dr. John Sutherland Bonnell of New York wrote to Graham: "The stand you took was very courageous and I believe truly Christian. Even *The Christian Century* had to take off its hat to you! I know that such a stand cost you a great deal in the matter of relations with some of the brethren in the South, but God will be able to use you even more effectively as the result." The extreme Northern liberals, however, misunderstanding Graham's work for conciliation, grumbled that he ought to have stood fast on the capitol steps, thereby rebuking the governor and risking a riot; besides, he had given a special platform seat to former Governor James Byrnes, a leader of the opposition to integration, and had not talked about segregation in his address.

Shortly before this, the integrated high school at Clinton, Tennessee, had been destroyed by a bomb. Drew Pearson, the well-known newspaper columnist, took the initiative of raising a fund for rebuilding. "It was rather difficult at that time," states Mr. Pearson, "because there was a lot of fear and a lot of opposition to integration. Among the few Southerners who did join enthusiastically was Billy Graham, who had taken a courageous stand." Graham served on the executive committee of Pearson's rebuilding fund, "The Americans Against Bombs of Bigotry," and on Sunday December 14, 1958, he addressed an integrated meeting of about 5,000 persons in the undamaged gymnasium of the bombed high school. "A very fine and inspiring sermon," was Drew Pearson's estimation. In his address Graham urged tolerance, forgiveness, cool heads and warm hearts; "hot heads and cold hearts never solved anything." As a Southerner he urged that neither integration nor segregation be allowed "to become our Gospel. Our Gospel must be Jesus Christ and the Cross." When at the close he gave the invitation, nearly two minutes passed before anyone responded. Then a young mother with a toddler in her arms went forward. Soon scores were coming forward, including a white racist who had vowed to wreck the meeting.

Little Rock became open to Billy Graham at last in September 1959, for two rallies. A week that had begun with yet another bombing incident ended with crusade meetings in War Memorial Stadium, which led the committee chairman, the Reverend W. O. Vaught, Jr., pastor of Immanuel Baptist Church, to write to Graham a week later: "There has been universal agreement in all the churches and out across the city that your visit here was one of the finest things that ever happened in the history of Little Rock. So very many people have changed their attitude, so many people have washed their hearts of hatred and bitterness, and many made decisions who had never expected to make such decisions." Six years later Dr. Vaught endorsed his verdict on Graham. "The influence of this good man," he writes, "was a real factor in the solution of our racial problems here in Little Rock."

Little Rock provides a prime example of Billy's message, that only Christ can turn racial hate into love, in the person of one of its inhabitants—Jimmy Karam. In 1957 Karam was a forty-four-year-old storekeeper and football coach, who gambled, drank and smoked heavily. He acquired notoriety as the man believed to have instigated the integration riots outside Little Rock's Central High School; pictures and descriptions of his activities had been featured in *Life* magazine.

Some months before the riots, on a visit to New York, he had been taken to hear Billy Graham at Madison Square Garden. "What sunk in," he recalls, "was Graham's saying that anybody, no matter how completely bad, can be made over by God." This message took two years to germinate. On April 9, 1959, thanks to his twelve-year-old daughter and to Dr. Vaught, her pastor, "the new life through Christ came into my heart." At the time of Graham's visit to Little Rock the following September—with Jimmy Karam as a crusade helper—a local reporter was quoted in *Time* as saying: "Many church people are convinced that it's the greatest conversion since Paul of Tarsus. Others still see Jimmy Karam under the sheep's clothing."

Karam himself affirmed at that time: "I have no hatred for anyone. We should get people on both sides to really accept Christ." In the next years the former segregationist led the fight for integration in Little Rock, and now travels all over America "telling the other Jimmy Karams," as he puts it, "about Jesus Christ who will wipe out their sins, make them born again and able to love and be loved."

When the Freedom Marches began in the nineteen-sixties, and Northern churchmen flocked to Southern cities to press the cause of integration and civil rights, Billy Graham declined to march. Instead he maintained his consistent stand for mutual tolerance, conciliation, and the necessity to strike at the root of the matter: "The race question will not be solved by demonstrations in the streets, but in the hearts of both Negro and white. There must be genuine love to replace prejudice and hate. This love can be supplied by Christ and only by Christ."

The 16th Street Baptist Church in Birmingham, Alabama, was destroyed by bombs, with the death of four Negro children, in September 1963. Once again Drew Pearson took the lead in raising funds for rebuilding, establishing America's Conscience Fund, with Governor Brown of California and Charles P. Taft of Cincinnati as co-chairmen. Billy Graham is one of the four honorary chairmen, all religious leaders, on the interfaith committee of distinguished persons such as Harry S. Truman. Graham offered to bring the Team for an integrated evangelistic rally in Legion Field Stadium on Easter Day, 1964, and the offer was accepted. In the opinion of George Harris, formerly of *Time* and *Life,* now a senior editor of *Look* magazine, who has covered many racial riots, Graham's going to Birmingham "took a good deal of courage, and was needed very badly there. The community leadership under the business men knew that they wanted a solution, knew where they wanted to go, but weren't sure they would have the community with them. Billy Graham could have a deeper impact than anybody else."

Bev Shea recalls "the feeling of apprehension in the city, and hearing privately from committee people that Dr. A. or Mrs. B. were timid about coming—they were with Billy, praying for Billy, but afraid of bodily injury." The segregationist "Citizens' Council" had called for the meeting's cancellation, and from among the black racists the late Malcolm X had uttered threats. Three hundred policemen were on hand, but the crowd of over 30,000, estimated to be about equally Negroes and whites, went out of their way to be friendly to one another.

"It is a wonderful thing to be gathered together like this in the city of Birmingham," Graham told the crowd, "in the name of Jesus Christ, on Easter Day. Somehow all our problems and difficulties seem not quite so great when we stand at the foot of the cross of Christ and hear Him say, 'Father, forgive them; for they know not what they do.' " Graham preached a straight address of love, repentance and faith, and the national press reporters were stunned at the response, as Negroes and whites streamed forward at the invitation.

Had Graham been a late jumper on the integration bandwagon, instead of for years an almost lone voice among American preachers, the achievement at Birmingham would have been impossible. Had he implied that a rally of witness could be a sufficient substitute for the still-delayed integration of the churches, it would have been superficial. But Graham was known for his emphasis on the need to integrate at worship: one of the themes of his article in *Reader's Digest* (August 1960) "Why Don't the Churches Practice the Brotherhood They Preach?" had been that 11 o'clock on a Sunday morning in America was the most segregated hour of the week.

But the Birmingham Easter rally would have been an empty gesture had not Graham helped men and women of both races to know Christ and the power of his Resurrection, and the active love of Christ which "transcends all law, all natural prejudices, all envy, all bitterness, all pride . . . a divine gift from God himself to all those who have been born of the Spirit."

In June 1964 Billy Graham received from the Negro George Washington Carver Memorial Institute its Supreme Award of Merit "for outstanding contribution to the betterment of race relations and human understanding." [1]

As the civil rights struggle continues, Billy Graham maintains his stand for conciliation and strikes at the roots of the evil, which lie deeper than the tragic legacy of history. The marchers have come in from the North, had their headlines and may have them again. Posterity alone can assess to what extent the marchers have aided the Southern Negro. Whatever the ultimate verdict, the immediate reality is that, when demonstrators depart, the communities must find a way to live together and the wounds must be healed. Billy Graham knows that. Thus, after the town of Selma broke into the news in the spring of 1965 while he lay in Hawaii recovering from respiratory trouble following the Hawaii crusade, he offered to hold an Easter rally there. Though this did not work out, Graham canceled engagements in England so that he could hold April meetings in Alabama, and he rearranged his early summer schedule in order to hold an integrated crusade at Montgomery, the state capital, in June. The invitation had come from the Ministerial Association and the Interdenominational Ministerial Alliance, and President Johnson personally advised Billy Graham to accept it. In every audience in Montgomery's rain-swept Cramton Bowl about one-third were Negroes, sitting wherever they liked, and the choir was half Negro, half white, entirely integrated. The outstanding documentary film of this crusade should prove on its release to be a powerful aid, in itself, to racial reconciliation in North and South.

Those who believed that marching was the only way to remove evils cried again that Billy Graham dragged his feet. After the Los Angeles riots of August 1965, Graham uttered a strong warning that political forces which cared nothing for the Negro might be exploiting the situation, and was lectured by *The Christian Century* for a "vague emotional outburst," as of "a man who knows something is dreadfully wrong but who hadn't the slightest idea what caused it."

A more sober judgment comes from the White House. On April 13, 1965, before Graham went to Alabama, President Johnson wrote

[1] In 1960 the President of Liberia had presented him with that country's highest medal for his contribution to African redemption and freedom.

to him: "You are doing a brave and fine thing for your country in your courageous effort to contribute to the understanding and brotherhood of the Americans in the South. In this instance, I am praying for your success and want you to know I am very proud of you."

---

31 · Crusade Is Involvement

If Sydney was a pattern crusade, that at Manchester in northern England in 1961 was not.

The Manchester-Liverpool area, densely populated and lying halfway between Glasgow and London, was an obvious site should Graham return. When, however, the Americans decided to explore numerous tentative invitations, they misjudged the relative geographical and religious situations and chose the cotton manufacturing city of Manchester in preference to the port of Liverpool, where they would have had a far stronger base among the churches. The Church of England, especially, was favorably disposed in Liverpool but decidedly dubious in Manchester. The crusade was aimed for all North-Central England, but the Americans did not appreciate how sharp is the physical barrier formed by the low north-south-running Pennine range, and they diffused their preparations over an area that has no true unity.

The Manchester Council of Churches declined to cooperate except on terms that had never been put to Graham anywhere in the world.

Some of the council believed that industrial workers could be reached for Christianity by dialogue only, not by mass-evangelism. Others felt that Manchester was not so spiritually poverty struck as to need a crusade, yet the great success of Sydney two years earlier (and Los Angeles two years later) was due largely to the very fact that both had a wealth of spiritual life on which to build. The Manchester Council was influenced strongly by Bishop Ted Wickham of Middleton, known for his work in industrial relations. Bishop Wickham believes, as he had already told Billy Graham forcefully at a 1960 seminar in Switzerland arranged by the World Council of Churches' commission on evangelism, that the workers did not want personal mercy but social righteousness; that the preaching of theological righteousness leaves only disillusion and disappointment once emotion has abated; and that individualistic evangelism had driven the workers out of the Church. Wickham's view is highly debatable, for a contrary argument can be put: that the one period in which the British industrial proletariat were deeply affected by Christianity was that which began with the "individualistic evangelism" of Whitefield and the Wesleys, and ended with the decline of Biblical preaching before the First World War.

The council announced that they would welcome and work with Graham only if he would share his preaching with three men who had quite different conceptions of evangelism. No names were officially offered, but the Manchester public understood that two of them were to be Donald Soper and George MacLeod, who had been Graham's loudest British critics.

By their conditions the council had in effect told Graham that he must jettison the lesson of more than a decade: that unequivocal and authoritative preaching of a plain New Testament message, backed by the strong cooperation of ministers prepared to bury theological disagreements, will bring blessing. Moreover from Detroit in 1953, through Glasgow, to Sydney in 1959, a Graham crusade had demonstrably reached the industrial working man whenever churches acted in the belief that it could. If Graham had agreed to the Manchester conditions, the resulting confusion of aims, the chaos of counseling after a different gospel each night, would have been an invitation to calamity.

Because of the council's refusal to endorse the invitation to Graham, cooperation was far less broad than was now normal in crusades. Nor as the preparation advanced did the Team's crusade directors and the executive committee work together as smoothly as had their counterparts of London and many other cities in the world. In retrospect most of the Americans' decisions were right. Two however were wrong. First, they used a publicity firm unfamiliar with Manchester. Secondly, instead of building an annex to the largest public hall (as was technically possible), they chose a steep, bleak outdoor stadium. When reminded that it generally rains in Manchester, even in May, the Americans talked of Australia and the thousands coming forward in the mud.

Manchester and northern England never reached the fervency of prayer that had preceded London, New York or Sydney. And whereas, here and there, a church would work unstintedly to reach the uncommitted, many felt that the crowds would flock anyway to hear Billy Graham.

Billy arrived in England, fell ill in London with a throat infection and high temperature, and was unable to open the crusade.

Leighton Ford substituted very acceptably. The Bishop of Manchester, attending the opening night, was impressed by the power and intelligence of so young a man's preaching. All the first week, in bitter cold and wet, Ford conducted the Manchester crusade. The shape and size of the stadium, the stiff steps making it a trial to the old or infirm; the miserable weather and consequent empty spaces; poor publicity and an indifferent press; and especially the absence of Billy Graham, combined to make it a hard toil. The actual attendance on even the worst night was greater than at London's Harringay arena in 1954; and for 30,000 or more to come out nightly for religion in Manchester was unprecedented. But such crowds did not fill the stadium, and thus were barely remarked upon. The majority were at least vaguely church-related, for except in a few outstanding Anglican parishes and nonconformist churches, Christians were shy of inviting nonchurchgoers to so cold a stadium where the preacher was not even Billy Graham.

The proportion of inquirers to attendance was high. "They came so quickly that we were embarrassed," says the head of the follow-up department. "It was amazing," added a committee member, "that so many did come forward, that sparks were struck in that chilly and damp atmosphere."

Billy arrived for the second week, still a sick man. (Fortunately the crusade chairman was a consultant surgeon, who kept an eye on his condition.) There was, however, no diminution in his message, and as Graham entered his second week (the crusade's third) the meetings were gathering momentum. The Bishop of Manchester and other church leaders, too late, were becoming increasingly committed, and had the crusade been extended it might have broken through. Graham's health, the weather, the empty standing space directly opposite the platform, militated against extension. The crusade ended after the originally planned three weeks.

Manchester was not a fiasco. Churches which had cooperated fully profited immeasurably, and others were brought new vision. Hundreds of lasting conversions can be traced back to the stadium itself or the landline relays across Britain. One Anglican clergyman recalls attending among 32,000 people, many of them standing under umbrellas in the pouring rain. "At the end of Billy Graham's address," he relates, "he stopped suddenly and said: 'I have been criticized for emotional appeal, for choirs singing softly and for artificially urging people to come forward. Tonight the choir will not sing. I will just say "Come forward," and I promise anyone who does that he will stand [being counseled] for anything up to twenty minutes in the deluge.' Twelve hundred people came forward," continues the clergyman. "I went away *convinced* that here was only one power— that of the Holy Spirit."

For all this, the Manchester crusade did not set northern England aflame or fire the nation, as had been the hope of the Team and of those who had invited them.

To people in the United States Manchester seemed a trivial episode in the ministry of Billy Graham. But it has a significance in his story as showing how the churches of a community should *not* regard a crusade. For despite all the discouraging physical factors, the basic reason for disappointment was not the weather, nor the unsuitable stadium, nor Billy's illness, but the failure of churches to involve themselves fully, from the start, in working beside a Team that has acquired unique experience through the years. As the veteran evangelist of the Church of Scotland Dr. D. P. Thomson puts it: "A minister must be humble enough, open enough in mind and spirit and heart, and concerned enough to be involved with his people in what is happening, even if he doesn't wholly approve of the technique used. The fact that he's involved with them means that he can carry through with them in a way that he cannot, however sympathetic he is, if he stands outside and merely waits to deal with the results."

Most ministerial hesitations arise from fears or understandable ignorance of the purpose and methods of the Graham Team. In earlier years the whole weight of preparation was thrown into a few months, building up to a climax of a crusade. The Team now feels (in the words of Bill Brown, one of the crusade directors) that the actual period of a crusade is "not any more important than that previous or following; perhaps nothing is as important as that which happens after: we are preparing people for an ongoing period of evangelism in their church."

Though England in 1961 had not yet realized that the secret of a crusade is the full involvement of clergy and church people, America was learning it fast.

With few exceptions the crusades of the early nineteen-sixties in the United States have shown more complete participation by churches and ministers, over a wider area, than in the fifties. More counselors are enrolling, larger audiences are attending the services, and there is closer follow-up. Crusades are increasingly looked upon as a beginning rather than a climax, and ministers take to heart the remark often made by Graham as he leaves a city: "When you think of the crusade, don't think of myself or the Team—think of the on-going work of the Lord."

The perspective of the years is too short for a true assessment of crusades since 1960, but almost certainly it will certify the typical im-mediate reaction, such as that voiced after the Miami crusade, held at the height of the tourist season of 1961. The religious editor of Miami *Daily News,* Louise Leyden, wrote: "The Crusade hit Miami Beach with an impact greater than did Hurricane Donna last fall. Never since the days of Carl Fisher, developer of Miami Beach, when his crew of men and elephants cut away the alligator-infested man-grove swamps and transformed the island into a beauty spot of the world, has this little sandy strip seen such a change in the lives of so many people."

The Miami crusade reached not only tourists and native Floridians but Cuban refugees. And, unexpectedly, thousands of vacationing students. The mayor of nearby Fort Lauderdale sent an urgent mes-sage to Billy Graham to come and address several thousand rowdy college students who had invaded the area. A platform was placed on the beach, where Graham stood with his back to the gentle surf. The students booed the mayor. During Anita Bryant's solo there were shouts of "We want Billy Graham." When Billy started his talk he asked, "What do you believe in?" "Sex!" shouted a voice. "Yes," re-plied Graham, "that's important. Without it we wouldn't be here today!" The crowd laughed, and from that moment were with him. He preached for more than an hour. "I've never had an audience lis-ten so," he recalls. "The only thing you could hear was the lapping of the sea behind. And all I did was to talk about Jesus."

Another of the crusades of 1961, at Philadelphia, saw the intro-duction of a new venture which has done much for the involvement of younger ministers.

The story behind this venture started in 1957. Lane Adams, the former night-club singer, had been stirred to the roots by his work among show people in the New York crusade of that year, when on special leave from his seminary. "I heard Billy preach, I counseled people immediately upon their decision, and then in the cold light of days after I would track the show people down and see what God had done in their hearts, and it was fantastic, this movement of the Spirit of God." When a journalist asked, "What has this crusade meant to you?" the gist of Adams' reply was, "It has floored me with the fact that Jesus Christ is alive and He's reaching out and transforming lives."

Thereafter Adams returned to Columbia Presbyterian Theological Seminary. When he next met Leighton Ford, a Columbia graduate, Adams suggested that more students at seminary should have the practical training that had come to both of them, through participating in evangelism on the Billy Graham scale. The evangelistic training activity provided by a seminary course, Adams argued, is inadequate. In the next three years Adams applied in his first pastorate, near Miami, the lessons he had learned in the New York crusade. He became convinced that too few discovered, while still students, the practical meaning of the Apostle Paul's words to pastor Timothy: "Do the work of an evangelist." "The ideal servant of God is not a lopsided wheel," mused Adams. "He's well rounded, he can evangelize, he can teach, he speaks prophetically, and he's a pastor at heart. All these things are not distinct gifts, but should be blended together."

Early in 1961 Adams asked the president of Columbia, Dr. Richards, for leave to raise money to enable students to share in the counseling preparation and service of a crusade, "not to make them little duplicates of Billy Graham, but to give them this practical know-how instead of just a lot of theory." Dr. Richards agreed with enthusiasm, and they then prayed together for the money Adams wished to raise. To their amazement it became available the next morning: one of the students, a young former textile manufacturer named Donald Munson, gave the seminary a substantial sum for the purpose.

Seven Columbia students went to the Philadelphia crusade of August–September 1961. Their reports vindicated Adams' faith in the project.

Meanwhile a similar scheme had begun through the initiative of a San Francisco industrialist, Lowell Berry. Back in 1958 Berry had been a member of the finance committee of the San Francisco crusade, though he was a liberal churchman who harbored doubts of the integrity of mass-evangelists and of the value of their work. What he saw of the management of the funds convinced him on the score of integrity. During the San Francisco crusade he himself went forward in commitment to Christ. Conscious now of a spiritual dimension of which he had been ignorant—a dimension brought to him through an evangelism which previously he had regarded with suspicion—he determined to help clergy and future clergy lose their mistrust of it, and to learn how to evangelize their own local congregations.

Like Lane Adams, Berry saw that this could be best done in the midst of a crusade. The ideas of Adams (and of others) and the generosity of Lowell Berry converged at the Chicago crusade of May–June 1962, when twenty-seven men from seven seminaries enrolled for a full-scale seminar of lectures and for work contributing to the preparation for and carrying out of the crusade.

Graham appointed Dr. Robert Ferm to develop the program. Ferm began with a seminar in evangelism linked to the El Paso crusade of November 1962. At Los Angeles (August 1963) a hundred students and younger clergy had Berry scholarships. The program is now a normal part of the schedule of any crusade held at times when students are free. Many who enroll are from theological seminaries which give little attention to mass evangelism.

Hundreds of students and younger clergy have now attended the seminars. Some of these, writes Ferm, have "witnessed for the first time the converting effect of Gospel preaching, and have for the first time counseled personally one who was at that moment making a life commitment. Having both seen and studied the evangelistic method, they return to their classes and to their churches with a new note in their preaching."

Billy Graham had thought he might never do a crusade in Chicago. He had declined the invitation of a sectional group in the mid-nineteen-fifties; in 1958 the Church Federation voted narrowly against a crusade. A strong evangelical committee pursued the matter. Billy "wrestled for nearly three years about going to Chicago, and even after I accepted I thought I'd done wrong, but decided to go ahead. After I was in the middle of the crusade I knew that it was of God, but it took that long for me to get that conviction."

The Church Federation never cooperated officially, but the leaders later acknowledged that in a city of much diversity and disunity of church life, the crusade proved to be a big advance in true ecumenicity. Chicago showed, indeed, on a city scale, the importance of Billy Graham to the highest good of the ecumenical movement.[1] Because of Graham's achievement and prestige and the clarity of his views, ecumenical church leaders in America (who generally ignore but seem unwilling to attack his views) cannot dismiss fundamental Biblical

[1] The Southern Baptist denomination is not a member of the World Council of Churches, but Billy Graham attended the Assembly at New Delhi in December 1961 as an observer. He missed the Evanston Assembly in 1954, where he was to speak, through illness.

doctrines in their search for a "jargon of communication" or a formula of union. History may well judge the crusades to be the present greatest single contribution in America to Christian unity at the local level—a unity founded not upon words but in action, a spontaneous result of involvement in evangelism.

This local-level unity is deepening as the Team further develops the methods of crusades. Ministers are now invited to attend a retreat some months before a crusade and another after it. Thus in June 1954, following the Canadian Maritime Provinces crusade, Billy Graham and Leighton Ford joined 300 ministers for a conference of evangelism at Dalhousie University in Nova Scotia, "high Anglicans and Pentecostalists kneeling on the campus grass and praying together."

But Chicago 1962, was far more than an exercise in unity.

The 40,000 seats at the new McCormick Place were filled every night for three weeks, with an overflow crowd besides. The teenage gang leaders from the South Side who threw away their sheath knives, the prisoners converted through listening to Billy or his associates speaking in the jails; the wide sweep of social background among the inquirers; the 116,000 people at the final rally in Soldier Field Stadium on a blazingly hot afternoon—all this looks as if the Chicago crusade will prove in perspective to be one of the greatest.

Yet Chicago's strongest impact on America arose from a near-disaster. The final rally at Soldier Field was video-taped to be the last of five telecasts from the Chicago crusade for later showing across the nation. Because an actual crusade service is much longer than the time available on television, the producer of the telecast always films only so much of the preliminaries as to provide him with a margin if Billy Graham's sermon proves to be shorter or longer than usual. The length of the sermon, until this last service at Chicago, had never varied from the average by more than a few minutes.

On that June Sunday afternoon at Soldier Field the heat reached 110 degrees. (The traffic at the approaches to the stadium was in chaos because of cars stalled by vapor lock.) Billy Graham stood in the full glare of the sun throughout his sermon, which to him, though not to his audience, seemed weak and ineffective. A heat headache worsened as he preached, and suddenly he believed he might collapse. He managed to give the invitation. The response was immediate and impressive. Billy returned at once to his hotel, thrilled but utterly weary, and retired to bed.

Back at Soldier Field the television unit filmed the movement of the inquirers, ran through the credits in the normal way, went to work on the editing—and discovered they were short seven minutes of footage. Seven minutes to fill, if television screens were not to go dark for seven minutes at next week's showing. Dick Ross, Cliff Barrow, Walter Bennett and Fred Dienert hurriedly conferred. Someone suggested bringing Billy to a studio next morning, but that would be out of sequence and an anti-climax. Then Cliff hit on the answer: bring Billy back to the empty stadium.

Cliff telephoned the hotel and reached T. W. Wilson, who had now joined the Team as Billy's personal assistant. T.W. reported that Billy lay exhausted in bed. When T.W. put the idea to him, Billy was dubious, but he brightened when told, truthfully, that it had been a great telecast.

When the last of the Chicago series was given its showing, therefore, viewers saw the great service and the sermon and the inquirers moving forward. As the credits came on the screen, many viewers reached for refreshments or began to leave their chairs. Suddenly the camera focused on the classical-style pillars high up on Soldier Field, then moved across empty benches, drab with inevitable litter. The camera moved to the platform, and there sat Billy Graham, black rings around his eyes, entirely alone.

"It has been about three hours since the benediction was pronounced," he said, looking straight at the camera, "and I have come back here to Soldier Field to talk to you. When the appeal was given, about 2,000 people came forward to receive Jesus Christ as their Lord and Savior. Now the stadium is empty. The breeze is blowing. I think this afternoon was the hottest that I have ever preached in. . . .

"I talked on Agrippa almost being persuaded to follow Christ. Some of you during this meeting have almost been persuaded to give your life to Jesus Christ, but you haven't done it. You are sitting there in the quietness of your home, you may be in a bar, you may be in some unique place that I don't even know about, watching right now, and God has spoken to you as you have seen the great crowd and as you heard the sermon and heard the singing; the spirit of God spoke to your hearts. . . .

"And as this stadium is empty now, your heart is empty; and yet Christ is willing to come in and fill it—to bring you a peace, a joy and a satisfaction that you have never known before. But more than that, to adopt you into His family. You become a child of God. The Bible teaches that history is going to a definite objective, and that objective is the way of Jesus Christ. His kingdom is ultimately going to triumph and you can be part of it, and the decision, the stepping over the line, can be right now as you give your heart and life to Jesus Christ.

"But just as Agrippa neglected or refused to repent and turn to God, so many of you are in danger of doing the same. But I'm going to ask you right now to do it. You don't have to be here in this big stadium. There's nothing about the mechanics of coming forward that saves anybody's soul. Coming forward is an open acknowledgment and a testimony of an inward experience that you have with Christ. But this inward experience with Christ, this encounter, is the most important thing. And that could happen to you right now wherever you are, whatever your condition, whatever your circumstance.

"But you say, 'Billy, I'm really too great a sinner. I've just been too bad, I've done too many things. I'm too big a hypocrite.' No, you're not too much a sinner. There is no sin too bad but what Christ can forgive. When He died on the cross He was dying for you. He took your place. Your sins were put on Him, not just the sins of this big crowd that we had today at Soldier Field, but your sins, your own sins were placed on Him.

"And now if by faith you will receive Him into your heart, He will forgive those sins and then you can note something of the power of His own resurrection. The same power that raised up Jesus Christ from the dead is available to you right now, to help you live a new life, if you will put your confidence and your faith in Him."

---

32 · *Too Big an Organization?*

The impact of those moments of watching Billy in empty Soldier Field, immediately following the great service, released a flood of mail.

From all over America, every television crusade brings to the Association hundreds of thousands of letters. The total of letters from viewers and listeners to the *Hour of Decision* in 1962 was 1,123,999. In 1964, just short of 2,000,000. When the Hawaii telecasts were shown in June 1965, over 800,000 letters came in a month.

The figures indicate the enormous size of Billy Graham's television ministry in North America. Although he may preach face to face to two million people in a year, it is through the coast-to-coast television crusades that he is having his widest influence. Few Americans have not seen Billy Graham on television. His face is one of the best known in the country, and his message reaches into American homes as has that of no other preacher in history.[1]

The hundreds of thousands of letters reveal the impact of the message. From Hollywood, California: "I watched you for the first time on your closing rally of the Hawaiian Crusades. This is the nearest I have been to church in 35 years. Next Sunday I expect to return to God. Thank you for starting me back on the right path." From Cleveland, Ohio: "I am 24 years old and my husband divorced me for a younger girl and left me with three children. I want to thank you for what you have done for me tonight as I watched your telecast." From Santa Monica, California: "I can't tell you how encouraging your message was to me tonight. It seemed to melt away my bitterness and give me such great hope. I am a young mother who just returned from the hospital after attempting suicide. My husband left me after 10 years for another woman. I hope now through your bringing me God's message I'll find the strength to go on." From Phoenix, Arizona: "I committed myself to God while watching you on my TV screen, and I need material to read as I am not a member of any church."

Most letters ask for a free New Testament or other literature that Billy offers on the screen. Many send gifts, many need a reply of detailed counsel. Two pastors, with secretarial staff, work full time as counselors at Minneapolis, reinforced by ordained men from other departments. In cases of emergency one of these men will telephone advice.

The radio and TV correspondence and the distribution of Christian literature would by themselves require a highly organized office, but in 1960 Billy Graham took another leap forward by the founding of *Decision* magazine.

To complement *Christianity Today,* "I felt we needed a popular magazine that would go to the ordinary farm wife, to the worker, which would present clear Christian teaching, be thought-provoking, devotional and evangelistic, with a breezy, easy-to-read style." It would also keep readers informed of the crusades.

Graham received little encouragement from many of his friends for so risky a venture as the launching of a two-color, illustrated magazine. But the plan was firm enough in 1958 for Billy to choose an

---

[1] Billy Graham has been among the top ten of Gallup Poll's "Most Admired Men" for eleven successive years since 1955. In 1965 his position was fourth, following Lyndon B. Johnson, Dwight D. Eisenhower, and Robert F. Kennedy.

editor, Dr. Sherwood Eliot Wirt, pastor of a Presbyterian church in Oakland, California, and author of *Crusade at the Golden Gate*.[1] Wirt holds a doctorate of philosophy from Edinburgh University and was a newspaper editor in Alaska before ordination. The first monthly number of *Decision* was issued in November 1960. Since no advertisements were to be carried, the magazine was an invitation to financial disaster for the Association.

Decision paid its way from the first issue. Circulation grew from an initial 253,000 to over 3,000,000 monthly by October 1965. (75,000 copies circulating in Britain and Australia, and smaller, less frequent editions in French, German and Spanish are included in the 3,000,000 figure.) The circulation is the highest of any religious periodical in America and has risen every month.

Decision is, Billy Graham remarks, "the first thing we've ever done that has never been criticized." Dr. Wirt, however, treasures a letter of criticism dated May 13, 1964, from Montreat: "The June issue of *Decision* has arrived. It has too much Billy Graham and too little of the Lord Jesus Christ. I told you in the beginning that I did not want this to become a propaganda sheet for me or the organization. Lately the trend has been to publicize and promote our various aspects of work to the detriment of its spiritual content.

"I am sure that you agree with me, and that this is your personal desire as well. I must decrease, and He must increase."

Decision brought growth of expenditure and staff but growth of funds too. The Association was now maintaining four major ministries in addition to the crusades: *Decision* magazine; the weekly radio *Hour of Decision;* the periodic television crusades; and World Wide Pictures of Burbank, California, under the presidency of Cliff Barrows. More than sixty evangelistic films are being shown free or made available at nominal rental cost throughout the world. A few titles circulate in commercial circuits in Asia and Africa and reach where no religious films normally go. Thus the folk of a town in Thailand or Ghana may one week see a Hollywood movie of sex or violence rampant and *Shadow of the Boomerang,* the feature story from the Australian crusade, the next.

Costs of the Billy Graham ministries have risen enormously and gifts just barely keep pace. In 1964 expenditure and income reached $10,000,000 of which nearly 6,000,000 represented subscriptions to *Decision* at $2 a year—scarcely enough to cover production and dis-

[1] The story of the Billy Graham San Francisco Crusade in 1958.

tribution costs. Nearly $2,750,000 was spent for TV and radio time, and related costs such as advertising and the free issue of New Testaments, *Daily Light, Living Letters* and other literature. The total expenditure on three nights of television in September 1964 (of the San Diego crusade) was $635,000.

Despite such costs, the Association has never ended a year in the red. Sometimes it had seemed likely, but funds always came in time. The need is lightly mentioned on radio by Graham, and more explicitly in occasional appeal letters. In 1964 the average amount of all gifts was $6.21. A gift of $1,000 or more is rare. The Association's support comes from moderate gifts of hundreds of thousands of people praying regularly for Billy Graham and his work. More large single gifts are made in connection with crusades, but these are sent to the crusade committee. The financing of crusades has nothing to do with the Association; indeed the Association contributes substantially to each crusade by paying the salaries of the Team members engaged in it.

The Association is governed by a board of directors (twenty-one in 1965), most of whom are professional and religious leaders. The integrity and soundness of its finances have been unquestioned except by the ignorant or malicious; even Dr. McLoughlin, who attacked Billy Graham on many grounds, paid tribute to this integrity. The Association has maintained a policy of using all income to support its ministries (and the opportunities are always more than can be met) and not to build up capital. It owns no property except the Minneapolis offices and a small office at Montreat.

The Grason Company, set up in 1950, handles demands for Team books and phonograph records, and for Billy Graham's radio-sermon leaflets, which circulate by the million. These could not be distributed by BGEA as a nonprofit association. Grason on the other hand is a taxable corporation, and after taxes any profits it may produce go to BGEA.

When the board was expanded in 1958 it raised the salaries of the Team to a level more in line with the increased cost of living and with the salaries of other American clergymen, and of faculty members of Christian colleges and theological seminaries. But when the board tried to raise Graham's salary from $15,000 to $25,000 they met stout resistance for five years. In 1963 he agreed to take $19,500 but refused to go over $20,000. There are, therefore, hundreds of church leaders, city pastors and seminary presidents who receive a higher salary than Billy Graham.

If the Minneapolis headquarters were not automated with the latest computers, processing machines and mailing equipment, *Decision* would never reach its 3,000,000 subscribers promptly. Nor would follow-up materials for crusades be on hand when needed in their thousands. Many opportunities for the Graham ministry would go by default, and half the television mail would lie unopened for months.[1]

George Wilson defines the Association's job as "to dispense the world's greatest product with the greatest economy to the greatest number of people as fast as possible." His penchant for using commercial jargon has sometimes inadvertently disguised the reality that he and the Minneapolis staff are a team of spiritually-minded Christians as intent on their mission as any group of missionaries in jungle huts. Numbers have risen from two in 1950 (George Wilson and a girl) to 400 by 1965, including technicians and janitors. They all begin the day with ten minutes of silent prayer and Bible reading, each at desk or machine. They gather at least once a week for a chapel service; prayer needs are often mentioned over the public-address system.

The character of the executives is exemplified by the words of Billy Graham at the funeral of George Edstrom, the office manager, who died suddenly after a heart attack in November 1964: "There were many times when I would grow a bit discouraged, there were times in my ministry when I put my foot in my mouth, got on the wrong side of something, and I would call up the office and if George Wilson wasn't there I would ask for George Edstrom; and he'd say, 'Don't worry about it, it's in the Lord's hands, it's all right.' And he was like oil all the time. There was something steady about him, he was always there when you needed him. And he was a man that walked with God."

Because the Association has grown to such size, with offices in six countries, the legend has arisen that Billy Graham himself has lost control, that a distinction should be drawn between the simplicity and holiness of the man and the methods and activities of the BGEA, a juggernaut exploiting his name. This view causes amusement among members of the Team and the staffs of the offices, who know exactly who is boss.

Billy Graham receives daily reports by telephone. Each month he

---

[1] Among the peculiar addresses which the U.S. post office department has managed to deliver to Minneapolis, Minnesota, have been: "Billy Graham, Many Apples, Minny Soda," "Many Helpless, Minn." "Billy Graham, Uncle Sam knows where," "c/o Archbishop of Canterbury."

runs his eye down the list of checks, large and small, paid out from every office, and asks for the detail of any he cannot understand.

The legend that Graham is merely a figurehead has arisen from the skill with which he leads by delegating authority, letting people make mistakes and accepting their mistakes. He can certainly rebuke: one former Team member recalls how Billy took him to pieces until he felt an inch high, "and then he threw his arms around me and immediately began building me up again." Should Billy Graham die, the Association's work will not end, for a procedure is drawn up for choosing a new president, and Team members will continue to hold crusades. In the early days Grady Wilson was the only associate evangelist. Now he has been joined by eleven others. When not assisting Billy Graham at major crusades the twelve are each working on their own. Because they are members of his Team, trained under Graham, they find response on a scale they had not experienced while traveling previously as independent evangelists.

As requests grew for associate crusades, Billy Graham appointed a Team coordinator and set up a Team office in Atlanta. Many North American cities too small for a full-scale crusade led by Graham have thus had similar preparation for crusades led by one of his twelve associates. All through the year several crusades are being held simultaneously. Billy Graham's touch thus reaches far more places than he can visit himself, though he does sometimes appear in such cities for a closing rally.

The associates form their own teams, generally on a temporary basis. Leighton Ford, however, working mostly in Canada, has built up a permanent team, and his crusades are already reaching, in size of audience and in response, a scale comparable to Billy Graham's own crusades of the mid-nineteen-fifties, but with the added depth of method that has come from the experience of the intervening years.

For Latin America, Africa and India Graham has appointed missionary associates to conduct crusades. Another variation is for the Team to work together overseas in a manner similar to the plan carried out in Australia: the associates each preaching in a different city for a week or more, while Billy Graham moves from one to the other, bringing each crusade to its climax. This was done in South America in 1962. Another variation in the carrying of the load occurred in 1963, when the associates stepped in effectively when Graham had to withdraw from the Orient crusade through illness.

The previous October Billy had returned from the second half of the South America crusade, unknowingly carrying a rare bacillus. He was at Dallas, Texas, in January 1963, for the annual Laymen's Leadership Institute (of which he had been co-founder seven years earlier) when he was troubled by a severe cough and was taken to Baylor Hospital for tests. Five days later he flew with T. W. Wilson to Washington for the Presidential Prayer Breakfast, at his own insistence against the specialist's better judgment.

After addressing the gathering, "Billy and President Kennedy," tells T. W. Wilson, "went across and talked a few minutes to the wives of the ambassadors and senators. And then we walked out the side door to the President's limousine." They chatted a few moments and said goodbye. By now Billy was running a high fever, the start of a pulmonary illness. He was sent to Hawaii to convalesce before the Orient crusade, but there the bacillus attacked the intestines. He entered St. Francis Hospital, Honolulu, and was obliged to withdraw from the imminent crusade.

It was here that the associate evangelists stepped in—one each for Manila, Hong Kong, Formosa and Japan—after a complete last-minute redesign of the crusade by Dan Piatt.

The illness proved that the Team was sufficiently firmly established to rise to a major emergency. It did more.

Both specialists, Dr. Richard Chang of Hawaii and Dr. Martin S. Buehler of Dallas, succeeded in convincing Billy of a truth which his father-in-law, Dr. Nelson Bell, had been urging upon him for years, though he had never really listened. In Dr. Buehler's words: "I talked to him very seriously about his failure to take care of himself physically, and insisted he take more time off to rest and relax. I explained to him that no human body or mind could take the tremendous burden that he was constantly imposing on himself."

Graham's recovery was complete. He went to Europe for crusades in Germany and France, in the early summer of 1963, a new man physically. Even insomnia returns only intermittently. He has had a share of illness since, but it has been kept down by his willingness to relax and the adoption of a physical fitness program which includes a two-mile run most days. He can say, as he told London clergy in March 1964, "I am in the best of health now of my entire life. I feel as if I have been released."

33 · *The Roots of a Man and Message*

Billy Graham had a habit of getting up early, shaving, and then returning to bed for another half hour or so of prayer or sleep. If Ruth looks into the bathroom in winter time she often finds him shaving in semi-darkness. When she switches on the light he looks up surprised and grateful—he had been too intent on whatever problem was on his mind! It is the same sometimes with his golf. Gary Player, the famous golfer, who has often played with Graham, writes:[1] "Billy Graham could be successful in any field he chose to undertake seriously, including golf, for which he has a great natural ability. But because his mind tends to wander onto weightier matters when he is playing, especially during crusades, he cannot give the concentration required to make him a more perfect golfer."

This preoccupation is symbolic of the constant load of responsibility, and the unceasing pressure. Nor can Graham ever know much private life. Even though he lives on a mountain the tourists find their way up. Belshazzar's successors, Peter the Alsatian and Heidi the Saint Bernard (who really was born on the St. Bernard Pass, and is decidedly grumpy to strangers) afford some protection, but Billy often returns tired from a meeting to find strangers on his door step. During the ensuing conversation only Ruth can remotely detect that he is frayed.

Graham has his share of visits from cranks and mental cases. Once when he was alone in the house except for small Ned, the study door burst open and a young man with a wild look dashed in shouting, "I've come to get you!" Before the fellow could land his blow Billy knocked him down, took him outside, held him on the ground and said, "Now what's your trouble?" The young man began to cry. At that moment an older man appeared and said the intruder was his son, who was crazy and determined to kill Billy, and that he had tried to stop him but feared for his own life. Billy prayed with them both as he held the boy, who was taken away quieted.

When Billy is known to be at home he has a steady flow of genuine inquirers from Buncombe County and far beyond, seeking advice or spiritual aid. Over the years he has led scores of individuals to Christ in his own study. If he did not have an unlisted telephone number he would spend most of the day answering serious and frivolous callers.

[1] In a letter to the author, November 13, 1965.

Dr. Bell, to whom many of these calls are diverted, has been told by a telephone supervisor that, on an average, fifty long-distance callers try to reach Billy Graham in every eight-hour period.

When Billy is traveling he is even more a prisoner of his ministry. He cannot eat in a public place in America without quick recognition, followed by people wanting his autograph, wanting to shake his hand, wanting to express gratitude. Fortunately he does not like his food too hot, for it nearly always gets cold. Where they do not pester him eating they approach in the lobby. Inevitably he has to travel with an aide and to eat privately wherever possible. When he visited Disneyland he gave up in half an hour because of his recognition by the crowd. At the New York World's Fair he had taken one of his sons to only three pavilions before the friendly mobbing drove him away. This impossibility of leading a normal life, together with the frequent absences from his family, are two of his hardest sacrifices. Occasionally he says to T. W. Wilson, "Wouldn't it be a tremendous relief just to have a little pastorate and preach three sermons on Sunday and visit a few people, and see lots of our families and play plenty of golf?"

Yet his graciousness to those who accost him is not simulated. A former associate recalls being deep in discussion with Billy in a hotel lounge when a strange woman interrupted their talk to tell Billy she prayed for him every day. The associate bridled at the interruption, but Billy leaped to his feet and chatted a few minutes with her. As he sat down again he remarked, "Just think, she prays for me every day. How very kind of her to tell me."

It has been a wonder to many how Billy keeps fresh and is such good company, with sense of humor unquenched—a welcome guest at the table of such diverse characters as film moguls and missionaries, financiers and hillbillies. As his friend Governor Frank G. Clement of Tennessee describes him: "He is a brilliant spark, full of drive, zeal and dedication, who inspires others to their best efforts. He walks with even step among the humble and moves with towering stature with the mighty." [1]

One part of the secret of Graham's poise is that he is an integrated, balanced personality. Beyond this, he is well-read, with a fund of general knowledge garnered from newspapers, magazines and a wide range of books. For some years he has had research assistance from one or other of his staff, not as a substitute for but as an extension of his own reading. The mass of digested or condensed books served up

[1] From a letter to the author, February 1, 1965.

to him sometimes inclines him in his addresses or writings to pile quotation upon quotation. But most of his research is done by himself. He has a large and growing library; he spends a remarkable portion of each day in study, digging and analyzing and absorbing until the material is part of him. It is the same when he is in conversation. Dr. Harold Ockenga says he knows no one "who can grasp more quickly an idea, absorb it, and let it become his own. You can talk with Billy and the next thing you know Billy is using the very idea; it has passed through his personality and has become spoken and expressed in his words. And he can get a point in a meeting, too. He'll be very intent. You watch him. He'll be very intent on listening for a moment, but he'll get that point, and he won't forget it."

Beyond all else Billy Graham studies the Bible, the supreme authority for his belief and action. Every day he reads five Psalms, covering the whole psalter in a month, and one chapter of Proverbs, the book that "shows us how to relate our own lives to our fellow men." He reads through a gospel each week, using commentaries and modern translations, and constantly returns to the Acts of the Apostles. He annotates throughout the Bible. "Sometimes His word makes such an impact on me that I have to put the Bible down and walk around for a few moments to catch my breath." He learns great stretches by heart.

Graham's Bible reading is soaked in prayer. He spends less time on his knees than in those early Florida days but he prays more, consciously or subconsciously. He prays when studying, discussing, preaching. At nights, if he cannot sleep and the weather is warm, he will often walk out under the stars to pray over problems or for people. He keeps a written list of intercessions he wishes to make so that they will not be edged out. Often the urge comes upon him to pray for an associate or a missionary friend, to learn later that the subject of his prayers was in need. A news report or a letter or a telephone call may also set him praying. Lorne Sanny, although he did not have opportunity to study Billy's prayer life at close quarters, gathered a correct impression "that he has mastered the art of praying without ceasing better than anybody I have known."

Billy has said, "I have so many decisions to make each day, and so many problems, that I have to pray all the time."

Prayer and Bible reading, inextricably intertwined, are the taproots of Graham's character and of his message. "My faith is grounded in a personal encounter with Christ, in a daily experience with him." As

Alan Redpath of Chicago and Edinburgh says, "Graham's public note of authority comes from his private walk and intimacy with God."

In the winter of 1963–64 Graham gave much of his time to American universities. This was not a new field for him; he had often spoken on college campuses and had held a notable mission at Yale in 1957. But he had not previously accepted invitations for an extended tour. The tour for this winter ranged from the Roman Catholic Belmont Abbey College, where he received a standing ovation from 2,000 priests, students and nuns, to Harvard University. Wherever he spoke, Graham left behind him, above all, a new respect for the evangelistic message. This was particularly noticeable in the panel discussions at Harvard, where students came with sneers, expecting whiffs of the sawdust trail, and left, as Akbar Haqq observed, "overwhelmed by the profundity of the Gospel." Cliff Barrows, sitting in the audience, heard an originally giggling student exclaim to his neighbor, "Oh, this is brilliant. I never expected this!" Billy himself feels that the discussion groups were "my greatest opportunity. If I have any gift at a university, it's not so much in the preaching as in the discussion groups."

Though without pretensions to be an "intellectual" Graham can meet with equality not only theologians but scientists. The English writer who on the strength of hearing him once or twice at a crusade dismissed him as preaching an alarmingly introverted gospel which never dares to face the complexities of scientific or psychological thought would be strongly contradicted by the numerous psychiatrists and scientists who are Billy Graham's friends. Whether or not these men accept his premises and conclusions, they know his interest in their disciplines, his fearlessness in exploring the implications of their findings. To Graham, the God and Father of Jesus Christ is the Creator of distant galaxies and infinitesimal electrons and the discerner of the deepest psychological twists of the human mind.

The charge is sometimes made against the crusades that though Billy Graham is personally sincere he puts across what is virtually an immense confidence trick, by the manipulation of crowds, the singing and the lights, to produce decisions in a whirl of emotion and a mental vacuum. This charge breaks down against the fact that similar results follow his university preaching and discussions.

Graham is essentially a preacher to the individual, whether in a crowd of one or twenty, of a hundred or a hundred thousand. He is vividly aware of the dangers of mass psychosis. He never preaches to evoke a crowd response but selects in his mind one unknown member of the audience and aims to each the whole of that man—his intellect, his conscience and his will.

Graham believes that he carries an imperative message which he must proclaim in such a manner that the simplest person can grasp its essentials. God has spoken, and neither Graham nor any man may arrogate to himself the right to alter or trim the message. The preacher is a messenger, not the author of the message. Furthermore the message is totally relevant to the times. The contemporary crisis —political, moral, psychological, scientific or theological—is a reflection of the unchanging human predicament.

Against the background of this human crisis Graham sets forth Christ, knowing that Christ's excellence, which is the standard by which God holds man accountable, will stand out in such contrast to man's imperfection that the conscience of the hearers will be awakened. And then Graham passes to Christ's death, by which man finds peace with God. He stresses "the love of God from the Cross saying to the whole world, 'I love you, I love you, I will forgive you.'" He does not try to explain the mystery of the atonement but declares it, as did St. Paul: "Christ sent me to preach the gospel, not with the wisdom of words, lest the cross of Christ should be made of none effect. . . . We preach Christ crucified, unto the Jews a stumbling block, and unto the Greeks foolishness; but unto them which are called, both Jews and Greeks, Christ the power of God and the wisdom of God."

Implicit and explicit in Graham's preaching is Christ's resurrection: having died for our sins, He rose again. Often a convert will say that the main effect of the sermon was a growing desire, an intense longing, to find the Christ whom Billy Graham knows so well. But Christ can be found only by repentance and faith, by being sorry for one's sin, recognizing that it was laid upon Him, and by committing oneself into His hands. "Come as a little child," Graham says, "not as a doctor of philosophy or a doctor of law, but come as a simple human being to the Cross and your life can be changed." True repentance and faith make possible the new birth.

Here the preaching reaches its core. Graham believes that every human being must be born again, even as Jesus told the intellectual, successful, devout Nicodemus, "You must be born again," by believing on Him who was lifted up to die. Graham urges a definite step of commitment because he considers that a deliberate and open act of faith, whether in a great crusade or in the presence of a single friend, or alone, is the normal way for a human to be born again. It is not, however, the only way. But the open commitment is not necessarily in itself the new birth, which is an encounter alone between the soul and God, and cannot be induced by human persuasion.

With each passing year there is less of Graham's persuasion and more dependence on the power of the Holy Spirit in his preaching. "I used to think that in evangelism I had to do it all," he told Harvard Divinity School in February 1964, "but now I approach evangelism with a totally different attitude. I approach it with complete relaxation. First of all, I don't believe any man can come to Christ unless the Holy Spirit has prepared his heart. Secondly, I don't believe any man can come to Christ unless God draws him. My job is to proclaim the message. It's the Holy Spirit's job to do the work. And so I approach it with a great deal of relaxation now." He drew an analogy from natural birth. "There's the moment of conception, there's nine months of gestation, there is birth. Now, I believe that of these people who come forward in our meetings to make a commitment, for some it is a moment of conception, for others it's another stage in gestation, for others it is birth into the Kingdom of God. And for many it's completely spurious and there's nothing to it. . . . When I see 100 or 500 people, or whatever number it may be, respond to an appeal to receive Christ, I know that in that group are certain people whose lives will be irrevocably changed from that moment on. And I have that confidence every time I preach."

The new birth is the entrance to the whole range of true Christian experience, a beginning, not an end. Graham's specialist calling is to be a spiritual obstetrician, an evangelist fulfilling the strictly limited human part in the miracle by which man enters into the life of Christ, so that by all the means of grace he may grow to Christian maturity. St. Paul says Christ gave some to be apostles, some prophets, some pastors and teachers, and some evangelists. Billy Graham believes "with all my heart as I look back on my life, that I was chosen to do this particular work as a man might have been chosen to go into East Harlem and work there, or to the slums of London like General Booth. I believe that God in His sovereignty—I have no other answer for this—sheer sovereignty, chose me to do this work and prepared me in His own way."

34 · Do the Converts Last?

In August 1963 Billy Graham held a crusade in Los Angeles, where he had first sprung to fame fourteen years before. The contrasts could hardly be greater.

The Team came at the invitation of the Southern California Council of Churches. More than 3,500 individual churches were involved in a whole year of preparation; 23,000 persons applied for the counseling classes, of whom about 15,000 completed the course; of these, 7,000 were selected as counselors and advisers. Some 1,800 ushers were trained, nearly 10,000 singers registered, and each night the choir would number between 3,000 and 5,000.

Twenty thousand church members called on 1,000,000 homes to invite attendance at the crusade. The fantastic statistics must be seen as the aggregate of individual effort. Moreover, Operation Andrew had been launched so effectively that nearly every individual present at the crusade was there either to help others, or was the individual responsibility of the Christian who had invited and prayed for him.

As the opening day drew near (and during the crusade's course) 80,000 Los Angeles women met for fifteen-minute prayer meetings in 10,000 homes in the morning, led by Cliff Barrows on specially recorded radio programs. People all over the world were praying too. "When I stood up to preach I could sense their prayers," Graham said at Harvard a few months later. "I'm convinced that when Christians of all races and many languages pray for one specific event, God answers. And, in spite of my failure and my crudeness and my limitations, God blesses it and something happens. I believe one of the secrets of success in our crusades has been this great prayer that has been organized."

The whole Graham Team came together at Los Angeles. As always, a crusade was not only the work of Billy but of a Team, alongside the churches. The original nucleus of 1949 was there: Billy, Grady Wilson, Cliff Barrows and Bev Shea.[1] Supporting them were the musical and office staffs and the eleven other associate and staff evangelists, including Akbar Haqq from India, Howard Jones back from Africa, and Fernando Vangioni from Latin America.

[1] An Englishman present at the opening services wrote: "It is very striking what a kindliness there is in Cliff Barrows' voice and manner. The same should be said of Beverly Shea. And as Beverly sings, every word comes over clearly."

Anticipation was at its zenith in Southern California when Billy Graham arrived in Los Angeles. At the ministers' breakfast he warned against false optimism and the belief that "we can *organize* spiritual revival. . . . The longer I work in crusades the more convinced I am that salvation is of the *Lord*. God must prepare hearts."

Instead of the circus style tent of 1949 the crusade was held in the Los Angeles Coliseum, America's largest stadium, used primarily for football and track meets, a vast oval with the tiers rising sheer from ground level. The platform had been placed so that one half of the stadium could be filled and the empty half would fade into the darkness when night fell soon after the start of each service. The platform was moved back as attendance rose.

The turnstiles registered 38,708 at the opening of the crusade. Thereafter, except on two very rainy nights, the attendance in the next three weeks hovered in the thirty or forty thousands, sometimes going up into the sixties. But at the final service 134,254 persons passed through the turnstiles, leaving an estimated 20,000 outside.[1]

Louis Zamperini, the convert of 1949, working among his tough gangs and in the prisons, found that "everybody is thrilled about Billy Graham. My non-Christian neighbors say, 'He gets up there and the minute the bell goes off he's fighting, fighting for the Lord.'" The crusade reached the other end of the social scale, too. Large numbers of the film colony came to the section specially reserved by the Hollywood Christian group, among them such stars as Randolph Scott, Jack Lemmon, Glenn Ford, Jane Russell and Debbie Reynolds. Miss Reynolds invited twenty top-ranking film stars to meet Billy Graham, together with the former English actress converted in the London crusade, Joan Winmill Brown, and her husband Bill Brown, the associate crusade director. "Mr. Graham was specially invited to answer questions," recalls Brown. "The first question was, 'What is sin?' The meeting lasted for about four hours, during which time Mr. Graham answered many questions and clearly presented the Gospel of Jesus Christ."

The crusade youth committee canvassed the beaches, amusement parks and tourist attractions such as Disneyland and Knott's Berry Farm. The youth nights were always highly attended; on one of them

[1] This 134,254 was the highest number recorded for any event at the Los Angeles Coliseum. The Coliseum officials later erected a bronze plaque recording the occasion, bearing in bas-relief Graham's head and an impression of the scene.

3,216 persons, including hundreds of young people, came forward. This was the highest figure for any night at any Graham crusade in the United States. It did not by much fall short of the aggregate of decisions recorded in the entire eight weeks of Los Angeles '49.

Despite the huge crowds, the reverent dignity of the Coliseum services was unforgettable. "I can't get over it," exclaimed comedian Jack Benny. "These people are so quiet! I have never seen anything like it."

Billy Graham's sermons were packed with teaching, and no hearer could fail to realize that the Christian life was not an escape from reality but an enlistment. On one of the youth nights he spoke frankly about sex. "There is nothing wrong with sex. God gave it to us for certain reasons. And it is to be used wisely, as creative energy. Before your marriage it will be a driving dynamo that will take you to the top, and after marriage it is to be used for fulfillment, for communication, and for propagation. But *only* within the bonds of marriage.

"And when temptation comes, accept the fact that it's normal to be tempted, that it's normal to have sex hunger. Accept that—but watch out—and then refuse to allow that sex power to be directed into forbidden channels. . . . Now, don't go so far in petting that you lose control. You punch the light switch, and the lights are going to come on. Hand the conflict over to Christ in the very beginning.

"You may be called a nonconformist. We're living in a period today when young people conform. We're afraid to be different. We all want to be independent, we're rebelling for independence, but we're scared to death to be independent. We want to be like every other person, we want to dress the same way, we want to talk the same way. Be a nonconformist, stand out. That's the kind of young people that Christ is looking for today—young people who will follow Him and serve Him, and march in His army. The whole world is exploding. God is looking for young people who will pay the price, who will dedicate and yield themselves in every aspect of their lives.

"I don't believe in this day that a young person can live clean and pure and wholesome without the help of Christ. I don't believe you can be the kind of a man or woman that Christ wants you to be without His help, and that is why you need to come to Him. That's why you need to receive Him, because the moment you receive Him He gives you a new nature and a power to live the kind of life that you should live."

Once again Billy Graham set forth the essentials of the Christian Gospel. And then he said: "I'm going to ask you to do something tough and hard. I'm going to ask you to get up out of your seat, hundreds of you, get up out of your seat, and come out on this field and stand here reverently. Say tonight, 'I do want Christ to forgive me, I want a new life, I want to live clean and wholesome for Christ. I want him to be my Lord and my Master.' God has spoken to you. You get up and come—we're going to wait right now—quickly—hundreds of you from everywhere."

And not another word. He stood back, arms folded, head bent in prayer. At once the flow began. As in Sydney or Chicago or scores of cities throughout the world, it looks from the platform like a mass movement; but far up in the stadium it is one here, another there—a deliberate, costly choice.

Since—as on most nights of the Los Angeles crusade—the choir does not sing the invitation hymn, "Just As I Am," the reverent hush is broken only by the tramp of feet moving slowly down the aisles and across the ramps over the race track and onto the grass. Billy Graham stands motionless, a distant figure barely discernible above the sea of people, young and old; waiting until the tide ceases to flow and he can address them briefly before the benediction is given and the counseling will begin, right there.

On the platform one night sat the German theologian, Professor Helmut Thielicke of Hamburg. He had come frankly critical. But that evening, as he admitted afterward in a generous letter to Graham, he saw that the question should not be, "What is wrong about Graham?" but, "What is lacking in me and in my theological colleagues in the pulpit and at the university lectern that makes Billy Graham so necessary?"

It became suddenly clear to Dr. Thielicke that the relationship between the theologian and evangelist was complementary: "We learn to see ourselves as various dabs of paint upon the incredibly vivid and colorful palette of God; we are led to humility and to gratitude that everything is not required of us, but that there is another one with his gifts at our side.

"The second offensive aspect," he added, "which I had always noted as far as your ministry was concerned, was also removed. I am speaking of the way in which you call people to come forward and to confirm their decision. It all happened without pressure and emotionalism (contrary to the reports which I had received up until now). It was far more the shepherd's voice, calling out in love and sorrow for the wandering ones.

"I saw them all coming towards us, I saw their assembled, moved and honestly decided faces, I saw their searching and their meditativeness. I confess that this moved me to the very limits. Above all there were two young men—a white and a Negro—who stood at the front and about whom one felt that they were standing at that moment on Mount Horeb and looking from afar into a land they had longed for. I shall never forget those faces. It became lightning clear that men *want* to make a decision. . . .

"The consideration that many do not remain true to their hour of decision can contain no truly serious objection: the salt of this hour will be something they will taste in every loaf of bread and cake which they are to bake in their later life. *Once* in their life they have perceived what it is like to enter the realm of discipleship. And if only this memory accompanies them, then that is already a great deal. But it would certainly be more than a mere memory. It will remain an appeal to them, and in this sense it will maintain its *character indelibilis.*"

Los Angeles '63 provides an opportunity to pause and look back over the years since Los Angeles '49. What has been the overall result, worldwide? Do the converts last?

Just short of one million (by the end of 1965) have "come forward." Though the figure may be somewhat affected by unreliable statistics for the earliest crusades, this possibility of error is more than balanced off by the unrecorded, unestimated tens of thousands brought to faith through Billy Graham films, television and radio. These nearly 1,000,000 persons include those whose commitment was one of rededication or restoration, and also a few committed Christians who came forward for help on a problem. The figure includes, too, as Graham frequently points out, those in whom the seed has fallen on stony or shallow earth, who bring no fruit to perfection. Graham personally dislikes statistics: "How can you put a reconciled home, a transformed drunkard, or a new selfless attitude, into a cold statistic?" They are kept only for the sake of accuracy and to prevent exaggeration by pressmen who do not appreciate that the crowd they see come forward is partly formed of counselors.

In the first years Graham worried a little as to whether converts lasted, but when he began to meet them wherever he went, his concern disappeared. All around the world people come up to him; he cannot go to a religious conference, a seminary, a church, or visit a mission field without strangers wanting to tell him they were converted through his ministry. He has been told it on the golf course and on the highway. Once he and Cliff were stopped by a policeman near Seattle in 1962 for exceeding a 25-mile speed limit. As the policeman recorded Cliff's name as driver he told them he had been converted in the Seattle crusade of 1951, "And I want you to know I've been going on with the Lord."

The suspicion that converts do not last is widespread but never sustained by those who study the evidence. The late Stanley High, asked by *Reader's Digest* to go to London a year after Harringay, warned Billy that he expected to be critical. Instead, he found that "a surprisingly large number of the converts are carrying on." His findings led him to investigate more fully. Ultimately he wrote in his book, *Billy Graham* (1956), that in every British or American city where a crusade had been held, there were individuals who had become "contagious Christians for whom life's most important business has become the spreading of that contagion. I have enough 'case histories' in my own notes not merely to fill a chapter, but to make a substantial start toward a book. Yet I knew that my inquiries hardly scratched the surface."

As High found, and it is even more true in the nineteen-sixties, the evidence is overwhelming. The files of the Billy Graham Evangelistic Association spill over with letters and testimonies. It is difficult to convey the impact of the evidence because a selection may seem to give a spurious impression.

The honest investigator is left in no doubt. Yet many people, within the church or outside, have made up their minds that Billy Graham converts do not last. In 1964 at the Church Army training college in Canada a "very important learned gentleman" was asked to say a few words at lunch about evangelism. He referred to the weakness of mass meetings such as those of Billy Graham and stated that there was little lasting result from "so-called decisions." "In thanking the speaker," relates Captain R. A. Taylor, director of the Church Army in Canada, "I was delighted to be able to look down our table and ask those to please stand who were converts at Toronto, 1955, or London. A good number of our students stood and were able to testify to the change in their lives which led them into full-time service as a result of those campaigns."

Another persistent but now untenable misconception was that most crusade converts were church related and mainly from the middle class of society. Since the early crusades were all in North America or Britain, a high proportion of converts with at least a nominal church relationship was inevitable, because only minorities of the population of these areas disclaim all church connection.

In any case, why should a new commitment by a nominal Christian be belittled? Many regular churchgoers need to discover a personal, compulsive faith in place of a comfortable conformity. Thousands of churchgoers are in the position described in a letter to Billy Graham on August 12, 1957, by George W. Cornell, who was covering the crusade for Associated Press: "When your New York crusade began, I would classify myself as one of those mental believers you often speak of, those who accept it all in the brain, but there it stops. It didn't burn and quicken and motivate. My own will ruled the game. It was a will chastened somewhat by living, and by a partially educated conscience, but it was my will, just the same. My will was king, not God. Your sermons, and that other element that comes through with them, soon had me backed in a corner, realizing my insufficiency, more and more keenly, as the nights went on."

Cornell told Billy how his conflicts and questionings were gradually resolved until "it was perfectly easy to step forward with no qualms or worries. . . . God, previously an important but remote truth, became an intimate presence, an infallible compass always at hand, so that the journey through this life is no longer muddled, vague and indefinite, but clear and plain."

Eight years later, George Cornell endorses this statement made in 1957.

By the mid-nineteen-sixties it is no longer possible to assert that crusade converts are mostly of one cultural background or ethnic group, for the same phenomena are found in whatever lands crusades are held. Robert O. Ferm, who made an extensive investigation in Asia in 1959, three years after the crusade, discovered that a large percentage of the converts whom he interviewed had received no previous Christian instruction; they had been reared in another religion or in none. Many persons whom Ferm met recalled that after their decision several days passed before the full meaning of the experience was clarified; but, as they impressed upon Ferm, "It was no less vivid or less permanent."

Ferm has interviewed, personally or by correspondence, nearly 14,000 converts from four continents, most of them several years after their decisions. His research has made clear not only that the crusades touch all strata of society, but that they do so evenly: the percentage of converts from each stratum approximates the percentage of that stratum within the community.

To break down his findings Ferm assessed statistically an imaginary 3,000 converts, on the basis of the percentages revealed by the 14,000. Of the 3,000, 46 per cent would be nonchurch prior to the crusade, 54 per cent would have been affiliated in various degrees. Five of the 3,000 would be of the "intellectual" professions (doctor, university professor, etc.), for Graham has seen the conversion of a steady trickle of such men as Dr. Fred Smith, the English-born professor of biochemistry at the University of Minnesota who died of cancer comparatively young in 1965, six years after his conversion.

Five of the 3,000 would be owners of businesses, of varying degrees of wealth; again, the crusades have been the means of transforming the lives and purses of more than a few millionaires.

Ferm's figures continue: three law enforcement officers, 46 school teachers; 325 would be sales or office staff personnel, or employed in skilled trades. No less than 355 would be semi-skilled or industrial workers—a high proportion in that automation is reducing the number who so describe themselves in any given community. In any event, the cry that "Billy does not touch the working man" would appear to be invalid.

Of the rest, the largest single group within the 3,000 figure is that of high school and college students: 1,800. Here lies a potentially valuable contribution by Graham which cannot be fully assessed for years after a crusade, until these young people have grown up. On the evidence of earlier crusades, many will be found in lay or full-time Christian service.

Statistics of course have their limitations. These figures do not, for example, allow for scores of "delayed action" conversions not included in the crusade figures because the persons did not come forward but were converted in the weeks or months after a crusade. And no one can reflect in statistics the possibly enormous aggregate influence of the converts themselves.

Nor do statistics reflect the influence on those who came to the point of decision and refused.

Billy Graham believes that "I have a responsibility and an obligation to give people the opportunity to decide 'Yes' or 'No,' and when a man deliberately faces Christ and turns Him down, he can never be the same again.... Jesus pushed the rich young ruler right in a corner. He had to decide. He decided 'No.' And it says, 'he went away and grieved.' People say, 'Those who leave our meetings and don't make a decision have emotional and psychological reactions.' Of course they do. When you face Jesus Christ and reject Him, you are going to have a disturbance. The rich young ruler was *grieved*. A psychologist can find a lot in that word 'grieved.'

"I think there should be no apology on this point. I read criticisms of our work both in Britain and in America, that many people go away psychologically disturbed. This is the work of the Holy Spirit. He is a disturber. Christ said, 'I didn't come to bring peace, but a sword.' He said, 'I came to divide families and communities and nations.' His Gospel is divisive."

Billy Graham has no doubt, on the evidence, that the crusades have won many thousands to Christ. Even if they had not, he must give his message. As with the Apostle Paul, "Woe is unto me, if I preach not the gospel." Billy quotes the words in the Book of Ezekiel: "I do send thee unto them; and thou shalt say unto them, Thus saith the Lord God . . . whether they will hear, or whether they will forbear."

Any assessment of the crusades must also take into account their many side effects. They have helped a return to Biblical preaching. They have brought a new concern for religion to the world's press. They have been an influence for church unity and racial reconciliation. And they have strengthened Christians in non-Christian lands, both by stimulating support and reinforcements from the West and by the impact of crusades held in Asia, Africa and South America.

But the primary effect—as well as the primary target—has been transformed lives, reckoned in their hundreds of thousands.

To go deeply into the evidence—whether documentary or face-to-face in the many countries involved—is to emerge with the conclusion best described in words used by Canon J. B. Phillips in the preface to his translation of the Acts of the Apostles, *The Young Church in Action:* "No honest reader can evade the conclusion that something very powerful and very unusual has happened. People are unquestionably being changed at the root of their being: cowards become heroes; sinners are transformed; fear, greed, envy and pride are expelled by a flood of something above and beyond normal human experience. For in the pages of this New Testament the cruel, the wicked, the evil minded and the Godless become filled with selfless love, with gay and generous courage. The critics of Christianity have got somehow to explain this."

35 · Unfinished Chapter

In April 1964 the New York World's Fair opened at Flushing Meadow, and with it the Billy Graham Pavilion.

The Vatican, the Orthodox churches, the New York City Protestant Council of Churches and several other religious organizations were already planning pavilions when George Wilson went to see the Fair director, Robert Moses, in 1962. Mr. Moses listened to George Wilson and on behalf of the Fair donated a site close to the main gate, and secured the services of the prize-winning architect Edward Durell Stone. The central feature of the Billy Graham Pavilion would be a wide-screen film theater showing a specially prepared Billy Graham film. To place the film on a parity with the visual attractions of the other exhibitions it was decided to shoot it in Todd-AO despite the heavy cost. For director of the pavilion Billy chose Dan Piatt. Piatt hesitated.

Before long, Billy Graham was hesitant himself. During his illness of early 1963 he doubted whether the Association could raise the money or find the personnel, and whether the technical difficulties could be overcome. He even wondered whether an evangelistic center in the midst of the Fair would draw more than a trickle of visitors. The problems seemed so insurmountable that Billy wrote to the BGEA board that the project was canceled. Dr. Edman of Wheaton told him that he was wrong, and referred him to the success of D. L. Moody's campaign during the Chicago World's Fair of 1893. Another board member, Carloss Morris, a Texas lawyer, wrote Billy, "Never make a decision when you're ill." Billy revoked the cancellation and invited Dan Piatt to stop in Hawaii for a time of rest and golf on his way home from reorganizing the Orient crusade.

"Before we reached the first green," says Dan, "he asked me again about coming to the World's Fair. In July 1963 I arrived on the scene and there was nothing but a hole in the ground—mud, dust and debris all over."

The twenty-eight-minute film, *Man in the Fifth Dimension,* was shot in California shortly before the Los Angeles crusade. In keeping with the theme of the Fair, the film looks at the marvels of the universe and life. Then, with Billy Graham as guide, it passes on to consider man's rebellion against his Creator and the way of reconciliation through Christ.

Throughout the fall and winter of 1963–64 Piatt was absorbed in problems of constructing the pavilion, until at times he felt no longer in the ministry. Trade unionists and executives, however, were learning the meaning of Christian witness. The first man to accept Christ through the ministry of the Billy Graham Pavilion was the Todd-AO representative. Another was the head of the electronics firm that installed the multi-language equipment, similar to the equipment he had installed at the United Nations. The worker sent by the firm that contracted to keep the lawns and building tidy, a Negro, had attended the New York crusade of 1957. "We really had to chase him off the job after eight hours each day," reports Piatt. "He said, 'I am really dedicated to the work going on here at the pavilion.' "

New York churches supplied the counselors. In the two six-month periods of the World's Fair in 1964 and 1965 the Billy Graham Pavilion, with its 117-foot high landmark of a tower which glittered with 4,000 gold-anodized discs, drew 5,000,000 visitors from 125 countries, to wander through the airy loggias, study the panels of color transparencies, which showed the different Graham ministries, and to take literature. More than a million visitors viewed the film, shown once an hour from ten in the morning until ten at night, in the theater seating about 350 people.

At every showing of *Man in the Fifth Dimension* Billy Graham on the screen gave the invitation to accept Christ. A steady flow of inquirers responded and went forward to the counseling room. Of many languages, they represented fifty-five countries from China to Peru and every American state. Included among them were most known occupations: doctor, psychologist, film producer, ski instructor, clergyman, airline pilot, soldier, ice-cream vendor, jujitsu instructor—even a lady who registered her profession as baby sitter.

Counselors' reports read like a survey of all the troubles, fears and hopes of men. Nor did this "miniature crusade," "Graham's World Crusade at Flushing Meadow," as pressmen called it, end in the counseling room. The pavilion staff, equipped with enormous maps and plans and directories, took endless trouble to refer every inquirer to a church in his home district.

With such a variety of peoples and range of occupations encountering Christ at the World's Fair, Dan Piatt has justification in saying, "I believe this World's Fair Crusade will turn out to be one of the greatest single evangelistic efforts in the history of the Billy Graham Association."

The regular crusades of 1964 were all within the United States. Columbus, located in the center of Ohio, drew delegations from every part of the state. With an extensive share-partner scheme, Columbus became the first crusade to meet its entire budget before the opening service. The offerings during the meetings therefore enabled three of the nights to be shown on television across the country. In Omaha, Nebraska, the proportion of inquirers to crusade attendance was double the previous average.

The most memorable, however, of the Billy Graham crusades of 1964 were the two at Boston.

For the first time since 1950 the Graham Team returned to New England, with its numerous Roman Catholics, Unitarians and Christian Scientists. The crusade filled Boston Garden for ten days. Not all the converts of 1950 could help: in one church all twelve had gone elsewhere as missionaries or pastors. The 1964 crusade concluded with a rally on Boston Common on September 27, attended by some 75,000, far more than had come to the similar rally in the same place in 1950. But ten days did not seem long enough for Boston, and Graham agreed to return after a short rest, giving up his intention of devoting October to writing.

The crusade resumed after hurried rearrangements. Though numbers were not so great as in September, the depth of attention and the high proportion of inquirers left the Team awed by the signs of the Spirit's movement. At the close of the crusade Billy and the Team did what he had regretted not doing after the second Boston crusade of 1950: they toured New England cities for meetings arranged at short notice. At Portland, Maine, 3,000 persons packed the municipal auditorium, but twice as many were thronging the plaza and the roped-off street beyond. Bev Shea sang to the crowds outside, and Billy, intending to give a greeting, was so inspired by the sight that he preached them a sermon.

One incident in the 1964 New England crusade was historic—the interview with Richard Cardinal Cushing.

The magazine of the Boston Roman Catholic archdiocese had been friendly even in 1950. In 1964 Cardinal Cushing issued a statement welcoming Graham, with "the prayer of Catholics in the Boston area that God will bless his preaching and crusade, and will lead many to the knowledge of Our Lord." Soon after Graham's second arrival in Boston he sent a message asking for an appointment with the Cardinal to express gratitude. When Graham reached the Cardinal's house on Wednesday morning, October 7, he found to his surprise that the popular, publicity-minded prelate had arranged the attendance of a full battery of reporters, television and news cameras and radio microphones.

"You do a great job," began the Cardinal. "I congratulate you, and I've listened to you many times on Sunday nights on radio." Graham thanked him for his kindness, and Cushing replied: "You're preaching Christ and Christ crucified. No one could listen to you without becoming a better Christian."

"Well, I feel that the great need of the world," replied Graham, "is the proclamation of the Gospel. We've defended it so long, and now we need to proclaim it. And the people are listening. I think that in the country today they are waiting for something. I feel it especially among the young people."

For forty-five minutes the Cardinal and the evangelist conversed in public. Graham spoke of the "new day of understanding and dialogue which is going to help bring about the renewal and the revival we believe is necessary." Cushing said: "You've made a great contribution to this ecumenical spirit, because you tossed a banner bearing the fact that Christians agree on more things than they disagree on." Graham spoke of Cushing's long years of working for a better attitude between Protestants and Catholics, and then the two talked together about the Ecumenical Council in Rome, of a common translation of the Bible, and of Pope John and Pope Paul.

Graham spoke again of being "a sort of spectator on the sidelines watching this work, because I'm so convinced that it's the work of the Holy Spirit. I'm just as amazed as anyone else that large crowds come to these meetings. I wonder when it will all be over. And yet God seems to increase it because our audiences in the last three or four years have been larger than ever before."

Cardinal Cushing turned to the reporters, and said, "I have never known of a religious crusade that was more effective. . . . Dr. Graham's crusade has something tremendously needed in our day and age. I only wish we had half a dozen men of his caliber to go forth and do likewise—that is, to preach Christ and Him crucified to the modern world."

The fall and winter of 1964–65 continued the round of addresses, broadcasting and writing in America, marred only by the attempt to force Billy Graham, by sheer weight of hundreds of thousands of telegrams and countless telephone calls, to endorse one or other candidate for President. Graham constantly receives requests to endorse books, labor unions, products, people and schemes of all sorts. All are declined because his mission is simply evangelism. The request made to him at election time in 1964 differed only in the importance of the matter to both political parties and the importunity with which it was presented, swamping the telephone lines at Minneapolis and Montreal.

At Christmas time Billy preached as usual to the corps of cadets at West Point and at Annapolis Naval Academy. A few weeks earlier he had been at The Citadel, the military college of South Carolina, and, in the words of its president, General Mark Clark, "He made a profoundly favorable impression on my cadets and me." General Clark "found it refreshing to discuss with him the great problems that face today's world." [1]

In February 1965 came the Hawaii crusade, and again the proportion of inquirers to attendance was high. Throughout 1965 Billy Graham worked in North America except for the difficult little crusade at Copenhagen, significant because nothing like it had ever occurred there before. At Houston, Texas, in November, a Billy Graham crusade was attended for the first time by a President of the United States in office.

Meanwhile, preparations were forging ahead for the Greater London crusade of June 1966.

Nearly three years earlier some sixty British laymen, among them peers, Members of Parliament, industrialists, doctors and lawyers, had met at a luncheon and signed a hand-lettered and decorated scroll inviting Billy Graham to hold a crusade in the spring of 1965, the tenth anniversary of Wembley.

There could be little disputing the evidence of the British churches' failure to maintain the momentum of 1954–1955. The temporary rise in churchgoing had again given way to a downward trend. Crime and illegitimacy were rising. A nation whose spiritual values had been choked by the affluence of the later nineteen-fifties was disheartened by fresh economic difficulties and political uncertainties. Moreover a comment in the *Daily Mail* at the close of Harringay: "The complacency of irreligion has been profoundly disturbed," had proved true. A strong, vocal, secularist or humanist movement, with a considerable following in the universities, was attempting to undermine

[1] Letter of General Mark W. Clark to the author, June 3, 1965.

Christianity's position as the traditional religion of the British people, by agitating for the abolition of Christian teaching in schools and for a reduction in the time allowed to Christian services and speakers on radio and television. The humanists asserted that Christianity's influence had been pernicious and that its moral standards were perverse.

The Church of England and the Free Churches, at the time of the 1963 luncheon meeting, were indeed more active than in 1954, overhauling their organization, studying reunion, stirring their members to renewed responsibility for churches overseas. But these activities made little impact on the masses in Britain. To them the church seemed increasingly irrelevant and dull.

The Anglican Archbishops, Michael Ramsey of Canterbury, who had succeeded Geoffrey Fisher, and Donald Coggan of York, were propounding the power and intrinsic value of historic Christianity. Yet the ear of the nation was more attuned to churchmen and professors whose intellectual search, as it filtered down to the ordinary television viewer or newspaper reader, appeared to have made the discovery that in this scientific age any authoritative proclamation of faith was childish; that God was not a Person who could be known, loved and obeyed; that He had never walked on earth, nor had Christ risen bodily from the dead; that the one absolute was love, and thus that a true morality must be uninhibited by traditional Christian chastity.

The time cried for another voice.

In the hope that Billy Graham would accept the London invitation an executive committee of laymen and clergy was formed under the chairmanship, as in 1954 and 1955, of Major-General Wilson-Haffenden. Harringay arena no longer existed; an outdoor stadium such as Wembley should be avoided because of the dangers of bad weather, until the crusade's climax. The committee approached the management of Earl's Court and learned that for the next two years the one period still unbooked was the month they wanted: June 1965.

In March 1964 Billy Graham, with T. W. Wilson, Cliff Barrows and Walter Smyth, visited London to make inquiries. The ship was delayed, so that from Southampton Billy had to drive direct to Lambeth Palace for his Sunday supper engagement with the Archbishop of Canterbury. In the course of the next five days Billy was received by the Prime Minister, Sir Alec Douglas-Home, by Harold Wilson, who was to become Prime Minister six months later, and by the

Bishops of London and Southwark, the two Anglican leaders most closely involved, both of whom expressed their support.

After his interviews and a long, frank discussion with the executive committee, Graham decided that he should not come in 1965 but the year after. Earl's Court rearranged its bookings accordingly to June 1966.

Before he returned to America, Billy Graham addressed 3,000 clergy and lay workers in Central Hall, Westminster.

In one of the preliminary speeches the Rector of All Souls', Langham Place, John Stott, quoted Archbishop Fisher's statement after Harringay: "Dr. Graham has taught us all to begin again at the beginning in our evangelism and speak by power of the Holy Spirit of sin and righteousness and of judgment." "If," said John Stott, "Dr. Graham taught us that ten years ago, we've largely forgotten the lesson and we need to learn it again. What is needed more than anything else in our nation today is simplicity and authority in the proclamation of the Gospel, in the power of the Holy Spirit."

In a vigorous address Graham met the clergy's questionings, touched upon all that his Team had learned since Harringay, spoke of the needs of the hour and concluded: "I believe if ever there was a time to unite and work together for Christ on this island it is now. I believe London could be touched. I don't believe it would solve all the problems—there are vast limitations as to what a crusade can do —but I believe it could bring about a proclamation of the Gospel that perhaps the whole nation might listen to again. That's in the hands of the Holy Spirit."

A far wider range of churches than in the previous crusades of 1954 and 1955 showed an appreciation of the crusade's possibilities. Four Team members arrived nearly eighteen months before the opening date to begin the mammoth task of speaking to every London clergyman, Anglican and Free Church, about involvement in the crusade. By November 1965 more than 3,000 of them had already had their questions answered. "The early resistance of some to the concept of mass evangelism," wrote Dr. Ferm that month, "has been gradually changed to a hopeful sense of anticipation. Hundreds of clergy have become involved and are involving their congregations in every phase of planning and preparation."

Earl's Court, the largest indoor arena in London, was being adapted to hold 27,000 for the crusade, including 7,000 watching in an annex by television. The crusade, despite its name, would not be limited to London, for closed circuit television over long distances was at last technically feasible, and other cities planned to join.

One notable event of the year was the publication of *World Aflame,* Graham's first major book since *Peace with God. World Aflame* sold over 34,500 copies before publication. In ninety days it passed 100,000, and in five months, by the first of February, 1966, its score was 440,000 copies sold. Another event was the release of *The Restless Ones,* the film dealing with the teenage problem and based on the recent Los Angeles crusade. *The Restless Ones* drew large audiences in America and in Britain, where it was aided by some violent criticism from a novelist. The number of young people who asked for counseling after the showings suggests that Billy Graham films may have an even greater future as a means of evangelism.

And this promise of a still greater future seems true also for the personal ministry of Billy Graham. By the evidence of the demands for crusades, his first forty-seven years have been merely a prelude and preparation for the years ahead. He has more invitations from different parts of the world than at any time in his ministry. Scores of cities on every continent seek to impress upon him that a crusade is urgent. The schedule for 1966 includes, together with the Greater London crusade, another in Berlin, followed by a World Congress of Evangelism, sponsored by *Christianity Today,* under Graham's leadership. In 1967 he has agreed to hold crusades in Puerto Rico, in Canada, and in two major cities of America. For a month in the summer of 1968 he has accepted an invitation by a widely representative group of clergy and laymen to return to New York for a crusade in the new, much larger Madison Square Garden now being erected over the remains of the old Pennsylvania Station. All New York churches are being invited to cooperate, and the closing rally will be in Shea Stadium. Meanwhile, Australia and New Zealand are waiting eagerly to know when Billy Graham will return.

Graham has more church cooperation and more aid from the press than ever before. One great change has been increasing Roman Catholic support, which could open a whole new era in the ministry of the Billy Graham Team. Meanwhile, Graham has again been urged by his friends to found a Christian university, and is closely exploring the possibilities of turning this long-time ambition of his into a reality. The Billy Graham Evangelistic Association continues to grow because of the incessant demand. And Graham is determined to keep it from growing. He is consolidating, and pulling back in some areas of its activities for fear that it might become an institution.

Billy Graham is all the more settled that his ministry should be simply an aid to the churches and never become the basis of a new denomination. He rejects pleas that he should found a movement, or take the leadership of the thousands of prayer groups and Bible study groups and "house churches" which are springing up spontaneously across the United States. Graham feels there are too many denominations already. "I am determined," he says, "to make whatever contribution I can, in and through the Church as it now exists."

He has unbounded opportunities. He has many temptations. Billy Graham is resolved to continue crusades for as along as he has the strength—a servant of God, the Church and his fellow men.

Notes on Sources

The principal sources are as follows:

(a) Some twenty hours of tape-recorded interviews with Billy Graham in 1964 and 1965.

(b) A transcript, running to about 80,000 words, of memories of his early life, tape-recorded by Graham in 1963. Part of this material (edited by Curtis Mitchell) was published in *McCall's* magazine in 1964.

(c) Tape-recorded interviews with about one hundred and fifty persons who were kind enough to give me unhurried time in North America, Europe, Australia and New Zealand. They include relatives, friends and colleagues of Billy Graham, organizers and helpers of crusades, opponents, converts, journalists and church leaders. In addition, witnesses I could not meet sent me tapes, memoranda or letters, and lent me papers. The transcripts of all my interviews run to a total of nearly half a million words.

(d) Billy Graham's private files, from 1946 up to and including 1959, with certain papers from subsequent years.

(e) The archives of the Billy Graham Evangelistic Association at Minneapolis, Minnesota.

(f) The millions of words of printed material from newspapers, magazines and books.

Since most of the unpublished sources are not accessible to scholars it seemed merely pretentious to litter this book with footnotes of references, or weary the reader by continually repeating "As So-and-So said in 1964." All unidentified quotations come from one or another of the private sources.

Index